CAMBRIDGE LIBRARY COLLECTION

Books of enduring scholarly value

British and Irish History, General

The books in this series are key examples of eighteenth- and nineteenth-century historiography which show how centuries of political, social and economic change were interpreted during the height of Britain's power. They shed light on the understanding of dynasty, religion and culture that shaped the domestic, foreign and colonial policy of the British empire.

Registrum sacrum Anglicanum

This 1858 work was the first major publication of William Stubbs (1825–1901), who later became bishop of both Chester and Oxford. Stubbs also published highly respected and influential works on the constitutional history of England and was considered an authority on ecclesiastical history. The present work consists of a thorough chronology of the succession of the bishops of England, beginning with the consecration of Augustine of Canterbury in 597 and continuing up to 1857. Each bishop's entry includes their see, their consecrators and the sources from which this information was drawn. Wherever possible, Stubbs endeavoured to consult the original sources, and thus he was able to present more accurate dates of consecration than were previously available. The appendices include a well-annotated list of suffragan, Manx and Welsh bishops, as well as an index of each bishop, ordered by see.

T0352197

Cambridge University Press has long been a pioneer in the reissuing of out-of-print titles from its own backlist, producing digital reprints of books that are still sought after by scholars and students but could not be reprinted economically using traditional technology. The Cambridge Library Collection extends this activity to a wider range of books which are still of importance to researchers and professionals, either for the source material they contain, or as landmarks in the history of their academic discipline.

Drawing from the world-renowned collections in the Cambridge University Library and other partner libraries, and guided by the advice of experts in each subject area, Cambridge University Press is using state-of-the-art scanning machines in its own Printing House to capture the content of each book selected for inclusion. The files are processed to give a consistently clear, crisp image, and the books finished to the high quality standard for which the Press is recognised around the world. The latest print-on-demand technology ensures that the books will remain available indefinitely, and that orders for single or multiple copies can quickly be supplied.

The Cambridge Library Collection brings back to life books of enduring scholarly value (including out-of-copyright works originally issued by other publishers) across a wide range of disciplines in the humanities and social sciences and in science and technology.

Registrum sacrum Anglicanum

*An Attempt to Exhibit the Course
of Episcopal Succession in England
from the Records
and Chronicles of the Church*

WILLIAM STUBBS

CAMBRIDGE
UNIVERSITY PRESS

CAMBRIDGE
UNIVERSITY PRESS

University Printing House, Cambridge, CB2 8BS, United Kingdom

Published in the United States of America by Cambridge University Press, New York

Cambridge University Press is part of the University of Cambridge.

It furthers the University's mission by disseminating knowledge in the pursuit of education, learning and research at the highest international levels of excellence.

www.cambridge.org
Information on this title: www.cambridge.org/9781108061193

© in this compilation Cambridge University Press 2013

This edition first published 1858
This digitally printed version 2013

ISBN 978-1-108-06119-3 Paperback

Registrum Sacrum Anglicanum.

AN ATTEMPT TO EXHIBIT THE

COURSE OF EPISCOPAL SUCCESSION

IN ENGLAND,

FROM THE

RECORDS AND CHRONICLES

OF

THE CHURCH.

BY

WILLIAM STUBBS, M.A.

VICAR OF NAVESTOCK,

AND LATE FELLOW OF TRINITY COLLEGE, OXFORD.

OXFORD:

AT THE UNIVERSITY PRESS.

M.DCCC.LVIII.

PREFACE.

THIS Book is offered as a contribution to Ecclesiastical History in the departments of Biography and exact Chronology. Its position in relation to the first of these, though humble, is sufficiently obvious: in regard to the latter it seems to require some apology. This must be found in the fact that it occupies and confines itself to a distinct ground not solely or exclusively appropriated by any similar work, and so is not intended to supersede the labour or to disparage the arrangement of any former collectors. A short notice of the sources of the information contained in it will suffice.

And, first, with regard to the Saxon period. This portion of the Record has been constructed from a comparison of the Ancient Lists of Bishops, with the scanty memoranda of the Anglo-Saxon Chronicle, Simeon of Durham, Florence of Worcester, and the Annotators. The results of this comparison have been carefully tested by the signatures of the Charters printed in Kemble's Codex Diplomaticus, and additional light has been thrown on them by the Profession Rolls at Canterbury: these valuable evidences, which are available up to the end of the 14th century, are the written declarations of obedience to the Metropolitical Church which were made by each Bishop at his consecration.

The later portion of the Record, from the consecration of Parker downwards, is an abstract of the records of the provinces of Canterbury and

York, which are lodged at Lambeth, the Vicar General's office in Doctors' Commons, and at York.

The second or medieval portion is a careful compilation, now for the first time attempted, from all the accessible sources. Of these sources a list will be given. A few general remarks on them may not be out of place or useless to students of the same subjects.

And first, as most accessible, stand the Collections towards English Church History, in which class the "Antiquitates" of Parker and Josselin, Godwin " de Præsulibus," Wharton's "Anglia Sacra," and Le Neve's " Fasti," are text books.

Next, and indispensably necessary to one who would refer to original records, are the unrivalled Manuscript Collections of Henry Wharton at Lambeth. This wonderful man died in 1695, at the age of 30, having done for the elucidation of English Church History (itself but one of the branches of study in which he was the most eminent scholar of his time) more than any one before or since. Contemporary and apparently in frequent communication with him was Matthew Hutton of Aynho, (he died in 1711,) whose valuable Collections are in the Harleian Library. They contain, among other transcripts, copies of several volumes of Wharton's MSS.

Bishop Kennett seems to have transcribed and digested the Collections of both these on ecclesiastical subjects, with additions from his own reading. These are in the Lansdowne Collection.

It was at first attempted to construct a Chronological Table from the above authorities, in conjunction with the printed Chronicles. But the many discrepancies of the latter, and the imperfect notes of the Collectors, who not collecting for this branch of the subject in particular, seldom exhausted their authorities or quoted them exactly, determined the editor to have recourse to original documentary evidence, and nowhere, if possible, to commit himself to a statement on second-hand testimony. With this view he has consulted a large number of the Registers and Records of various sees, and as many of the Chronicles preserved in Manuscript in our National and Academic libraries, as seemed likely to afford any information. With respect to the Chronicles, a list of those from which information was actually gained, will be enough. Of the Episcopal Registers to be found in the several Cathedrals, which are of course less accessible, the chief features are these:

Every Bishop kept (and still keeps) a register of all his official acts. The first page generally contains the account of his consecration or appointment; then follow the bulls and other privileges which he received from the Popes. The bulk of each volume is occupied with the records of institutions to benefices, acts of consistory courts, and lists of persons ordained; to which in many instances important wills are annexed. This may be considered as an adequate description of the general run of registers. There are however frequent exceptions. Those of Canterbury and York contain proceedings with the Suffragans, records of Convocations and Councils, and a vast number of letters on public business. The Register of William of Wykeham is the model of the record of a statesman Bishop, and a most valuable storehouse of notices of public interest, summonses to Parliament, and miscellaneous official and personal acts. Others contain copies of more ancient documents, which were perishing when transcribed, and are now lost. Nor are the materials only worthy of remark; the arrangement also is various: some are patterns of neatness, especially the early ones of York, and those of Winchester generally; others are confused and scanty, the Canterbury ones being by no means the best, which is very unfortunate, considering their importance. Several are lost, among them the larger portion of Cardinal Beaufort's, which seems to have come after his death into the King's hands and may possibly be found some day. It must have contained very much of historical importance at a period not much illustrated by historians, and especially on the subject before us. The condition however of the existing ones is very good, and altogether they form a curious and by no means exhausted mine of information to a careful inquirer.

From these and similar sources the following tables are framed: in most cases the evidence they afford is direct and particular, in some few the date and circumstances have to be derived from indirect indications. These (which are in the text printed in Italics) will be found chiefly during the troubled times of Richard II, when, notwithstanding the statute of

Provisors, each appointment of a Bishop received its confirmation at Rome, where most, if not all, of the unrecorded consecrations probably took place : others during the wars of the Roses, and up to the close of the 15th century. For the latter period the dates have been fixed with reference, 1st, to the time at which the licences for consecration were issued by the Convent of Canterbury, which in most cases was during the week preceding the appointed Sunday : 2nd, to such scattered notices of the filling up of preferments vacated by consecration as could be found in various Registers; and 3rd, to the computation of the pontifical years of the several Bishops as given in existing Instruments. It is hoped that in all these cases the dates given will be found correct when examined by the light of further evidence. Similar historical and chronological tests have been applied to every date in this portion of the Record, and if the results in some instances are different from those given by older authorities, no particular has been set down without careful calculation and consideration.

The thanks of the Editor are offered to all who have kindly procured him access to Records, especially to Felix Knyvett, Esq. of Lambeth, the Rev. A. P. Stanley and the Hon. D. Finch of Canterbury, the authorities at the Vicar General's office and S. Paul's, Mr. Wooldridge of Winchester, Chancellors Harrington of Exeter and Melvill of S. David's, Egerton V. Harcourt, Esq., and the Rev. W. V. Harcourt of York, the Rev. J. Raine, Junior, of Durham, the Rev. Geo. Gilbert of Grantham, the Bishop of Carlisle, W. T. Alchin, Esq., and the Deputy Registrars of Worcester, Hereford, Lichfield, Chichester, Rochester, Norwich, Wells, and Salisbury.

It is perhaps necessary to add, that throughout the work the beginning of the year is placed on the first of January.

NAVESTOCK,
January 25, 1858.

LIST OF AUTHORITIES.

I.—COLLECTIONS, HISTORICAL AND BIOGRAPHICAL.

1.—PRINTED BOOKS.

(α) *Church History.*

1. Parker or Josselin, Antiquitates Eccl. Britannicæ. Ed. Drake. London, 1729.
2. Godwin de Præsulibus Angliæ. Ed. Richardson. Cambridge, 1743.
3. Wharton, Anglia Sacra. London, 1691.
4. Le Neve, Fasti Ecclesiæ Anglicanæ. London, 1716.
5. Wood, Athenæ Oxonienses. Lond. 1691.
6. Wilkins, Concilia Magnæ Britanniæ et Hiberniæ.
7. Rymer, Fœdera et Acta Publica.
8. Wadding, Annals of the Minorites.
9. Br. Willis, English and Welsh Cathedrals.
10. Gallia Christiana. Paris, 1716, &c.
11. Farlati Illyricum Sacrum. Venice, 1751.
12. Perceval on the Apostolic Succession. London, 1841.
13. Keith's Scotch Bishops. Edinb. 1824.
14. Ware's Ireland. London, 1705.
15. Cotton's Fasti Ecclesiæ Hibernicæ. Dublin.
16. Mason and Lindsay on the Episcopate.
17. Dugdale's Monasticon. (New Edition.)
18. Kemble's Codex Diplomaticus Anglo-Saxonum. London, 1839–1848.
19. Ussher's Antiquitates Eccl. Britannicarum. Dublin, 1639.
20. Prynn's Records.

(β) *Local and Biographical Memoirs, &c.*

1. Battely and Somner's Canterbury.
2. Drake's Eboracum.
3. Wharton's Bishops of London and S. Asaph. London, 1695.
4. Wharton and Pegge's Suffragans. Lond. 1785.
5. Bloomfield's Norfolk.
6. Thomas's Worcester.
7. Custumale Roffense.
8. Registrum Roffense.
9. Textus Roffensis.
10. Hunter's See of Somerset. Lond. 1840.
11. Pedler's See of Cornwall. Lond. 1856.
12. Godwin's See of Wells.
13. Haddan's Notes on Bramhall's Works.
14. Strype's Cranmer, &c.
15. Le Neve's Protestant Archbishops.
16. Pegge's Life of Weseham.
17. Lewis's Lives of Peacock and Fisher.
18. Churton's Life of Smith. Oxford, 1800.
19. Budden and Chandler's Lives of Wainfleet ; v. y.
20. Duck and Spencer's Lives of Chicheley ; v. y.
21. Lowth's Life of William of Wykeham. London, 1758.

2.—MANUSCRIPTS.

1. Henry Wharton's. Lambeth.
2. Matthew Hutton's. Harleian.
3. White Kennett's. Lansdowne.
4. Cole's. B. M. Additional. 5798–5887.
5. Cotton's. Cleopatra E. 1, &c.

6. Tanner's and Sancroft's. Bodleian.
7. Torre's. York Chapter House.
8. Ducarel's Abstracts of Canterbury Registers. B. M. Additional 6062–6113.
9. Rymer's MSS. Add. 4573–4630.

II.—ORIGINAL AUTHORITIES.

1.—HISTORIANS.

(a) *Printed Books.*

a. Monumenta Historica Britannica. Ed. Hardy. London, 1848.
    Anglo-Saxon Chronicle.
    Asser.
    Bede's Ecclesiastical History.
    Henry of Huntingdon.
    Florence of Worcester.
    Simeon of Durham.
b. Twysden, Decem Scriptores. Lond. 1652.
    Simeon of Durham.
    John of Hexham.
    Ralph de Diceto.
    Bromton.
    Gervas.
    Thomas Stubbs.
    William Thorne, &c.
c. Gale and Fulman. Oxford, 1684–1687.
    Annals of Margam.
    Annals of Waverley.
    Annals of Wikes.
    Annals of Mailros.
    Heddi's Life of Wilfrid.
    History of Ely.
    History of Ramsey.

d. English Historical Society.
    Walter of Hemingburgh. Lond. 1848.
    William of Newburgh. Lond. 1856.
    Nicolas Trivet. Lond. 1845.
    Adam Murimuth. Lond. 1846.
    Florence of Worcester. Lond. 1848.
e. Camden Society. London.
    Chronicle of Peterborough. 1849.
    Chronicle of Rishanger. 1840.
    Liber de Antiquis Legibus. Chron. Majorum. 1846.
    Chronicle from 1377 to 1461. 1856.
    Machyn's Diary. 1847.
f. Surtees' Society. Durham.
    Scriptores Historiæ Dunelmensis, viz. Coldingham, Graystanes and Chambre. 1839.
g. Hearne's Publications.
    Annals of Dunstaple. 1733.
    Monk of Evesham. Oxford, 1729.
h. Roger of Hoveden. London, 1596.
i. Roger of Wendover. London, 1640.
j. Matthew Paris. London, 1640.
k. Matthew of Westminster. London, 1570.

l. Chronicle of Lanercost. Edinb. 1839.
m. Chronicle of Battle Abbey. Lond. 1846.
n. Eadmer, Historia Novorum. Migne. Paris, 1853.
o. William of Malmsbury. Paris, 1855.
p. Letters of Lanfranc. Paris, 1854.
q. Letters of Anselm. Paris, 1853.

r. Letters of Thomas à Becket, &c. Par. 1854.
s. Pertz, Monumenta Germaniæ Historica. Adam of Bremen. Hanover, 1826, &c.
t. Ordericus Vitalis. Paris, 1619.
u. Chronicon Manniæ. Copenhagen, 1786.
v. Langebek, Scriptores Rerum Danicarum. Copenhagen, 1774, &c.

(β) *Manuscripts.*

Annals 1195–1316	Add. B. M. 5444.
—— 1307–1339 (Chandos)	Lansd. 791.
—— of Tewkesbury	Cotton. Cleop. A. 7.
—— of Dover	Cotton. Julius. D. 5.
—— of Lewes	Cotton. Tiberius. A. 10.
—— of Hagnebie	Cotton. Vespasian. B. 11.
—— of Evesham	Harl. 229.
—— of Southwark	Cotton. Faustina. A. 8.
—— of Rochester and S. Bennet of Hulme	Cotton. Nero. D. 2.
Robert of Redding	Harl. 685. Lansd. 791.
Polistoire of Canterbury	Harl. 636.
Continuation of Gervas	C. C. C. 438.
Obituary of Canterbury (John Stone)	C. C. C. 417.
Eulogium	Cotton. Galba. E. 7.
Continuation of the Polychronicon	Bodleian. Digby. 201.
Ditto, by John Malvern	C. C. C. 197.
Benedict Abbat	Harl. 4321.
Peter of Yckham	Harl. 4323.
Chronicle of Canterbury	Cotton. Galba. E. 3.
Birchington, by Bishop Reade	Cotton. Julius. B. 3.
Ralph de Diceto	Arundel. 220.
John of London	Heralds' College. 20.

2.—RECORDS.

(α) *Printed Books of the Record Commissions.*
(β) *MSS. Public Records at the Rolls' Office.*
(γ) *Miscellaneous Records.*

Vatican Papers	B. M. Additional. 15,351–15,400.
Collection of Precedents	Harl. 862.
State Papers	Vitellius. B.
Register of S. Stephen's Westminster	Faustina. B. 8.

(δ) *Episcopal and other Registers.*

I. Canterbury.   1. Archbishops.   Begin 1279.

    (1) Lambeth.

Peckham.	Whittlesey.	Bouchier. (Imperf.)
Winchelsey. (Also	Sudbury.	Morton. (Ditto.)
Lambeth MS. 244)	Courtenay.	* Dean. (Ditto.)
Reynolds.	Arundel.	Warham. (Ditto.)
Mepeham.	Chicheley.	Pole.
Islip.	Stafford.	Cranmer, &c. down
Langham.	Kemp.	to the end of Potter.

    (2) Vicar General's Office, Doctors' Commons.   From Herring to the present time.

  2. Prior and Convent.

    (1) Rolls of professions of obedience made by the Bishops at their consecration, frequently endorsed with the date and circumstances of the consecration.

    (2) Letters of licence to Bishops elect to be consecrated out of the Metropolitical Church, to which the privilege was secured by immemorial usage and charters of S. Thomas and S. Edmund.

    (3) Miscellaneous Letters on the same subject.

    (4) Registers containing copies of the above, and other memoranda.

    (5) Registers of the Acts of the Prior and Convent during vacancies of the see.

II. London.   1. Bishops.   Begin 1306.   Abstracts. MSS. Harl. 6955, 6956.

Baldock.	Walden.	Gilbert.	Barons.
Gravesend.	Clifford.	Kemp.	Fitz James.
Sudbury.	Kemp.	Hill.	Tunstall.
Courtenay.	Gray.	Savage.	Stokesley.
Braybrook.	Fitzhugh.	Warham.	Bonner.

  2. Dean and Chapter.   MSS. Hutton. Harl. 6955, 6956.

III. Winchester.   Bishops.   Begin 1282.

Pontoise.	Stratford.	Beaufort.	Langton.
Woodlock.	Orlton.	Wainfleet.	Fox.
Sendale.	Edendon.	Courtenay.	Gardiner.
Asser.	Wykeham.		

An elaborate Index of the Winchester Registers made by W. T. Alchin, Esq., of the City of London Library, is in that gentleman's possession.

---

* The Editor, when searching for the Will of Bishop Wells of Sidon, was so fortunate as to discover the portion of Archbishop Dean's Register which contains the Bulls of his appointment and his proceedings with the Suffragans, in the Book " Blamyr" in the Prerogative Office. The existence of this fragment appears to have been unknown to Godwin, Wharton and Le Neve, and had probably never been noticed by Antiquaries, although duly entered in the Catalogue of Wills.

IV. **Ely.** Begin 1336. Abstracts in Cole's MSS. B. M. Add. 5824–7.

Montacute.	Arundel.	Bouchier.	Alcock.
De Lisle.	Fordham.	Gray.	West.

V. **Lincoln.** Abstracts in Hutton's MSS. Harl. 6950–4. Begin 1217.

VI. **Lichfield. Bishops.** Begin 1296.

Langton.	Skirlaw.	Booth.	Smith.
Northburgh.	Scroop.	Boulers.	Blyth.
Stretton.	Heyworth.	Hales.	

VII. **Wells. Bishops.** Stafford, Beckington and Stillington. The Registers begin in 1309, and there are full Abstracts among the Hutton MSS. Harl. 6964–6968.

VIII. **Salisbury. Bishops.** Reg. Neville and Blyth. The Registers begin in 1297. Abstracts, Harl. 6979 and 80.

IX. **Exeter. Bishops.** Begin 1257. Abstracts, MSS. Hutton. 6979–80.

X. **Norwich. Bishops.** Begin 1299.

Salmon.	Bateman.	Courtenay.	Lyhert.
Ayermin.	Percy.	Wakering.	Goldwell.
Bek. (Also	Spencer.	Alnwick.	Nykke.
Harl. 4720.)	Tottington.		

XI. **Worcester. Bishops.** Begin 1268.

Giffard.	Bransford.	Clifford.	Gigliis II.
Gainsbrough.	Thoresby.	Peverell.	Medicis.
Reynolds.	Brian.	Morgan.	Ghinucci.
Maidstone.	Barnet.	Polton.	Latimer.
Cobham.	Whittlesey.	Bouchier.	Bell.
Orlton.	Lynn.	Carpenter.	Heath.
Montacute.	Wakefield.	Alcock.	Pates.
Hemenhale.	Winchcomb.	Morton.	

XII. **Hereford. Bishops.** Begin 1275.

Cantilupe.	Courtenay.	Spofford.	Audley.
Swinfield.	Gilbert.	Beauchamp.	Castello.
Orlton.	Trevenant.	Boulers.	Mayhew.
Charlton.	Mascall.	Stanbery.	Fox.
Trilleck.	Lacy.	Milling.	Skip.
Charlton.	Polton.		

There are extracts by Mr. Reynolds, registrar, communicated by Adam Ottley to Henry Wharton, MS. Lamb. 585, also Harleian 4056 and 6979.

XIII. Chichester.　Bishops.　Begin 1397.

Reade.	Story.	Sherborn.	Day.
Praty.	Fitz James.	Sampson.	

XIV. Rochester.　Bishops.　Begin 1319.

Heath.	Bottlesham.	Brown.	Fitz James.
Sheppey.	Bottlesham.	Wells.	Fisher.
Whittlesey.	Young.	Lowe.	Hilsey.
Trilleck.	Langton.	Savage.	

XV. York.　1. Archbishops.

Gray.	Greenfield.	Waldby.	Booth.
Giffard.	Melton.	Scroop.	Rotherham.
Wickwane.	Zouch.	Bowet.	Savage.
Romain.	Thoresby.	Kemp.	Bainbridge.
Newark.	Neville.	Booth.	Wolsey.
Corbridge.	Arundel.	Neville.	Lee.

2. Dean and Chapter.

(1) Acta Capituli, from the close of the thirteenth century.

(2) Registrum Magnum Album ; a great collection of documents, precedents, and charters. A similar volume of smaller size is in the British Museum ; MS. Lansdowne. 402.

(3) Register during the vacancies of the see. A copy of part of this in MS. Galba. E. 10.

M. Hutton (MS. 6969-6972) made an imperfect abstract of the York Registers. Also Dodsworth. Bodl. MS. MS. Cotton. Vitellius. A. 2. contains Constitutiones Eccl. Ebor.

XVI. Carlisle.　Bishops.　Begin 1292.

Halton.　Ross.　Kirkby.　Welton.　Appleby.

The rest of the Registers before the Reformation are lost. Extracts made at the end of the 16th century by Bishop Robinson are in MS. Lansdowne 721.

XVII. The Registers of Durham also are mostly lost : nor have the existing ones, which have been examined very kindly by the Rev. James Raine, junior, furnished any information for the present work. They are those of Kellaw, Bury, Hatfield, Langley, Fox and Tunstall.

XVIII. Those of S. David's, extracts from which are in MS. Tanner. Bodl. 145, began in 1397, but are lost : nor have the other Welsh Cathedrals any remains of the Records before the 16th century. Bangor begin 1512, S. Asaph 1538, Llandaff 1660.

The Liber Landavensis, an ancient Register of Llandaff, is printed by the Welsh Manuscripts Society. Llandovery, 1840.

ABBREVIATIONS MADE USE OF IN THIS WORK.

Chr. S. .... Saxon Chronicle.

G. P. .... Gesta Pontificum.

C. between the name and the See .... Cardinal.

A. S. C. .... Anglo-Saxon Chronicle.

A. O. .... Athenæ Oxonienses.

A. S. .... Anglia Sacra.

C. D. .... Codex Diplomaticus.

P. R. C. .... Profession Roll, Canterbury.

d. .... died.

res. .... resigned.

dep. .... deposed.

P. A. .... Protestant Archbishops.

Perceval, A. S. .. Perceval on the Apostolical Succession.

Reg. P. & C. ... Register of Prior and Convent.

Reg. D. & C. .. Register of Dean and Chapter.

Subs. .... Subscriptions to Charters in the Codex Diplomaticus.

F. Wig. .... Florence of Worcester.

S. D. .... Simeon of Durham.

N. B. In the column of Consecrators, the see of the Archbishop of Canterbury is not expressed, only the Christian name. The common plan of denoting a Bishop by placing his Christian name before the modern name of his see, has been adopted for convenience. The Editor, however, gives no opinion as to the propriety of the usage.

In all cases in which only one name appears in the column of Consecrators, it is to be understood that at least two other Bishops joined in the rite, whose names are not given by the Authorities, but implied in the general formula "assistentibus aliis Episcopis," which for the sake of brevity is omitted.

COURSE OF EPISCOPAL SUCCESSION

IN ENGLAND.

NOTE.—P. R. C. stands for Profession Roll of Canterbury. Dates, &c. in Italics are in the Saxon portion probable conjectures ; in the latter portions careful deductions from evidence.

× signifies that the event referred to took place between the years mentioned : 711 × 714 means between 711 and 714.

DATE OF CONSECRATION.	NAME.	SEE.	CONSE-CRATORS.	AUTHORITIES, &c.
597 Nov. 16 Arles	S. Augustine, d.604. May 26	Canterbury	Vergilius Arles	W. Thorn. 1760. Bede i. 27. ii. 3. Lingard. A. S. C. i. 367.
604	Mellitus, d.624. Ap. 24	London, Canterbury 619	Augustine	Bede ii. 3. Chr. S. 604.
604	Justus, d.627.Nov.10	Rochester,Canterbury 624	Augustine	Bede ii. 3. Chr. S. 604. subs. 604. Ap. 28.
604	Laurentius, d.619. Feb. 2	Canterbury	Augustine	Bede ii. 3. subs. 604. Ap. 28.
624	Romanus, d. 627.	Rochester	Justus	Bede ii. 8. Chr. S. 616.
625 July 21 Canterbury	Paulinus, d.644. Oct.10	York, Rochester 633.	Justus	Bede ii. 9. Chr. S. 625.
627 Lincoln	Honorius, d.653. Sep. 30	Canterbury	Paulinus	Bede ii.18. Chr.S.627.
630	Felix, d.647. Mar.8	Dunwich	Honorius	Bede ii. 15.
634 Genoa	Birinus, d.650. Dec. 3	Dorchester	Asterius Milan	Bede iii. 7. Chr. S.634.

DATE OF CONSECRATION.	NAME.	SEE.	CONSE-CRATORS.	AUTHORITIES, &c.
635	Aidan, d.651. Aug.31	Lindisfarne	Irish Bishops	Bede iii. 3. The chief Irish Bishops were : Tomian, Armagh, 623 –661. Columban, Meath, d. 651. Croman, Ferns, d. 675. Diman, Connor, d. 656. Baithan, Clonmacnoise, d. 663. Bede ii. 19, and Ware.
644	Ithamar	Rochester	Honorius	Bede iii.14.F.Wig.644.
647	Thomas, d. 652.	Dunwich	Honorius	Bede iii.20.F.Wig.647.
650	Agilbert	Dorchester Paris 664	French Bishops	Bede iii.7. Chr. S.650. F. Wig. 650.
651	Finan, d. 661.	Lindisfarne	Irish Bishops.	Bede iii.25.F.Wig.651.
652	Bertgils, or Boniface, d. 669.	Dunwich	Honorius	Bede iii.20.F.Wig.647.
654 Lindisfarne	Cedda, d. 664. Oct.26	London	Finan and two Bishops	Bede iii. 22.
655 Mar. 26 Canterbury	Deusdedit, or Frithona, d. 664. Jul. 14	Canterbury	Ithamar	Bede iii. 20. Chr.S.655.
655	Damian, d. 664	Rochester	Deusdedit	Bede iii. 20.
656	Diuma, d. 658	Mercia	Finan	Bede iii.21. A.S.I.424.
658	Ceollach, res. 659	Mercia	Finan	Bede iii.21. A.S.I.425.
659	Trumhere, d. 662	Mercia	Finan	Bede iii. 21 and 24.
661	Colman, res.664. d.676	Lindisfarne	Irish Bishops	Bede iii. 25.
662	Jarumnan, d. 667	Mercia	Irish Bishops	Bede iii. 24.

Date of Consecration.	Name.	See.	Conse-crators.	Authorities, &c.
662	Wina, d. 675	Winchester Dorchester 663 London 666	French Bishops	Bede iii. 7.
664	Tuda, d. 664	Lindisfarne	South Irish Bishops	Bede iii. 26.
664	Ceadda, d. 672. Mar. 2	York Lichfield 669	Wina and two British Bishops	Bede iii. 28. Chr. S. 664. Bede iv. 3.
664 Compiegne	Wilfrid, d. 709. Oct. 12	York, 669–678 Restored 686–692 Leicester, 692–705 Hexham, 705–709	Agilbert and 11 Bishops	Bede iii. 28. iv. 12, 13. Heddi. V. Wilfr. ch. 12. 44, &c.
668 Mar. 26 Rome	Theodore, d. 690. Sep. 19	Canterbury	P. Vitalian	Bede iv. 1. v. 8.
669	Putta, d. 688	Rochester Hereford, 676	Theodore	Bede iv. 2. F. Wig. 676. 688.
669	Bisi	Dunwich	Theodore	Bede iv. 5. F. Wig. 673.
670	Leutherius, d. 676.	Dorchester	Theodore	Bede iii. 7. Chr. S. 670. F. Wig. 670. subs. 676.
672	Winfrid, dep. 675.	Lichfield	Theodore	Bede iv. 3. F. Wig. 672.
673	Bedwin	Elmham	Theodore	Bede iv. 5. F. Wig. 673. subs. 693.
673	Etti	Dunwich	Theodore	Bede iv. 5. F. Wig. 673.
675	Saxulf, d. 691.	Lichfield	Theodore	Bede iv. 6. F. Wig. 675. Heddi c. 44. subs. 676.
675	Erkenwald, d. [693] Ap. 30	London	Theodore	Bede iv. 6. F. Wig. 675. subs. 676–692.
676	Cuichelm, res. 678.	Rochester	Theodore	Bede iv. 12. F. Wig. 676.
676 London	Headda, d. 705. July 7	Winchester	Theodore	Bede iv. 12. Chr. S. 676. F. Wig. 676. subs. 676–701.

Date of Consecration.	Name.	See.	Conse- crators.	Authorities, &c.
678 York	Bosa, d. 705. Eadhed, res. 678. Eata d.[686] Oct.26	York Lindsey Hexham, 678–681. Lindisfarne, 678–685. Hexham, 685, 6.	Theodore	Cf. Malms. G. P. iii. Heddi c. 52. Bede iv.12. Chr.S.678. F.Wig. 677.
678	Gebmund	Rochester	Theodore	Bede iv.12. subs. 693.
680	Bosel, res. 691.	Worcester	Theodore	F. Wig. 680.
680	Cuthwin	Leicester	Theodore	F. Wig. Catalogue.
680	Ethelwin	Lindsey	Theodore	Bede iv. 12.
681	Trumwin, res. 686.	Whithern	Theodore	Bede iv.12.Chr. S.681. F. Wig. 681.
681	Trumbert, dep. 684.	Hexham	Theodore	Bede iv.12. Chr.S.681. F. Wig. 681.
685 Mar. 26 York	Cuthbert, d.687.Mar.20	Lindisfarne	Theodore and seven Bishops	Bede iv.28. Chr.S.685. F. Wig. 685.
687 *Aug.* 25	John, res. 718. d.721. May 7	Hexham York 705.	[*Theodore*]	Bede v. 2. Chr. S. 685 –721.
688	Eadbert, d. 698. May 6	Lindisfarne		Bede iv. 29. F. Wig. 688.
688	Tyrhtel	Hereford		F.Wig. 688. subs.693.
691	Hedda	Lichfield		Subs. 693–706.
692	Oftfor	Worcester	Wilfrid	Bede iv.23.F.Wig.691. subs. 693.
693	Suidbert	Friesland	Wilfrid	Bede v. 11.
693 June 29 Lyons	Brihtwald, d. 731. Jan. 9	Canterbury	Godwin Ly- ons	Bede v. 8. Chr. S. 693. F. Wig. 693. subs. 693–706.
693	Waldhere	London		V.Bede iv.11.subs.704.
693	Ecgwin d.717.Dec.30	Worcester		F.Wig. 692.
693	Tobias d. 726	Rochester	Brihtwald	Bede v. 8. subs. 706.

DATE OF CONSECRATION.	NAME.	SEE.	CONSE-CRATORS.	AUTHORITIES, &c.
698	Eadfrith, d. 721.	Lindisfarne		F. Wig. 699.
705	Daniel, res. 744	Winchester d. 745	Brihtwald	Bede v.18. F.Wig. 705. subs. 705–737.
705	Aldhelm, d. 709. May 25	Sherborn	Brihtwald	Bede v. 18. F.Wig. 705.
693 × 706	Nothbert	Elmham		Subs. 706. F.Wig. Catal.
680 × 706	Eadgar	Lindsey		Bede iv. 12. subs. 706.
704 × 706	Ingwald, d. 745	London		Bede v. 23. subs. 706–737.
709	Eadbert	Selsey		Bede v. 18.
709	Forthere	Sherborn		Bede v. 18. Chr. S. 709 and 737. subs. 712–737.
709	Acca, dep. 732, 3.	Hexham d. 740. Oct. 20		Bede v. 20. Chr. S. 710. Sim. D. 740.
710	Torthere	Hereford		F. Wig. 710. subs. 727.
717	Wilfrid, d. 743 or 745	Worcester		Bede v. 23. F.Wig. 717. subs. 718–743.
718	Wilfrid, d. 732	York	John	Bede v. 6. F.Wig. 721.
706 × 731	Heatholac	Elmham		Bede v. 23.
675 × 731	Astwulf	Dunwich		Aldberht. Bede v. 23.
709 × 714	Eolla, d. before 731	Selsey		Bede v. 18. subs. 714.
721	Aldwin or Wor, d. 737	Lichfield		Bede v. 23. subs. 727–736.
724	Ethelwold, d. 740	Lindisfarne		Bede v. 23. F.Wig. 721. Sim. D. 740. A.S. i. 696.
706 × 731	Kinbert, d. 732.	Lindsey		Bede iv. 12. Sim. D. 732.
727	Eadulf	Rochester	Brihtwald	Bede v. 23. Chr. S. 727. F.Wig. 726. subs. 735 –738.
727 × 731	Wahlstod	Hereford		Bede v. 23.
730	Pecthelm, d. 735	Whithern		Bede v. 23.
731 June 10 Canterbury	Tatwin, d.734. July 30	Canterbury	Daniel Ingwald Eadulf Aldwin	Bede v. 23. Chr. S. 731. F.Wig. 731. subs. 732.

DATE OF CONSECRATION.	NAME.	SEE.	CONSE-CRATORS.	AUTHORITIES, &c.
733	Alwig, d. 750	Lindsey	Tatwin	Cont.Bede. Sim.D.733. subs. 737–747.
733	Sigga, or Sigfrid	Selsey	Tatwin	Cont.Bede. Sim.D.733. subs. 737–747.
734	Egbert, d.766.Nov.19	York	[Tatwin]	Chr. S. 734. Sim. D. 735.
734 Sep. 8	Frithbert, d.766. Dec.23	Hexham	Egbert	F. Wig. 739. Sim. D. 734.
735	Nothelm, d.740.Oct.17	Canterbury	[Egbert]	Chr.S.736. F.Wig.734. subs. 738.
735 Aug.14 York	Frithwald, d.763. May 7	Whithern	Egbert	F. Wig. 735. Sim. Dun. 764.
736	Cuthbert, d.758.Oct.26	Hereford Canterbury740	Nothelm	Sim. D. 736. subs. 737 –758.
736	Ethelfrith	Elmham	Nothelm	Sim. D. 736.
736	Herewald	Sherborn	Nothelm	Sim. D. 736. subs. 737 –759 and *766.
737	Huitta,	Lichfield		Sim. D. 737. subs. 747 –749.
737	Torthelm, or Totta	Leicester d. 764		Sim. D. 737. subs. 747 –758.
740	Cynewulf, res. 780	Lindisfarne d. 782.		S. Dun. 740.
741	Podda	Hereford	Cuthbert	F.Wig. 741. subs. 747.
741	Dunno	Rochester	Cuthbert	Chr.S.741. F.Wig.741. subs. 747.
736 × 758	Eanfrith	Elmham		Subs. 758.
743	Milred, d. 775	Worcester		F. Wig. 743. subs. 743 –774.
744	Hunferth	Winchester		Chr.S.744. F.Wig.744. subs. 747–749.
745	Ecgwulf	London		S. Dun. 745. subs. 747 –759, and *766.
731 × 747	Eardred, or Eardulf	Dunwich		Malms. G. P. Lib. i. Council of Cloveshoo.
†747	Eardulf	Rochester		Subs. 747–765.

* Dates marked with an asterisk refer to doubtful Charters.

† The signatures to the Council of Cloveshoo in 742 are fabricated. Those to the Council of 747 are given in Malmsbury G. P. lib. i. With regard to the Bishops of Dunwich nothing is known. I have inserted their names at such intervals as seemed probable from their position in the Catalogues.

DATE OF CONSECRATION.	NAME.	SEE.	CONSE-CRATORS.	AUTHORITIES, &c.
750	Eadulf	Lindsey		S. Dun. 750. subs. 758.
752	Hemele	Lichfield		A. S. i. 428.
754	Kinheard	Winchester		Chr. S. 754. F. Wig. 754. subs. 755–759 & *766.
747 × 758	Hecca	Hereford		Subs. 758.
	Cuthwin	Dunwich		F. Wig. Catalogue.
759 Sep. 29 Canterbury	Bregwin, d. 765. Aug. 25	Canterbury	[*Egbert*]	Chr. S. 759. F. Wig. 759. subs. 762–764. A. S. ii. 75.
763 July 17 Aelfetee	Petwin, d. 776. Sep. 19	Whithern	Egbert	Chr. S. 763. F. Wig. 763.
764	Eadbert	Leicester		Sim. D. 764. subs. 764 –781.
765	Cuthfrith	Lichfield		S. Dun. 765. subs. 767
	Wighed	London		F. Wig. Catalogue.
758 × 770	Ceadda	Hereford		Subs. 770. C. D. 1009 ?
747 × 765	Aluberht	Selsey		F. Wig. Catalogue.
747 × 765	Osa	Selsey		Subs. 765–770.
766 Feb. 2	Jaenbert, d. 790. Aug. 11	Canterbury	[*Egbert*]	Chr. S. 763. Sim. Dun. 765. subs. 765–789.
767 Ap. 24	Ethelbert, or Coena	York, d. 780		Chr. S. 766. Sim. Dun. 767.
	Alhmund, d. 781. Sep. 7.	Hexham	[*Jaenbert*]	
	Aldberht	London		Subs. 775–785.
	Ceolwulf, d. 796	Lindsey		Subs. 767–794.
768	Hadwin	Machni (Mayo) ?		S. Dun. 768.
768	Berhthun	Lichfield		A. S. i. 428. subs. 774 –777.
765 × 775	Diora	Rochester		Subs. 775–781.
773	Leuferth	Mayo ?		S. Dun. 773.
775	Weremund	Worcester		F. Wig. 775. subs. 775.
777	Tilhere	Worcester		F. Wig. 778. subs. 777 –780.
777	Aldberht	Hereford		Subs. electus 777–781.
777 June 15 York	Ethelbert d. 797. Oct. 16	Whithern Hexham 789	Ethelbert	Chr. S. 777. F. Wig. 778. S. Dun. 777.
766 × 778	Ethelmod	Sherborn		Subs. 778–789.

Date of Consecration.	Name.	See.	Conse-crators.	Authorities, &c.
766 × 778	Ethelhard	Winchester		F. Wig. Catalogue.
766 × 778	Ecgbald	Winchester		Subs. 778–781.
	Aldberht	Dunwich		F. Wig. Catalogue.
779	Higbert, archbp. 785	Lichfield		Electus 779. subs. Arch. 785–801.
	Ecglaf	Dunwich		F. Wig. Catalogue.
770 × 780	Gislehere	Selsey		Subs. 780–781.
758 × 781	Ethelwulf	Elmham		Subs. 781.
Before 781	Heardred	Dunwich		Subs. 781–789.
780	Eanbald, d. 796. Aug. 10	York	Ethelbert	Chr. S. 780. F. Wig. 781. Sim. Dun. 780.
781 Oct. 2 Wulfswell	Tilbert, d. 789	Hexham	Eanbald	Chr. S. 780. F. Wig. 779.
781 Sockburn	Higbald, d. 802. May 25	Lindisfarne	Eanbald	Chr. S. 780. F. Wig. 799. Sim. D. 781.
781	Heathored, d. 798	Worcester		F. Wig. 781. subs. 781 –798.
781 × 785	Unwona	Leicester		F. Wig. 785. subs. 785 –799.
781 × 785	Dudda	Winchester		F. Wig. Catalogue.
781 × 785	Kinbert	Winchester		Subs. 785–801.
781 × 785	Totta	Selsey		Subs. 785.
781 × 785	Esne	Hereford		Subs. 785.
781 × 785	Weremund	Rochester		Subs. 785–803.
781 × 785	Alheard	Elmham		Subs. 785–811.
785 Corbridge	Aldulf	Migensis *Mayo ?*	{ Eanbald Tilbert Higbald	Sim. Dun. 786. Council of Cealchythe.
785 × 788	Ceolmund	Hereford		Subs. 788–793.
785 × 789	Wiohthun	Selsey		Subs. 789–805.
785 × 789	Eadgar	London		Subs. 789.
790	Aelhun, d. 797	Dunwich		Subs. 790–793.
791 July 17 Hearrahaleh	Badulf	Whithern	{ Eanbald Ethelbert	Chr. S. 791. F. Wig. 791. Sim. D. 790.
793 July 21	Ethelhard, d. 805. May 12	Canterbury		F. Wig. 790 and 793. subs. 793–805.
789 × 793	Kenwalch	London		Sim. D. 791. subs. 793.
793	Denefrith	Sherborn	Ethelhard	P. R. C. subs. 794–796.

DATE OF CONSECRATION.	NAME.	SEE.	CONSE-CRATORS.	AUTHORITIES, &c.
793	Eadbald	London		Chr. S. 794.
794	Heathobert, d. 801	London		Subs. 798–799.
793 × 798	Utel	Hereford		Subs. 798–799.
796	Eadulf	Lindsey	Ethelhard	P. R. C. Electus 796. subs. 796–836.
796 Aug. 14 Sockburn	Eanbald	York	{ Ethelbert Higbald Baldulf	Chr. S. 796. fl. 808. Ep. P.Leo III. Mansi, 13. 974.
797 Oct. 29 Wduford	Heardred	Hexham	{ Eanbald Higbald	Chr. S. 797.
798	Tidferth	Dunwich	Ethelhard	P. R. C. Chr. S. 797. subs. 798–816.
798	Deneberht, d. 822. F.W.	Worcester	Ethelhard	P. R. C. F. Wig. 798. subs. 801–817.
796 × 801	Wigbert	Sherborn		Chr. S. 812. subs. 801–816.
801 × 803	Aldulf	Lichfield		Subs. 803–814.
800	Wulfhard	Hereford	Ethelhard	P. R. C. subs. 801–822.
800 Ettingaham	Eanbert, d. 806 or 814	Hexham	Eanbald	R. Hexham, c. 299. Chr. S. 806.
802	Alhmund	Winchester		Subs. 803–805.
802	Osmund	London		Subs. 803–805.
802	Werenbert	Leicester		Subs. 803–814.
803 June 11 Bigwell	Egbert	Lindisfarne	{ Eanbald Eanbert Badulf	F.Wig. 802. Sim. Dun. 803.
†803 or 4	Beornmod	Rochester	Ethelhard	P.R.C. Chr.S.801,802. F.Wig.802. subs.805 –842.

† After a careful examination of the Chronology of the Saxon Chronicle, I am obliged, notwithstanding the arguments in the Introduction to the Mon. Hist. Brit., to conclude that there is an error of two or three years in many of the entries from 794 to 851. This will appear from a comparison of the true dates of the mutilation of P. Leo (799, Chr. S. 797), and the deaths of Charlemagne (814, Chr. S. 812), and Leo (816, Chr. S. 814): of the dates assigned by the Charters to the death of Ethelhard (805, Chr. S. 803), accession of Ceolwulf (822, Chr. S. 819), Council of Cloveshoo (825, Chr. S. 822), second reign of Withlaf (830, Chr. S. 828), death of Egbert (838–9, Chr. S. 836), and the death of Osmod at Carrum (Chr. S. 833), who appears as a witness in 835. This will account for the dates assigned to Archbishops Feologild and Ceolnoth. If those of the Chr. S. be correct, we must suppose that these were consecrated successively as coadjutors to Wulfred, a view which possibly may be supported by C. D. 225.

Date of Consecration.	Name.	See.	Conse-crators.	Authorities, &c.
805 [*Aug.*3]	Wulfred, d.832. Mar.24	Canterbury	*Aldulf Werenbert Denebert Eadulf Wulfhard Alheard Tidferth Osmund Alhmund Wiohthun Wigbert Beornmod*	Compare the Charters C. D. 190 and 196, from which it would appear that Wulfred was consecrated between the 1st and 6th of August, in the Council of Acle. Chr. S. 803–829. subs. 805 Aug. 6 to 831 Aug. 28.
806	Tidferth	Hexham		806–821. Ang.S.i.699.
805 × 811	Ethelwulf	Selsey		Subs. 811–816.
805 × 811	Ethelnoth	London	Wulfred	P. R. C. subs. 811–816.
805 × 811	Wigthen, d. 833 or 836	Winchester	Wulfred	P. R. C. subs. 811–828.
After 808	Wulfsy	York		812 (Richardson.)
811 × 814	Sibba	Elmham		Subs. 814–816.
815	Herewin	Lichfield	Wulfred	P. R. C. subs. 816–817.
816	Hrethun	Leicester	Wulfred	P. R. C. subs. 816–839.
816 × 824	Hunferth	Elmham	Wulfred	P. R. C. Subs. 822–825.
818	Ethelwald, d. 828 or 831	Lichfield		A.S.i.431.Chr.S.828.
816 × 824	Ceolbert	London	Wulfred	P. R. C. subs. 824–839.
816 × 824	Cenred	Selsey		Subs. 824–838. fl. 852. Chr. S.
816 × 824	Weremund	Dunwich		Subs. 824.
821	Heathored	Lindisfarne		F.Wig. 819. Sim. Dun. c. 13.
822	Eadbert	Worcester	Wulfred	P. R. C. F. Wig. 822. subs. 822–845.
823	Beonna	Hereford		Subs. 824–825.
824	Heahstan, d. 867	Sherborn		Chr.S.823. F.Wig.816. subs.electus 824–862.
816 × 824	Humbert, d.870.Nov.20	Elmham		Subs. 824–838. Asser. 856. S.D. 870.

DATE OF CONSECRATION.	NAME.	SEE.	CONSE-CRATORS.	AUTHORITIES, &c.
825	Wilred	Dunwich		Electus 825. subs. 825 –845.
825	Herefrith, d. 833 or 836	Winchester	Wulfred	Chr. S. 833. subs. 825 –826. Coadjutor to Wigthen ?
828	Humbert	Lichfield	Wulfred	P. R. C.
825 × 831	Eadulf	Hereford	Wulfred	P. R. C. subs. 836.
830	Egred	Lindisfarne ·		S. Dun. 830.
832 June 9	Feologild, d.832. Aug.29	Canterbury		Chr. S. 829. Cf. Note p. 9.
833 Aug. 24	Ceolnoth, d. 870. Feb. 4	Canterbury		Chr.S.830. F.Wig.830. subs. 833–868. Cf. Gervas, 1643.
833 × 836	Edmund, or Eadhun	Winchester	Ceolnoth	P. R. C. subs. 836–838.
833 × 836	Kynferth	Lichfield	Ceolnoth	P. R. C. subs. 836–841.
837	Cuthwulf	Hereford		Subs. 838–857.
837	Wigmund	York		Sim. Dun. c. 78.
838	Berhtred	Lindsey	Ceolnoth	P. R. C. subs. 839–869.
838	Helmstan	Winchester	Ceolnoth	P. R. C. subs. 838–841.
839 × 840	Aldred	Leicester		F. Wig. Catalogue.
840	Ceolred	Leicester	Ceolnoth	P. R. C. subs. 840–869.
844	Tatnoth	Rochester	[Ceolnoth]	Electus 844: subs. 845.
841 × 844	Tunberht	Lichfield	Ceolnoth	P. R. C. subs. 844–857.
845	Eanberht, d. 854	Lindisfarne		F. Wig. 845. S. Dun. 846.
848	Aelhun, d. 872	Worcester		F. Wig. 848. subs. 848–869.
852	Swithun, d. 862. July 2	Winchester	Ceolnoth	P. R. C. subs. 858–862. A. S. i. 202.
854	Wulfhere, d. 900	York		S. Dun. 854, and c. 79.
854	Eardulf, d. 899	Lindisfarne [Chester le Street 883]	Wulfhere	F. Wig. 854. S. Dun. 854 & 883.

Date of Consecration.	Name.	See.	Conse-crators.	Authorities, &c.
839 × 860	Deorwulf	London	Ceolnoth	P. R. C. subs. 860–862.
852 × 860	Gutheard	Selsey		Subs. 860–862.
845 × 862	Weremund (Badenoth ?)	Rochester		Subs. 860–862. A. S. i. 331.
857 × 866	Mucel	Hereford		F. Wig. Catalogue.
862	Alfred	Winchester	Ceolnoth	P. R. C. subs. 868–871.
857 × 866	Deorlaf	Hereford	Ceolnoth	P. R. C. subs. 866–884.
857 × 866	Eadbald	[Mercia]		Subs. 866.
857 × 866	Wulfsy	[Mercia]		Subs. 866.
862 × 868	Cuthwulf	Rochester		Subs. 868.
	Swithulf	London		F. Wig. Catalogue.
866 × 869	Eadbert	[Lichfield]		Subs. 869–875.
868	Heahmund, d. 871. Chr. S.	Sherborn		Subs. 868–870.
845 × 870	Ethelwald	Dunwich	Ceolnoth	P. R. C.
870	Ethelred, d.889.June30	Canterbury		Chr. S. 870. Called Bishop of Wiltshire. subs. 871–875.
872	Etheleage	Sherborn		Subs. 871 × 878.
873 June 7	Werefrith, d. 915	Worcester	Ethelred	F. Wig. 872. subs. 873–904.
872 × 877	Tumbert	Winchester		Subs. 877.
875 × 880	Wulfred	[Lichfield]		Subs. 880–888.
879	Denewulf, d. 908. Chr. S.	Winchester		F. Wig. 879–909. subs. 882–904.
868 × 880	Swithulf, d. 897	Rochester		Chr. S. 897. subs. 880.
869 × 888	Alheard, d. 895–7	Dorchester		Chr. S. 897. subs. 888.
872 × 889	Wulfsy, or Alfsy	Sherborn		Subs. 889–892.
888	Cynemund	Hereford		Electus 888. subs. 888.
890	Plegmund, d. 914. Aug.2	Canterbury		Chr. S. 890–923. subs. 895–910. d. 914. F. Wig.
892 × 900	Asser	Sherborn		Subs. 900–904.
	Heahstan, d. 898–900	London		Chr.S.898. F.Wig.900.

Date of Consecration.	Name.	See.	Conse- crators.	Authorities, &c.
898	Wulfsy	London		Subs. 901–910.
900	Ethelbald	York		Sim. Dun. 900.
900	Cutheard, d. 915	Chester le Street		F. Wig. 900.
888 × 901	Eadgar	Hereford		Subs. 901–930.
889 × 901	Wigmund	[Lichfield]		Subs. 901–909.
862 × 904	Wighelm	[Selsey]		Subs. 904–909.
897 × 904	Ceolmund	Rochester		Subs. 904–909.
†909	Frithstan, res. 931	Winchester, d. 933. Sep. 10		Subs. 909–929.
	Beornege	Selsey		Subs. 926–929.
	Ceolwulf	Dorchester		
	Athelm, d. 923. Jan. 8	Wells	Plegmund	F. Wig. 914.
		Canterbury 914		
	Eadulf	Crediton		Subs. 926–934.
	Ethelstan	Ramsbury		Subs. 910.
	Ethelward	Sherborn		Subs. 910.
915	Tilred	Chester le Street		F. Wig. 915.
915	Ethelhun	Worcester		F. Wig. 915.
910 × 918	Werstan	Sherborn		F. Wig. Catalogue.
918	Ethelbald	Sherborn		Fl. Wig. 918.
922	Wilferth	Worcester		F. Wig. 922.
914	Wulfhelm d. 942. Feb. 12	Wells Canterbury 923	Athelm	Cons. 914. F. Wig. Chr. S. 925. subs. 923–941.
909 × 926	Kynferth	Rochester		Subs. 926–931.
923	Elphege	Wells	Wulfhelm	Subs. 930–937.

† The division of the Wessex dioceses, and the consecration of the seven Bishops by Pleg-mund, are a crux in chronology. Ethelred, archbishop of Canterbury, is said to have been Bishop of Wiltshire (Chr. S. 870), and before that Wigthen and Herefrith seem to have divided the administration of Winchester, the latter perhaps acting as coadjutor. That the diocese was divided in 909 is certain from charters, and that the division originated the dioceses of Wells, Ramsbury (Corvinensis), and Crediton, is agreeable with probability and tradition. There is nothing unlikely in the consecration of seven Bishops together, nor in the circum-stance that tradition should record such an event. The difficulties have arisen from attempts of late writers to fill in the outline of the tradition. The names of Werstan, Bishop of Sher-born, and Ethelstan, Bishop of Cornwall, are commonly inserted. I believe that Werstan is merely a corrupt reading of Ethelstan, and that Ramsbury, and neither Sherborn, Crediton, nor Cornwall, was his diocese: and that Ethelward, whose signature appears in Charters of 909, and who Godwin says was a son of king Alfred, was the Bishop of Sherborn who succeeded Asser (Cf. Liber de Antiquis Legibus, page 212). V. Malmsb. G. R. lib. ii. c. 129. A. S. i. 554.

Date of Consecration.	Name.	See.	Conse-crators.	Authorities, &c.
909 × 926	Elfwin, or Ella	Lichfield		Subs. 926–935.
910 × 926	Heahstan	London		F. Wig. Catalogue.
910 × 926	Theodred	London		Subs. 926–951.
918 × 926	Sigelm	Sherborn		Subs. 926–932.
909 × 926	Winsy	Dorchester		Subs. 926–934.
925 × 927	Odo, d.959. June 2	Ramsbury Canterbury 942	Wulfhelm	Subs. 927–959. A. S. ii. 80.
928	Wigred, d. 944	Chester le Street		F. Wig. 928. Sim. D. 925. Other suffragans of York are, Earnulf 929. Columban 929. Escbert 929–931. Eadward 931. Sexhelm 931.
904 × 928	Rodewald	York		Subs. 928–930.
929	Kinewold	Worcester		F. Wig. 929–957. subs. 930–957.
930	Tidhelm	Hereford		Subs. 930–934.
Before 931	Kinsy	Berkshire [*Lichfield* 949]		Subs. 931–934. & 949 –963. V. C. D. 1129. Cf. A. S. i. 804.
924 × 931	Conan	Cornwall		Subs. 931–934.
931	Wulfhun	Selsey		Subs. 931–940.
931	Wulfstan, d.956. Dec.26	York		Subs. 931–955. Stubbs 1698.
931 May 29	Beornstan, d.934. Nov.1	Winchester		Chr. S. 931. subs. 931–934.
933	Alfred, d.941–943.	Sherborn		Subs. 933–943. F. Wig. 941.
933	Burrhic	Rochester		Subs. 934–946.
934	Elphege, d.951.*Mar.*12	Winchester		Chr. S. 934–951. subs. 933–951.
934	Ethelgar	Crediton		Subs. 934–953.
938	Wulfhelm	Wells		Subs. 938–955.
934 × 939	Wulfhelm	Hereford		Subs. 939–940. also 934 ?
935 × 941	Wulfgar	Lichfield		Subs. 941–948.
941	Alfric	Hereford		Subs. 941–951.
943	Wulfsy	Sherborn		Subs. 943–958.
940 × 944	Alfred	Selsey		Subs. 944–953.

DATE OF CONSECRATION.	NAME.	SEE.	CONSE-CRATORS.	AUTHORITIES, &c.
942	Alfric	Ramsbury		C. D. 1151. Mon. Hist. Brit. 620.
942 × 952	Osulf, d. 970.	Ramsbury		Subs. 952–970.
944	Uhtred	ChesterleStreet		F. Wig. 944.
942 × 956	Eadulf	Elmham	Odo	P. R. C. subs. 956–964.
947	Sexhelm	ChesterleStreet		F. Wig. 944.
†946 × 949	Beorhtsy	[Rochester] ?		Subs. 949–951.
950	Oskytel, d.971. Nov.1	Dorchester York 958		Chr. S. 971. subs. 952–969.
951	Alfsin	Winchester Canterbury 959		F. Wig. 951–959. subs. 952–958.
953	Elfwold, d. 972	Crediton		F. Wig. 953. subs. 953–970.
Before 953	Leofwin	Lindsey Dorchester 958		Subs. 953–965.
951 × 953	Wulfstan	London		
951 × 953	Brihthelm	London		Subs. 953–959.
951 × 955	Daniel	[Rochester, or Selsey]		Subs. 955–959.
956	Brihthelm, d. 973	Wells		Electus 956. subs. 956–973.
957	Ealdred, d. 968	ChesterleStreet		A. S. i. 700. F. Wig. 968.
957 Canterbury	Dunstan, d.988.May 19	Worcester London 959 Canterbury 960	Odo	F. Wig. 957–959. subs. 958–988. Cant. 960. Oct. 21.
958	Elfwold, d. 978	Sherborn		Chr.S. 978. F.Wig. 958. subs. 961–975.
931 × 967	Comoere	Cornwall		Subs. "Temp. R. Edgar."
960	Brihthelm, d. 963	Winchester		Subs. 960–961.
961	Elfstan	London		Subs. 961–995.

† Several Bishops, whose Sees can only be guessed, subscribe between 930 and 970, e. g. Alfred 933–934, (Lindsey or Elmham): Brihthelm 938, (Wessex): Beorhtsy, Daniel, Ethelwald 945–949, (Elmham, or possibly he was a suffragan of York during the disgrace of Wulfstan. Cf. Stubbs 1699, C. D. 1154, &c.) Wulfric 963–970 perhaps is Elfric of Elmham. I have ventured with great diffidence to differ from Wharton (A. S. i. 804) about the Bishops of Lichfield.

Date of Consecration.	Name.	See.	Conse-crators.	Authorities, &c.
961	Oswald, d.992.Feb.29	Worcester York 972	Dunstan	F. Wig. 960. subs. 961–991.
961 × 964	Elfstan	Rochester		Subs. 964–995.
958 × 963	Eadhelm	Selsey		Subs. 963–979.
963 Nov.29	Ethelwold d.984. Aug.1	Winchester	Dunstan	Chr. S. 963. subs. 964–984.
964	Winsy	Lichfield		Subs. 964–973.
951 × 973	Athulf	Hereford		Subs. 973–1012.
968 York	Elfsy, d. 990	ChesterleStreet	Oskytel	F. Wig. 968. Sim. Dun. c. 26.
964 × 975	Elfric	Elmham		F. Wig. Catalogue.
Before 967	Wulfsy	Cornwall		Subs. 967–980.
970	Elfstan, d. 981	Ramsbury		Subs. 974–980.
973	Elphege	Lichfield		Subs. 975–1002.
973	Sideman, d.977. Ap.30	Crediton		Chr. S. 977. subs. 974–975.
973	Kineward, d.975. Jun.30	Wells		Chr. S. 975. subs. 975.
963 × 972	Gucan	Llandaff	⎰ Dunstan Ethelwold Elfwold Oswald Brihthelm ⎱	Lib. Landav.
965 × 974	Eadnoth	Dorchester		Subs. 975.
964 × 975	Theodred	Elmham		Subs. 975.
975	Sigar	Wells		F. Wig. 975. subs. 979–995.
975 × 979	Escwy	Dorchester		Subs. 979–1002.
977	Elfric	Crediton		F. Wig. 977. subs. 979–985.
978	Ethelsy	Sherborn		F. Wig. 978. subs. 979–990.
980 May 2	Ethelgar d. 989. Dec. 3	Selsey Canterbury 988	Dunstan	Chr. S. 980–988. F. Wig. 980. subs. 980–988.
981	Wulgar	Ramsbury		Chr. S. 981. subs. 982–984.
Before 982	Theodred	Elmham		Subs. 982–995.

Date of Consecration.	Name.	See.	Conse-crators.	Authorities, &c.
984 Oct. 19 Canterbury	Elphege, or Godwin, d.1012.Ap.19	Winchester Canterbury 1005. Nov.16	Dunstan	Chr.S.984–1006–1012. subs. 985–1009.
985	Siric, d.994. Oct.28	Ramsbury Canterbury 990	Dunstan	Chr. S. 990. subs. 985–994.
988	Elfwold	Crediton		Subs. 988–1008.
989	Ordbriht	Selsey		F. Wig. 988. subs. 990–1008.
990	Elfric, d.1005.Nov.16	Ramsbury Canterbury 995. Ap. 21	Siric	Chr. S. 994–1005. Subs. 994–1005.
990	Aldhun, d. 1018.	ChesterleStreet		F.Wig. He removed the see to Durham 995.
992	Wulfsy	Sherborn		Subs. 993–1001.
992	Aldulf, d.1002.May6	Worcester York 995		Chr.S.992. F.Wig.992. Electus A. 995. subs 994–1001.
980 × 993	Ealdred	Cornwall		Subs. 993–1002.
995 × 1005	Bledri, d. 1022	Llandaff	Elfric	Lib. Landav. Diceto 461.
995	Godwin	Rochester		Subs. 995–1046.
995	Elfstan	Elmham		Subs. 997–1001.
996	Wulfstan	London	Elfric	Chr. S. 996. subs. 997–1003.
Before 997	Sigeferth	Lindsey		Subs. 997–1004.
997	Elfwin	Wells		Subs. 997–998.
999	Living, or Elfstan, d.1020.Jun.12	Wells Canterbury 1013		Chr. S. 1013–1019. subs. 999–1019.
1001	Alfgar, d.1021.Dec.25	Elmham		Subs. 1001–1018. res. 1016. A.S. i. pag. ult.
1001	Ethelric	Sherborn		Subs. 1002–1009.
1002	Alfhelm	Dorchester		Subs. 1002–1005.
1002 × 1004	Godwin	Lichfield		Subs. 1004–1008.
1003	Wulfstan, d.1023.May28	Worcester and York	[*Elfric*]	Subs. 1004–1022. Stubbs 1700.
1004	Elfwin	London		Subs. 1004–1012.
1005	Kenulf, d. 1006	Winchester		F. Wig. 1006.

Date of Consecration.	Name.	See.	Conse-crators.	Authorities, &c.
1005	Brihtwold, d. 1045	Ramsbury		Chr.S.1006.F.Wig.995. subs. 1005–1045.
1006	Eadnoth, d. 1016	Dorchester	[*Elphege*]	Hist. Ramsey, 69. F.Wig.1016.subs.1012.
1006	Ethelwold	Winchester		F. Wig. 1006. subs. 1007–1012.
1009	Elmer	Selsey		F. Wig. 1009. subs. 1012–1031.
1008 × 1012	Eadnoth,	Crediton		Subs. 1012–1019.
1009 × 1012	Ethelsie	Sherborn		Subs. 1012–1014.
	Brihtwy	Sherborn		?
	Godwin	Rochester		Subs. 1046.
1012	Ethelstan, d.1056.Feb.10	Hereford		Subs. 1012–1052.
1013	Ethelwin	Wells		Subs. 1018–1023.
	Brihtwin	Wells		Subs. 1018.
1014 Feb.16 York	Elfwy	London	[*Wulfstan*]	Chr. S. 1014. subs. 1015–1035.
1014	Alfsin, d. 1032	Winchester		F. Wig. 1015. subs. 1014–1033.
1016	Ethelric, d. 1034	Dorchester		Subs. 1020–1033.
1016	Alwin	Elmham		Subs. 1019–1022.
1016	Leofsin, d.1033.Aug.19	Worcester		F. Wig. 1016. subs. 1016–1022.
1017	Elmer	Sherborn		Subs. 1020–1022. W.Thorn 1783.
1002 × 1018	Burwold	Cornwall		Subs. 1018.
1020 Nov.13 Canterbury	Ethelnoth, d.1038.Oct.29	Canterbury Pall 1022.Oct.7	Wulfstan	Chr. S. 1020. subs. 1020–1033.
1020	Leofgar	Lichfield		A. S. i. 432.
1020 Winchester	Edmund, d. 1040	Durham	Wulfstan	F. Wig. 1020.
1022	Bernhard	Scania	Ethelnoth	Ad.Bremen. Pertz. Vol. 9. p. 325.
	Reinhert	Fionia	Ethelnoth	
	Gerbrand	Roskilde	Ethelnoth	Subs. 1022.
1023 Canterbury	Elfric Puttoc, d.1051.Jan.22	York Worcester 1040–1	Ethelnoth	Chr. S. 1023. F. Wig. 1023.subs.1033–1049.
1023	Brihtwy	Sherborn		Subs. 1023–1045.

DATE OF CONSECRATION.	NAME.	SEE.	CONSE-CRATORS.	AUTHORITIES, &c.
1026	Brihtmar, d. 1039	Lichfield		Subs. 1026–1033.
1027	Living, d.1046.Mar.23	Crediton Worcester 1038 Cornwall ?		F. Wig. 1031. [1027 ?] Chr. S. 1038. subs. *1026–1045.
1027 Oct. 1 Canterbury	Joseph, d. 1043	Llandaff	Ethelnoth	Lib. Landav. Diceto 467.
1027	Merewit, d.1033. Ap.12	Wells		Subs. 1031–1032. Malms. Hist. Glast.
1023 × 1030	Elfric, d. 1038	Elmham		Chr. S. 1038.
1032	Alwin, d.1047.Aug.29	Winchester		Chr. S. 1032. subs. 1033–1046.
1032	Ethelric, d.1038.Nov.3	Selsey		Subs. 1032–1033.
1033 Jun. 11	Duduc, d.1060. Jan.18	Wells		Hunter's See of Somerset, p. 15, 16.
1033	Brihteag, d.1038.Dec.20	Worcester		Chr. S. 1033. subs. 1033.
1034	Eadnoth, d. 1050	Dorchester		Subs. 1042–1046.
[1035]	Eadsige, d.1050.Oct.29	[S. Martin's] Canterbury 1038	[Ethelnoth]	Chr. S. 1038. subs. 1035–1050. Cf. Battely's Canterbury. Codex Dipl. 1323–1325.
1035	Elfweard, d.1044. Jul.27	London		Subs. 1038–1042.
1038	Elfric	Elmham		Subs. Temp. R. Edw.
1039	Wulfsy, d. 1053. Oct.	Lichfield		Subs. 1039–1053. F. Wig. 1039.
1039	Grimketel, d. 1047	Selsey		Chr. S. 1038. subs. 1042–1046.
1041	Eadred, d. 1041	Durham		Sim. Dun. 1042.
1042 Jan. 11 York	Ethelric, res. 1056 d.1072.Oct.15	Durham		Chr. S. 1041 and 1072. Consecrated to York.
1043 Apr. 3 Westminster	Stigand, dep. 1070 Apr. 11	Elmham Winchester 1047 Canterbury 1052	Eadsige Elfric &c.	Chr. S. 1043. subs. 1046–1065. Pall 1058. Obit. Feb. 22.

DATE OF CONSECRATION.	NAME.	SEE.	CONSE-CRATORS.	AUTHORITIES, &c.
1044	Ealdred, d. 1069. Sep. 11	Worcester York 1061		Subs. 1044–1065.
1044	Siward, d. 1048. Oct. 23	Upsal, (suff. for Cant.)	Eadsige	Chr. S. 1044.
1044	Robert, exp. 1052. Sep. 14. d. 1070	London Canterbury 1051	[*Eadsige*]	Subs. 1046–1050.
1045	Herman, d. 1078. Feb. 20	Ramsbury Sherborn 1058		Chr. S. 1045. subs. 1045–1065.
1045	Elfwold, d. 1058	Sherborn		Subs. 1046–1050.
1046	Leofric, d. 1072. Feb. 10	Crediton Exeter 1050		Chr. S. 1044. subs. 1046–1065.
1047	Ethelmar, dep. 1070	Elmham		Subs. 1055.
1047	Heca, d. 1057	Selsey		Chr. S. 1045–7. subs. 1050.
1050	Ulf, exp. 1052	Dorchester		Chr. S. 1046, 9–1050. subs. 1050–1052.
1051	William, d. 1075	London	Robert	Subs. 1061–1065. Chr. S. Mon. H. Brit. 445.
1051	Kinsy, d. 1060. Dec. 22	York		Chr. S. 1053. Stubbs 1700.
1053	Wulfwy, d. 1067	Dorchester		Chr. S. 1053. He and Leofwin went abroad for Consecration. Chr. S.
1053	Leofwin, d. 1067	Lichfield		Chr. S. 1053.
1053	Magswem	Glasgow	Kinsy	Stubbs 1700.
1056	Leofgar, d. 1056. Jun. 17	Hereford		Chr. S. 1056.
†1056 May 26 London	Herewald, d. 1104. Mar. 6	Llandaff	Kinsy	Lib. Landav. Cf. Godwin.

† Ralph de Diceto states that the following consecrations of Welsh Bishops took place at Canterbury: Chevelliauc and Libiau of Llandaff, and Lunverd of S. David's, by Archbishop Ethelred; Bledri of Llandaff, and Tramerin and Elnod of S. David's, by Elfric; and Herewald of Llandaff by Lanfranc. R. de D. Twysden, c. 451. 461. 483. In his MS. History of the Bishops (MS. Arundel 220) he assigns Bedreu of Llandaff, and Tremerin and Elnod of S. David's,

DATE OF CONSECRATION.	NAME.	SEE.	CONSE-CRATORS.	AUTHORITIES, &c.
1056	Ethelwin, d. 1071	Durham		Chr. S. 1056.
1058	Ethelric, dep. 1070	Selsey	Stigand	Chr. S. 1058.
1058	Siward, d. 1075	Rochester	Stigand	Chr. S. 1058.
1053 × 1060	John	Glasgow	Kinsy	Stubbs 1700.
1061 Ap. 15 Rome	Giso, d. 1088	Wells ⎫		History of the See of Somerset. Camden Soc.
	Walter, d. 1079	Hereford ⎬ P. Nicolas II.		p. 16. F. Wig. 1061.
‡1062 Sep. 8 York	Wulfstan, d. 1095. Jan. 18	Worcester	Ealdred	Chron. S. 1062. F. Wig. 1062.
1067	Remigius, d. 1092. May 7	Dorchester	Stigand	P. R. C.
1070 May 30	Walkelin, d. 1098. Jan. 3	Winchester	Armenfrid B. of Sion	Flor. Wig.
1070	Stigand, d. 1087	Selsey Chichester 1075		Flor. Wig.
1070	Herfast	Elmham Thetford 1075		Flor. Wig.
‖1070 Aug. 29 Canterbury	Lanfranc Pall 1071 d. 1089. May 24	Canterbury ⎧	Will. London W. Winchest. Giso Wells W. Hereford H. Sherborn S. Rochester R. Dorchester H. Elmham Stig. Selsey	Malms. G. P. Lib. i. Flor. Wig. Gerv. 1653. Chr. S. 1070.

to Siric, and Bleduc of S. David's to Ethelnoth. The Liber Landavensis gives Elfric as the consecrator of Bledri and Kinsy of Herewald, A.D. 1059. The dates of the Canterbury Roll, given in Richardson's Godwin, are inconsistent with each other.

‡ S. Wulfstan, in his Profession, (MS. Cotton Cleopatra E. 1) states that during the Pontificate of Stigand some of the Bishops elect had sought consecration at Rome, some in France, and some from the comprovincial Bishops.

‖ The following changes of the Episcopal Sees took place shortly after the Conquest, partly in consequence of a decree of the Council of London in 1075. Malms. G. P. Lib. i. 1475. (ed. Migne) : Sherborn and Ramsbury to Old Sarum 1075, to Salisbury 1219 ; Wells to Bath 1088, Selsey to Chichester 1075 ; Lichfield to Chester 1075, to Coventry 1095 ; Dorchester to Lincoln 1095 ; Elmham to Thetford 1075, to Norwich 1094.

DATE OF CONSECRATION.	NAME AND SEE.	CONSECRATORS.	AUTHORITIES, &c.
1070 Canterbury	Thomas York Pall 1071 d. 1100. Nov. 18	Lanfranc	P. R. C. Malms. G. P. Lib. i. F. Wig. 1070.
1071 Winchester	Walcher Durham d. 1080. May 14	Thomas York	Ralph. A. C. Dec. Scriptores 1744. Flor. Wig. 1072. Hoveden 1071.
1072 London	Osbern Exeter d. 1103	Lanfranc	P. R. C. Chron. Sax. Gervas 1654.
1072 Gloucester	Peter Lichfield d. 1085	Lanfranc	Chr. S. Gervas 1654.
1074 London	Patrick Dublin d. 1084. Oct. 10	Lanfranc	P. R. C. Chr. S. Gervas 1654.
1075	Hugh d'Orivalle, London, d. 1085. Jan. 12	Lanfranc	P. R. C. Chron. S.
1076 S. Paul's	Arnostus, Rochester d. 1076	{ Lanfranc { Thomas York	P. R. C. Wilkins Conc. i. 369.
1077. Mar. 5 York	Ralph, Orkney	{ Thomas York { Wulstan Worcester { Peter Chester	Lanfranc. Epp. 11 & 12. (5 Non. Mart.) Chr. S. Stubbs 1709.
1077. Mar. 19 Canterbury	Gundulf, Rochester, d. 1108. Mar. 7	Lanfranc	P. R. C. and Chr. S. V. Gundulfi. D'Achery on Lanfr. ed. Migne. 93, and Ang. Sac. ii. 279. 280. 291.
1078	Osmund, Sarum, d. 1099. Dec. 3	Lanfranc	P. R. C.
1079. Dec. 29 Canterbury	Robert de Losing, Hereford, d. 1095. June 26	Lanfranc	P. R. C. Flor. Wig. ii. 13. Sim. Dun. 210. Gervas 1654.
1081. Jan. 3 Gloucester	William de S. Carilepho, (S. Calais) Durham, d. 1096. Jan. 1	{ Thomas York { Wulst. Worcester { Osbern Exeter { Giso Wells { Robert Hereford	Chr. Sax. Flor. Wig. ii. 16. Sim. Dun. 49. 211. Hist. Dun. Scr. iii. p. 156. Hoveden.

Date of Consecration.	Name and See.	Consecrators.	Authorities, &c.
1085 Canterbury	Donagh ô Haingly Dublin, d. 1095	Lanfranc	P. R. C.
1086 Canterbury	Robert de Limesey, Lichfield, d. 1117. Sept. 1 William de Beaufeu, Thetford, d. 1091	} Lanfranc	P. R. C. Chron. Sax. Gervas 1654.
1086 [Apr. 5] Winchester	Maurice, London, d. 1107. Sept. 26	{ Lanfranc Thomas York	P. R. C. Ordained priest by Lanfranc. Chichester, March 14. Ep. Lanfr. 24.
1087 Canterbury	Gosfrid, Chichester, d. 1088. Sept. 25	Lanfranc	P. R. C. Gerv. 1654.
1088 July Canterbury	John of Tours, Bath, d. 1122. Dec. 29	Lanfranc	P. R. C. Gervas 1654. Hunter's Bishopric of Somerset, p. 21.
1091	Ralph Luffa, Chichester, d. 1123. Dec. 24	Thomas York	P. R. C. Stubbs 1707. Orderic V. x. 2.
1091	Herbert de Losing, Thetford, d. 1119. July 22	Thomas York	P. R. C. Stubbs 1707. Removed to Norwich 1094. Apr. 9.
1092	Hervè le Breton, Bangor, Ely 1109, d. 1131. Aug. 30.	Thomas York	Stubbs 1707.
1093 Dec. 4 Canterbury	S. Anselm, Canterbury, d. 1109. Apr. 21	{ Thom. York Maur. London Walk. Winchester Gund. Rochester Osm. Sarum Robert Hereford Robert Lichfield John Bath Ralph Chichester Herbert Thetford	Eadmer 372. Sim. Dun. 219. Flor. Wig. ii. 33. Hoveden 1094.

DATE OF CONSECRATION.	NAME AND SEE.	CONSECRATORS.	AUTHORITIES, &c.
1094 [*Feb.* 12] Hastings	Robert Bloett, Lincoln, d. 1123. Jan. 10	Anselm Walk. Winchester Gund. Rochester Osm. Sarum John Bath William Durham Ralph Chichester Ralph Coutances	P. R. C. Eadmer 376. Battle Abbey was consecrated Feb. 11. Chr. Mon. de Bello 1095. Chr. S. 1094.
1096 Apr. 20 Winchester	Samuel ô Haingly, Dublin, d. 1121. July 4	Anselm and four Bishops	P. R. C. Eadmer 393.
1096 June 8 S. Paul's	Gerard, Hereford, York 1101, d. 1108. May 21 Samson, Worcester, d. 1112. May 5	Anselm Thom. York Maur. London Gund. Rochester Herbert Norwich	P. R. C. Eadmer 393. Gervas 1660. They were ordained priests the day before. Cons. June 15. Flor. Wig. ii. 40.
1096 Dec. 28 Canterbury	Malchus, Waterford,	Anselm Gund. Rochester Ralph Chichester	P. R. C. Eadmer 396.
1099 June 5 London	Ralph Flambard, Durham, d. 1128. Sept. 5	Thom. York	Flor. Wig. ii. 44. Sim. Dun. 60 & 224. Stubbs 1709.
1101 × 1108	Roger, Orkney	Gerard York	Stubbs 1710.
1107 Aug. 11 Canterbury	William de Giffard, Winchester, d. 1129. Jan. 25 Roger, Sarum, d. 1139. Dec. 4 William Warelwast, Exeter, d. 1136 Reinhelm, Hereford, d. 1115. Oct. 27 Urban, Llandaff, d. 1133	Anselm Gerard York Ralph Durham Robert Lichfield John Bath Ralph Chichester Herbert Norwich Robert Lincoln	P. R. C. Eadmer 466. Sim. Dun. 230. F. Wig. ii. 56. Gervas 1660. Hoveden 1107. Stubbs 1711.

DATE OF CONSECRATION.	NAME AND SEE.	CONSECRATORS.	AUTHORITIES, &c.
1108 July 26 Pagham	Richard de Beames, London, d. 1127. Jan. 16	Anselm Will. Winchester Ralph Chichester Roger Sarum Will. Exeter	P. R. C. Eadmer 473. Sim. Dun. 231. Gervas 1660. Hoveden 1108. Flor. Wig. ii. 59.
1108 Aug. 9 Canterbury	Ralph d'Escures, Rochester, Canterbury 1114. Apr. 26 d. 1122. Oct. 20	Anselm Rich. London Will Winchester Ralph Chichester	P. R. C. Eadmer 474. Sim. Dun. 231. Gervas 1660. Hoveden 1108. Flor. Wig. ii. 59.
1109 .June 27 S. Paul's	Thomas, York, d. 1114. Feb. 24	Richard London Will. Winchester Ralph Durham Herb. Norwich Ralph Rochester Herv. Bangor	Eadmer 482. Sim. Dun. 232. Flor. Wig. ii. 60. Hoveden 1108. Stubbs 1712.
1109 Aug. 1 York	Turgot, S. Andrew's d. 1117. Aug. 31.	Thomas York	Sim. Dun. 232. Stubbs 1713. Flor. Wig. ii. 60.
1109 × 1114	Michael, Glasgow	Thomas York	Stubbs 1713.
1109 × 1114	Wimund, Man	Thomas York	Stubbs 1713. W. Newburgh. i. 24.
1109 × 1114 York	Ralph Nowell, Orkney	Thomas York	Stubbs 1713.
1115 June 27 Canterbury	Theulf, Worcester, d. 1123. Oct. 20	Ralph Richard London John Bath Ralph Chichester Herbert Norwich Herv. Ely Roger Sarum	P. R. C. Eadmer 493. Flor. Wig. ii. 68. Sim. Dun. 236. Gervas 1660.
1115 Sept. 19 Westminster Abbey	Bernard, S. David's, d. 1147	Ralph Will. Winchester John Bath Robert Lincoln Roger Sarum Urban Llandaff Giles Limerick	P. R. C. Eadmer 495. Flor. Wig. ii. 68. Gervas 1660.

DATE OF CONSECRATION.	NAME AND SEE.	CONSECRATORS.	AUTHORITIES, &c.
1115 Dec. 26 Canterbury	Geoffrey de Clive, Hereford, d. 1120. Feb. 3 Ernulf, Rochester, d. 1124. Mar. 15	Ralph Will. Winchester Ralph Chichester Herbert Norwich Bern. S. David's	P. R. C. Eadmer 496. Sim. Dun. 237. Gervas 1660. Hoveden 1115. Flor. Wig. ii. 68.
1119 Oct. 19 Rheims	Thurstan of Bayeux, York, d. 1140. Feb. 5	P. Calixtus II.	Sim. Dun. 240. Ord. Vit. xii. 21. Eadmer 504. Hoveden. 1119.
1120 Apr. 4 Westminster	David the Scot, Bangor, d. 1139	Ralph Richard London Robert Lincoln Roger Sarum Urban Llandaff	P. R. C. Cont. Flor. Wig. ii. 74. Gervas 1660.
1121 Jan. 16 Lambeth	Richard, Hereford, d. 1127. Aug. 15	Ralph Richard London Robert Lincoln Urban Llandaff Bern. S. David's Ernulf Rochester	Cont. Flor. Wig. ii. 75. Gervas 1660.
1121 Mar. 13 Abingdon	Robert Peche, Lichfield, d. 1127. Aug. 22	Ralph Will. Winchester Will. Exeter Urban Llandaff Bern. S. David's	Eadmer 519. Cont. Flor. Wig. ii. 76. Gervas 1660.
1121 June 12 Canterbury	Everard, Norwich, dep. 1145 d. 1150. Oct. 15	Ralph Ernulf Rochester Richard Hereford Robert Lichfield	P. R. C. Cont. Flor. Wig. ii. 76. Gervas 1660.
1121 Oct. 2 Lambeth	Gregory, Dublin, d. 1161. Oct. 8	Ralph Richard London Robert Lincoln Roger Sarum David Bangor Ever. Norwich	P. R. C. Cont. Flor. Wig. ii. 77. Gervas 1660.
1123 Feb. 18 Canterbury	William de Corbeuil, Canterbury, d. 1136. Nov. 21	Richard London Will. Winchester Roger Sarum Bern. S. David's Ernulf Rochester	Chr. S. 1123. Cont. Flor. Wig. ii. 77. Sim. Dun. 248. Gervas 1662.

Date of Consecration.	Name and See.	Consecrators.	Authorities, &c.
1123 July 22 Canterbury	Alexander, Lincoln, d. 1148	William and four Bishops	P. R. C. Cont. Flor. Wig. ii. 78. Sim. Dun. 250. Gervas 1663.
1123 Aug. 26 S. Paul's	Godfrey, Bath, d. 1135. Aug. 16	William	P. R. C. Cont. Flor. Wig. ii. 78. Gervas 1663.
1125 Apr. 12 Lambeth	Seffrid Pelochin, Chichester, deposed 1145, d. 1151	William Thurstan York Richard Hereford Urban Llandaff Bern. S. David's David Bangor Ever. Norwich	P. R. C. Cont. Flor. Wig. ii. 79. Gervas 1663. H. Huntingdon. A. S. ii. 700.
1125 May 24 Canterbury	Simon, Worcester, d. 1150. Mar. 20 John, Rochester, d. 1137. June 22	William Rich. Hereford David Bangor Godfrey Bath Seffr. Chichester	P. R. C. Cont. Flor. Wig. ii. 80. Gervas 1663.
1128 Jan. 22. Canterbury	Gilbert the Universal, London, d. 1134. Aug. 10	William Seff. Chichester John Rochester	P. R. C. Cont. Flor. Wig. ii. 89. Gervas 1663.
1128 York	Robert, S. Andrew's	Thurstan York Ralph Durham Ralph Orkney John Glasgow	Ang. S. ii. 237. Cont. Flor. Wig. ii. 89.
1129 Nov. 17 Canterbury	Henry of Blois, Winchester, d. 1171. Aug. 8	William	P. R. C. Chron. S. & Cont. Flor. Wig. ii. 91. Sim. Dun. 256. Gervas 1663.
1129 Dec. 22 Canterbury	Roger de Clinton, Lichfield, d. 1148. Apr. 16	William	P. R. C. Cont. Flor. Wig. ii. 91. Gervas 1663.
1131 June 28 Oxford	Robert de Bethune, Hereford, d. 1148. Apr. 16	William	V. Ang. S. ii. 307. & 321. P. R. C. Cont. Flor. Wig. ii. 92. Gervas 1663.

DATE OF CONSECRATION.	NAME AND SEE.	CONSECRATORS.	AUTHORITIES, &c.
1133 Aug. 6 York	Geoffrey Rufus, Durham, d. 1140. May 6 Adelulf, Carlisle, d. 1156	Thurstan York	John of Hexham 257. Hist. Dun. 62. Stubbs 1720.
1133	Gilaldanus, Whithern	Thurstan York	Stubbs 1720.
1133 Oct. 1 Lambeth	Nigel, Ely, d. 1169. May 30	William	Rich.Eliens.Ang.S.i.619. P. R. C. Gervas 1663.
1136	Robert, Bath, d. 1166 Aug. 31	Henry Winchester	Cont. Flor. Wig. ii. 95.
[1137]	[*John, Rochester, d. 1142*]	[*Henry Winchester*]	[V. Ang. S. i. 343. John Hexham 265.]
1138 Dec. 18 Westminster	Robert Chichester, Exeter, d. 1155 Mar. 28	Alberic Ostia Alex. Lincoln &c. &c. (17 Bishops)	Cont. Flor. Wig. Gervas 1346 & 7.
1139 Jan. 8 Canterbury	Theobald, Canterbury, d. 1161. Apr. 18	Alberic Ostia Henry Winchester Roger Sarum Simon Worcester Seffrid Chichester Roger Lichfield Alex. Lincoln Robert Hereford Robert Exeter	Rich. Hexham 328. John Hexham 264. Gervas 1349 & 1665. Diceto 507. M. Paris. 77.
1140	Maurice, Bangor, d. 1161 Aug. 12 Uhtred, Llandaff, d. 1148	Theobald Robert Hereford Robert Exeter	P. R. C. Cont.Flor.Wig. ii. 124. Gervas 1665.
1140	Patrick, Limerick,	Theobald	P. R. C.
1141	Robert de Sigillo, London, d. 1151	Theobald	P. R. C. Cont. Fl. Wig. ii. 131.

DATE OF CONSECRATION.	NAME AND SEE.	CONSECRATORS.	AUTHORITIES, &c.
1142	Jocelin de Bailleul, Sarum, d. 1184. Nov. 18	Theobald	P. R. C.
1142	Ascelin, Rochester, d. 1148. Jan. 24	Theobald	P. R. C.
1143 Lambeth	Gilbert, S. Asaph,	Theobald Robert London Asc. Rochester	P. R. C. Gervas 1359.
1143 June 20 Winchester	William de S. Barbe, Durham, d. 1152. Nov. 24	Hen. Winchester Alex. Lincoln Seff. Chichester Sim. Worcester Roger Lichfield Robert Hereford Robert Bath Ad. Carlisle Urban Llandaff Joc. Sarum	Hoveden. 1142. Thorn 1803. (List of Bps.) Cont. Sim. Dun. 64. (7 Bps.) John Hexham 271. (9 Bps.)
1143 Sept. 26 Winchester	Will. Fitz Herbert, York, d. 1154. June 8.	Henry Winchester Ralph Orkney	W. Newburgh i. 17. John Hexham 273.
1146 Canterbury	William de Turbe, Norwich, d. 1174. Jan. 17	Theobald	P. R. C. Gervas 1361 & 1665.
1147 Aug. 3 Canterbury	Hilary, Chichester, d. 1169. July 19	Theobald Nigel Ely Robert Bath Will. Norwich	P. R. C. Gervas 1665.
1147 Dec. 7 Treves	Henry Murdac, York, d. 1153. Oct. 14	P. Eugenius III.	J. Hexham 276. Stubbs 1721.
1148 Mar. 14 Canterbury	Walter, Rochester, d. 1182. July 26 Nicolas ap Gurgant, Llandaff, d. 1183. July 6	Theobald Nigel Ely Robert Exeter Maur. Bangor	P. R. C. Gervas 1665.

Date of Consecration.	Name and See.	Consecrators.	Authorities, &c.
1148 Sept. 5 S. Omer's	Gilbert Ffolliott, Hereford, London 1163 d. 1187. Feb. 18	Theobald Theod. Amiens Nic. Cambray	P. R. C. Gervas 1364 & 1665.
1148 Dec. 19 Canterbury	Robert de Chesney, Lincoln, d. 1167. Jan. 26 David Fitz Gerald, S. David's, d. 1176. May 8	Theobald Hilary Chichester Walt. Rochester Gilb. Hereford Pat. Limerick	P. R. C. Gervas 1365 & 1665.
1149 Oct. 2 Canterbury	Walter Durdent, Lichfield, d. 1160. Dec. 7	Theobald Robert London Walt. Rochester Nic. Llandaff	P. R. C. Gervas 1367 & 1665.
1151 Mar. 4 Canterbury	John de Pageham, Worcester, d. 1158.	Theobald Hilary Chichester Walt. Rochester	P. R. C. Gervas 1367.
1152 Feb. 24 Lambeth	Geoffrey Arthur, S. Asaph, d. 1154	Theobald Will. Norwich Walt. Rochester	P. R. C. Gervas 1367 & 1665.
1152 Sept. 28 Canterbury	Richard de Beames, London, d. 1162. May 4	Theobald Hilary Chichester Walt. Rochester Gilb. Hereford	P. R. C. Gervas 1370 & 1665.
1153 Dec. 20 Rome	Hugh de Puisac, Durham, d. 1195. Mar. 3	P. Anastasius IV. William York	Gervas 1375. Coldingham III. Newburgh i. 26. Ann. Waverley 158.
1154	Richard, S. Asaph	Theobald	P. R. C. Gervas 1665.
1154 Oct. 10 Westminster Abbey	Roger de Pont l'Evêque, York, d. 1181. Nov. 26	Theobald Richard London Nigel Ely Robert Bath Will. Norwich Walt. Rochester Gilbert Hereford Robert Lincoln John Worcester	Gervas 1376 & 1665. Diceto 529. Newburgh i. 32.

Date of Consecration.	Name and See.	Consecrators.	Authorities, &c.
1154 Dec. 19 Bermondsey	Christian, Whithern, d. 1186. Oct. 7	Hugh Rouen Roger York	Chron. S. Cruc. Ang. S. vol. i. 161. & ii. 235.
1155 June 5 Canterbury	Robert Warelwast, Exeter, d. 1160	Theobald Nigel Ely Joc. Sarum Hil. Chichester Walt. Rochester	P. R. C. Gervas 1378. Diceto 530.
1158	Alfred, Worcester, d. 1160. July 31	Theobald	Diceto 531.
1160	Geoffrey, S. Asaph, res. 1175	Theobald	P. R. C. Gervas 1665.
1161 Canterbury	Richard Peche, Lichfield, d. 1182. Oct. 6	Walt. Rochester	P. R. C. Gervas 1381. Diceto 532.
1162 Canterbury	Bartholomew, Exeter, d. 1184. Dec. 15	Walt. Rochester	P. R. C. Gervas 1381. Diceto 532.
1162 June 3 Canterbury	Thomas à Becket, Canterbury, d. 1170. Dec. 29	Hen. Winchester Nigel Ely Robert Bath Jocelin Sarum Will. Norwich Hilary Chichester Walt. Rochester Nic. Llandaff Gilbert Hereford Robert Lincoln Dav. S. David's Geoff. S. Asaph Richard Lichfield Bart. Exeter	Gervas 1383 & 1669. Diceto 533.
1163 Dec. 22 Canterbury	Robert of Maledon, Hereford, d. 1167. Feb. 27	Thomas	P. R. C. N. Trivet. 54. Gervas 1385 & 1670.
1164 Aug. 23 Canterbury	Roger Fitz Count, Worcester, d. 1179. Aug. 9	Thomas	P.R.C.Ann.Tewkes.MSS. Diceto 536. Gervas 1389 & 1670.

DATE OF CONSECRATION.	NAME AND SEE.	CONSECRATORS.	AUTHORITIES, &c.
1174 Apr. 7 Anagni	Richard, Canterbury, d. 1184. Feb. 16	P. Alexander III.	Gervas 1426. Diceto 580.
1174 June 23 S. Jean de Maurienne	Reginald Fitz Jocelin, Bath, Elect to Cant. 1191, d. 1191. Dec. 26	Richard Pet. Tarentaise	P. R. C. Diceto 581. Gervas 1429 & 1764.
1174 Oct. 6 Canterbury	Richard Toclive, Winchester, d. 1188. Dec. 22 Geoffrey Riddell, Ely, d. 1189. Aug. 21 Robert Ffolliott, Hereford, d. 1186. May 9 John Greenford, Chichester, d. 1180. Apr. 26	Richard Reg. Bath	P. R. C. Gervas 1428 & 1674. Diceto 582.
1175 Oct. 12 Westminster	Adam, S. Asaph, d. 1181	Richard	P. R. C. Gervas 1432 & 1674. Diceto 587.
1175 Dec. 14 Lambeth	John of Oxford, Norwich, d. 1200. June 2	Richard	P. R. C. Cont. Flor.Wig. ii.154. Gervas 1674. Diceto 588.
1176 Nov. 7 Canterbury	Peter de Leia, S. David's, d. 1198. July 16	Gilbert London Walter Rochester Roger Worcester	P. R. C. Gervas 1434 & 1674. Diceto 595.
1177 May 22 Amesbury	Guy Rufus, Bangor, d. 1190	Richard Bart. Exeter John Norwich Reg. Bath Ad. S. Asaph	P. R. C. Gerv. 1674. Bened. Abb. MS. Harl. 4321. Bromton 1119. Diceto 598.
1180 Aug. 10 Lambeth	Baldwin, Worcester, Canterbury 1185, d. 1190. Nov. 19	Richard	P. R. C. Gervas 1457 & 1674.
1180 Nov. 16 Canterbury	Seffrid, Chichester, d. 1204. Mar. 17	Richard	P. R. C. Gervas 1457.

DATE OF CONSECRATION.	NAME AND SEE.	CONSECRATORS.	AUTHORITIES, &c.
1182 Dec. 19 Lisieux	Waleran, Rochester, d. 1184. Aug. 29	Richard	P. R. C. Gervas 1464 & 1674. Diceto 615.
1183 July 3 Angers	Walter of Coutances, Lincoln, Rouen 1186, d. 1207. John, S. Asaph, d. 1186	Richard	P. R. C. Gervas 1464 & 1674. Diceto 615 & 618. 692. Hoveden. 1183. "Ann. Cestrenses. penes T. Mostyn. Eq. Aur." MSS. Hutton.
1183 Sept. 25 Canterbury	Gerard la Pucelle, Lichfield, d. 1184. Jan. 13	Richard Reg. Bath Bald. Worcester Peter S. David's Wal. Rochester	P. R. C. Gervas 1465 & 1674.
1185 Sept. 29 Canterbury	Gilbert Glanville, Rochester, d. 1214. Jun. 24	Baldwin Reg. Bath Peter St. David's Seff. Chichester	P. R. C. Gervas 1477 & 1678. Diceto 629.
1186 Aug. 10 Lambeth	William Saltmarsh, Llandaff, d. 1191. William de Vere, Hereford, d. 1199. Dec. 24	Baldwin	P. R. C. Gerv. 1678. Diceto 630.
1186 Sept. 21 Westminster	Hugh of Grenoble, Lincoln, d. 1200. Nov. 17 William Northall, Worcester, d. 1190. May 3	Baldwin	P. R. C. Gerv. 1678. Diceto 631.
1186	Reiner, S. Asaph, d. 1224	Baldwin	P. R. C. Gerv. 1678.
1186 Oct. 5	John Fitz Luke, Exeter, d. 1191. June 1	Baldwin	P. R. C. & Gerv. 1678. Diceto 631.
1188 Jan. 31 Lambeth	Hugh Nonant, Lichfield, d. 1198. Mar. 27	Baldwin Gilbert Rochester	P. R. C. Gerv. 1520 & 1678.

Date of Consecration.	Name and See.	Consecrators.	Authorities, &c.
1189 Sept. 17 Pipewell	John, Whithern	John Dublin Fulmar Treves Concord Enaghdun	Hoveden 1189. Bromton 1162.
1189 Oct. 22 S. Catherine's, Westminster	Hubert Fitz Walter, Sarum, Canterbury 1193, d. 1205. July 13 Godfrey de Lucy, Winchester, d. 1204. Sept. 11	Baldwin *Hugh Lichfield* *Peter S. David's* *Gilbert Rochester* *Reg. Bath* *H. Durham*	Diceto 649. Gerv. 1678 & 1550, &c. Ann. Waverley 163. Ann. Margam. 10.
1189 *Nov.* 19 *Rome*	*Bernard,* *Ragusa,* *Carlisle* 1203	P. *Clement III.*	*Farlati. Illyricum Sacrum.* vi. 83. Bull. Nov. 25.
1189 Dec. 31 Lambeth	William Longchamp, Ely, d. 1197. Jan. 31 Richard Fitz Neal, London, d. 1198. Sept. 10	Baldwin	P. R. C. Gerv. 1564. Diceto 651.
1191 May 5 Canterbury	Robert Fitz Ralph, Worcester, d. 1193. July 14	William Ely Godf. Winchester Reg. Bath Seff. Chichester Gilb. Rochester Hugh Lichfield	P. R. C. Diceto 660. Gerv. 1568.
1191 Aug. 18 Tours	Geoffrey Plantagenet, York, d. 1212. Dec. 18	Bart. Tours Henr. Bayeux and 8 other Bps.	Giraldus. Ang. S. ii. 388. Diceto 663. Newburgh iv. 17.
1192 Sept. 20 Rome	Savaric, Bath, d. 1205. Aug. 8	Alb. C. Albano	P. R. C. Diceto 668.
1193 Dec. 12 Canterbury	Henry de Soilli, Worcester, d. 1195. Oct. 24 Hen. of Abergavenny, Llandaff, d. 1218. Nov. 12	Hubert	P. R. C. Gerv. 1681. Ann. Southwark. MS. A. Domersham. Ang. S. i. 579.
1194	Henry Marshall, Exeter, d. 1206. Nov. 1	Hubert	P.R.C. Feb. 10 × Mar. 29. Hoveden 1194. Gerv. 1681.

DATE OF CONSECRATION.	NAME AND SEE.	CONSECRATORS.	AUTHORITIES, &c.
1194 June 5 S. Catherine's, Westminster	Herbert le Poor, Sarum, d. 1217. Feb. 6	Hubert	P. R. C. Wendover & Paris 176. Gerv. 1588 & 1681. Diceto 673.
1195 Apr. 16	Alban, Bangor, d. 1196. May 19	Hubert	P. R. C. Gerv. 1681. Ann. Southwark. MS.
1196 Oct. 20 Ham Abbey, Stratford	John of Coutances, Worcester, d. 1198. Sept. 24	Hubert	P. R. C. Gerv. 1597 & 1681. Diceto 693. Wendover & Paris 181 Ann. Southwark. MS.
1197 Mar. 16 Westminster	Rob. of Shrewsbury, Bangor, d. 1213	Hubert	P. R. C. Gerv. 1681. Ann. Southwark. MS. Chr. Mert. MSS. Whart.
1197 Apr. 20 Rome	Philip of Poitou, Durham, d. 1208. Apr. 22	P. Celestine III.	Diceto 697. Coldingham xii.
1198 Mar. 8 Westminster	Eustace, Ely, d. 1215. Feb. 3	Hubert and nine Bishops	P. R. C. Diceto 701. Gerv.(Mar.1)1601&1681. Cont. Flor. Wig. ii.163. Ann. Southwark MS.
1198 June 21 Canterbury	Geoffrey Muschamp, Lichfield, d. 1208. Oct. 6	{ Hubert { Gilbert Rochester	P. R. C. Gerv. 1603 and 1681. Diceto 703.
1199 May 23 Westminster	William de S. Mere l'Eglise, London, res. 1221. Jan. 26, d. 1224. Mar. 27	{ Hubert Ph. Durham Godf. Winchester John Norwich Seff. Chichester Gilb. Rochester Sav. Bath Hen. Llandaff Hen. Exeter Herb. Sarum Eust. Ely Geoff. Lichfield Hugh Lincoln John Dublin	P. R. C. Gerv. 1681. Diceto 705. (Number of Bishops). Hoveden 1199. (Names)

DATE OF CONSECRATION.	NAME AND SEE.	CONSECRATORS.	AUTHORITIES, &c.
1200 June 4 Rome	Mauger, Worcester, d. 1212. July 1	P. Innocent III.	Diceto 706. Gerv. 1681.
1200 Sept. 24 Westminster	John de Gray, Norwich, d. 1214. Oct. 18 Giles de Bruce, Hereford, d. 1215. Nov.17	Hubert Will. London Gilb. Rochester Reiner S. Asaph Hen. Llandaff Hen. Exeter Herb. Sarum Rob. Bangor Eust. Ely Geoff. Lichfield	P. R. C. Diceto 707. Gerv. 1681. Ann. Southw. MS.
1203 Aug. 24 Westminster	William de Blois, Lincoln, d. 1206. May 10.	Will. London Gilb. Rochester Henry Exeter Sav. Bath Herb. Sarum Geoffrey Lichfield Giles Hereford	P. R. C. Giraldus.Ang.S.ii.600. Wendover & Paris 209. Ann. Southw. MS.
1203 Dec. 7 London	Geoffrey de Henlaw, S. David's, d. 1214	Hubert Will. London Gilb. Rochester Henry Exeter Maug. Worcester Will. Lincoln Maurice Cork	P. R. C. Ann. Menev. Ang. Sacra ii. 650. Gerv. 1681.
1204 July 11 Westminster	Simon de Wells, Chichester, d.1207	Hubert	P. R. C. Gerv. 1681.
1205 Sept. 25 Rome	Peter des Roches, Winchester, d. 1238. June 9	P. Innocent III.	Ann. Winton. 305. Trivet 176. Ann. Southwark MS.
1206 May 28 Reading	Jocelin Troteman, Bath, d. 1242. Nov. 19	Will. London Rein. S. Asaph Hen. Llandaff, Hen. Exeter Herb. Sarum Rob. Bangor Eust. Ely Maug. Worcester John Norwich Sim. Chichester	P. R. C. Wendover & Paris 214. Ann. Waverley 169. Ann. Southw. MS.

DATE OF CONSECRATION.	NAME AND SEE.	CONSECRATORS.	AUTHORITIES, &c.
1207 June 17 Viterbo	Stephen Langton, Canterbury d. 1228. July 9	P. Innocent III.	Wendover & Paris 223.
1209 Dec. 20 Melun	Hugh Wallis, Lincoln, d. 1235. Feb. 7	Stephen	P. R. C. Cont. Flor. Wig. ii. 168. Wendover & Paris 229.
1214 Oct. 5 Canterbury	Walter de Gray, Worcester, York 1215, d. 1255. May 1 Simon of Apulia, Exeter, d. 1223. Sept. 9	Stephen Will. London Pet. Winchester Rein. S. Asaph Eust. Ely Joc. Bath Hugh Lincoln	P. R. C. Wendover & Paris 275. Ann. Southw. MS. Cont. Gervas. MS.
1215 Jan. 25 Reading In Capellâ Infirmariâ	Richard le Poor, Chichester, Sarum 1217, Durham 1229, d. 1237. Apr. 15 William of Cornhill, Lichfield, d. 1223. Aug. 19	Stephen	P. R. C. Wendover & Paris 275. Ann. Waverley 180. Ann. Southw. MS. Cont. Gerv. MS.
1215 Feb. 22 Osney	Benedict de Sansetun, Rochester, d. 1226. Dec.	Stephen	P. R. C. Polistoire MS. Ann. Southw. MS. Cont. Gervas. MS. Ann. Roff. (Nero D. 2.)
1215 June 21 Staines	Martin or Cadogan, Bangor, d. 1241. Apr. 11 Gervas, S. David's, d. 1229	Stephen	Ann. Southwark MS. Prynn iii. 30. P. R. C.
1216 July 3 Perugia	Silvester of Evesham, Worcester, d. 1218. July 16	P. Innocent III.	Ann. Wig. Ang. S. i. 483. Ann. Tewkesbury MS.
1216 Dec. 18 Gloucester	Hugh de Mapenore, Hereford, d. 1219. Apr. 13	Silv. Worcester Sim. Meath Rein. S. Asaph Hen. Llandaff Gerv. S. David's	Ann. Wig. Ang. S. i. 483. Chron. Evesham. MS. Ann. Waverley. 183.

DATE OF CONSECRATION.	NAME AND SEE.	CONSECRATORS.	AUTHORITIES, &c.
1217 July 2 Gloucester	Richard de Marsh, Durham, d. 1226. May 1	Walt. York	Ann. Waverley. 183. Graystanes i.
1218 Jan. 7 Canterbury	Ralph de Wareham, Chichester, d. 1222. Apr. 15	{ Will. London Jocel. Bath Ben. Rochester	P. R. C. Reg. Roffense.
1218 Oct. 7 Westminster	William de Blois, Worcester, d. 1236. Aug. 18	Stephen	P. R. C. MS. Add. 5444. M. Westm.
1219 Feb. 24 York	Hugh, Carlisle, d. 1223. June 4	{ Walt. York Rob. Waterford	Hardy's Le Neve. Close Rolls i. p. 392.
1219 Nov. 3 Canterbury	Hugh Ffolliott, Hereford, d. 1234. July 26 William of Goldclive, Llandaff, d. 1230. Jan. 28	} Stephen	P. R. C. MS. Add. 5444. Wendover & Paris 309.
1220. Mar. 8 Westminster	John Pherd, Ely, d. 1225. May 6	Stephen	MS. Add. 5444. Ang. S. i. 635.
1220 Lambeth	Luke Netterville, Dublin, d. 1227. Apr. 17	Stephen	Ware.
1221 Apr. 25 Westminster	Eustace Fauconberg, London, d. 1228. Nov. 2	{ Ben. Rochester Jocel. Bath Richard Sarum Will. Lichfield Ralph Chichester John Ely	P. R. C. MS. Add. 5444. Ann. Southwark MS. Wendover & Paris 313.
1222 May 29 Rome	Pandulf Masca, Norwich, d. 1226. Sept. 16	P. Honorius III.	Ang. S. i. 410. Ann. Waverley 187.
1224	Walter Mauclerc, Carlisle, res. 1246, July 13, d. 1248. Oct. 28	Walter York	Wendover & Paris 317. Waverley 188. Dec.7.1223 × May6.1224
1224 Apr. 14 Rome	Alexander Stavenby, Lichfield, d. 1238. Dec. 26	P. Honorius III.	P. R. C. Waverley 188. Wendover & Paris 322. Ann. Southwark. MS. Cont. Gervas. MS.

DATE OF CONSECRATION.	NAME AND SEE.	CONSECRATORS.	AUTHORITIES, &c.
1224 Apr. 21 London	William Brewer, Exeter, d. 1244. Oct. 24 Ralph Neville, Chichester, d. 1244. Feb. 1	Stephen	P. R. C. Wendover & Paris 322. Waverley 188. Ann. Southwark. MS.
1225 June 29 Westminster	Geoffrey de Burgh, Ely, d. 1228. Dec. 8 *Abraham, St. Asaph,* d. 1233	Stephen	P. R. C. Ann. Wig. A. S. i. 487. Waverly 189. Ann. Southwark. MS.
1226 Dec. 20 Westminster	Thomas Blunville, Norwich, d. 1236. Aug. 16	Stephen	P. R. C. Waverley 189. Wendover & Paris 336. Ann. Southwark. MS.
1227 Apr. 25 Palace at Canterbury	Henry Sandford, Rochester, d. 1235. Feb. 24	Stephen Peter Winchester William Exeter	P. R. C. Ann. Roff. A. S. i. 348. Wendover & Paris 337.
1229 May 27 Wilton	Robert Bingham, Sarum, d. 1246. Nov. 3	Jocel. Bath Will. Worcester Alex. Lichfield	P. R. C. Wendover & Paris 363. Waverley 192. Chron. Dover. MS.
1229 June 10 Canterbury	Roger Niger, London, d. 1241. Sept. 29 Hugh Norwold, Ely, d. 1254. Aug. 6	Jocel. Bath Hen. Rochester	Cont. Fl. Wig. ii. 175. Wendover & Paris 363. Waverley 192. Cont. Gervas MS. Chron. Dover MS.
1229 June 10 Canterbury	Richard Grant, of Wethershed, Canterbury, d. 1231. Aug. 3	Hen. Roch Jocel. Bath	Chron. Dover MS. &c.
1230 Dec. 1 Merton	Elias de Radnor, Llandaff, d. 1240. May 13	Richard	P. R. C. Ann. Tewkesbury MS.
1231 Feb. 9 Canterbury	Anselm le Gras, S. David's, d. 1247	Richard	P. R. C. Cont. Gervas MS.

DATE OF CONSECRATION.	NAME AND SEE.	CONSECRATORS.	AUTHORITIES, &c.
1234 Apr. 2 Canterbury	Edmund Rich, Canterbury, d. 1240. Nov. 16	Roger London Peter Winchester Jocelin Bath Will. Worcester Will. Exeter Ralph Chichester Henry Rochester Robert Sarum Hugh Ely Luke Dublin John Ferns	Reg. D. & C. S. Paul. MSS. Hutt. Harl. 6955. Cont. Fl. Wig. ii. 176. Wendover & Paris 397. Hemingburgh i. 290.
1234 Nov. 12 Canterbury	Robert of Maidstone, Hereford, res. 1239. Dec. 17	Edmund	P. R. C. Waverley 196.
1235 June 17 Reading	Robert Grostête, Lincoln, d. 1253. Oct. 10 Hugh, S. Asaph, d. 1240	Edmund Roger London Jocelin Bath Robert Sarum Hugh Ely Robert Hereford	P. R. C. Wikes 43. Waverley 196.
1235 Sept. 2 York	Gilbert, Whithern, d. 1253	Walter York	Chron. Mailros 202.
1237 May 3 Viterbo	Walter Cantilupe, Worcester, d. 1266. Feb. 12	P. Gregory IX.	P. R. C. Ann. Wigorn. A.S.i.490. Wikes 43. M. Paris. 438.
1237	Richard, Bangor, d. 1267	Edmund	P. R. C.
1238 Nov. 21 S. Gregory's, Canterbury	Richard of Wendover, Rochester, d. 1250. Oct. 12	Edmund Roger London Ralph Chichester Hugh Ely Robert Lincoln	P. R. C. Add. MS. 5444. Waverley 198. Ann. Roff. A. S. i. 349. Chron. Dover. MS.
1239 Sept. 25 S. Paul's	William de Raley, Norwich, Winchester 1244, d. 1250. Sept. 1	Edmund	P. R. C. Waverley 200. M. Paris. 515. Ann. Southwark MS.

Date of Consecration.	Name and See.	Consecrators.	Authorities, &c.
1240 July 1 Guildford	Hugh Pateshull, Lichfield, d. 1241. Dec. 8	Edmund	P. R. C. Wikes 44. M. Paris. 532.
1240 Boxgrave	Howel ap Ednevet, S. Asaph, d. 1247	Edmund	Letter in Reg. Cant.
1240 Sept. 30 Westminster	Albert of Cologne, Armagh, d. 1247	Walter Worcester	M. Paris. 538.
1240 Dec. 23 S. Paul's	Peter d'Acquablanca, Hereford, d. 1268. Nov. 27	Walter Worcester Walter York	M. Paris. 546. Wikes 44.
1241 June 9 Gloucester	Nicolas Farnham, Durham, res. 1249. d. 1258	Walter York	Graystanes. v. (May 26) Ann. Dunelm. MS. Ann. Tewkesb. MS.
1244 Sept. 11 Reading	Roger, Bath, d. 1247. Dec. 21	Will. Winchester	P. R. C. M. Paris. 649. Trivet. 234. Wikes 45. Waverley 205.
1244 Oct. 9 Trinity, Aldgate	Fulk Bassett, London, d. 1259. May 20	Will. Winchester	P. R. C. M. Paris. 650. Ann. Winton. A.S.i.309. Chron. Majorum. 10. Wikes 45. Waverley 205.
1245 Jan. 15 Lyons	Boniface of Savoy, Canterbury, d. 1270. July 18	P. Innocent IV. *P. Hereford* *Rob. Lincoln*	Chron. Dover. MS. Cont. Fl. Wig. ii. 179. M. Paris. 661. MS. Cotton Galba E. 3.
1245 Feb. 19 Lyons	Roger Weseham, Lichfield, res. 1256. Dec. 4 d. 1257. May 20	P. Innocent IV. *P. Hereford* *R. Lincoln*	P. R. C. Cont. Fl. Wig. ii. 180. M. Paris. 661.
1245 Feb. 19 Carrow, Norwich	Walter Suffield, Norwich, d. 1257. May 18 William de Burgh, Llandaff, d. 1253. June 11	*Fulk London*	P. R. C. and Letters in Reg. Cant. Waverley 206. Cont. Fl. Wig. ii. 180. Ann. MS. Arundel 220.
1245 Mar. 5 Lyons	Richard Wych, Chichester, d. 1253. Apr. 3	P. Innocent IV.	P. R. C. Ann. Wigorn. A.S.i.492. Waverley 206. M. Paris. 661.

Date of Consecration.	Name and See.	Consecrators.	Authorities, &c.
1245 Oct. 22 Reading	Richard Blondy, Exeter, d. 1257. Dec. 26	Fulk London	P. R. C. and Letters. M. Paris. 686.
1247 July 14 Wilton	William of York, Sarum, d. 1256. Jan. 31	Fulk London	P. R. C. Wikes 47. Ann. Winton.A.S.i.309.
1247 Oct. 13 S. Agatha's, Richmond	Silvester Everdon, Carlisle, d. 1254. May 13	Walter York	Chr. Lanercost. M. Paris. 739.
1248 June 14 Lyons	William Button, Bath, d. 1264. Apr. 3	P. Innocent IV.	P. R. C.
1248 July 26 Canterbury	Thomas Wallensis, S. David's, d. 1255. July 11	Robert Lincoln	P. R. C. Ann. Menev. A. S. ii. 650. Wikes 47.
1249	Anian, S. Asaph, d. 1266	{ Walt. Worcester Richard Bangor Richard Meath	P. R. C. Ann.Wigorn.A.S.i.493. Hist. Evesham MS.
1249 Dec. 5 York	Walter Kirkham, Durham, d. 1260. Aug. 9	Walter York	Graystanes vi. Wikes 47. M. Paris. 769.
1251 Apr. 9 Lyons	Laur. de S. Martin, Rochester, d. 1274. June 3	Boniface	P. R. C. Ann. Roff. A. S. i. 350.
1254 Jan. 11 Canterbury	John de la Ware, Llandaff, d. 1256. June 30 John Bishop, or Climping, Chichester, d.1262.	Boniface Fulk London Walt. Worcester William Bath	P. R. C. Ann. Tewkesbury MS.
1254 May 17 New Temple, London	Henry Lexington, Lincoln, d. 1258. Aug. 8	Boniface Fulk London Walt. Worcester Walt. Norwich William Bath	P. R. C. Ann. Wint. A. S. i. 310. Chron. Dunstaple. M. Paris. 887.
1255 Feb. 7 S. Agatha, Richmond	Thomas Vipont, Carlisle, d. 1256. Oct. Henry, Whithern, d. 1293. Nov. 1	Walt. Durham	Chron. Lanercost. Wikes 49.

DATE OF CONSECRATION.	NAME AND SEE.	CONSECRATORS.	AUTHORITIES, &c.
1255 Aug. 15 Belley	William de Kilkenny, Ely, d. 1256. Sept. 22	Boniface Arn. Tarentaise John Belley	P. R. C. M. Paris. 909.
1256 July 23 York	Sewall de Bovill, York, d. 1258. May 10	Walt. Worcester Walt. Durham	Ann. Wint. A. S. i. 310. Wikes 50. Reg. Album Ebor. MS. Stubbs 1725. Hemingburgh i. 302.
1256 Rome	Richard de Carew, S. David's, d. 1280. Apr. 1	P. Alexander IV.	P. R. C. Ann. Menev. A. S. ii. 650.
1257 Jan. 7 S. Paul's	William de Radnor, Llandaff, d. 1266. Jan. 9	Boniface Walt. Worcester Walt. Norwich	P. R. C.
1257 Mar. 11 Canterbury	Giles Bridport, Sarum, d. 1262. Dec. 13	Boniface Walt. Worcester Walt. Norwich William Bath	P. R. C. Cont. Gerv. MS. Ann. Wint. A. S. i. 310.
1257 Oct. 14 Rome	Hugh Belsham Ely, d. 1286. June 15	P. Alexander IV.	P. R. C. Chron. Dover. MS.
1258 Mar. 10 Canterbury	Roger Longespée, de Meulan, Lichfield, d. 1295. Dec. 16 Walter Bronscomb, Exeter, d. 1280. July 22 Simon de Wanton, Norwich, d. 1266. Jan. 2	Boniface Giles Sarum William Bath	P. R. C. Ann. Burton. M. Paris. 960. Wikes 52. Cont. Gerv. MS. Chron. Dover MS.
1258 Apr. 14 Bermondsey	Robert de Chause, Carlisle, d. 1278 Sept.	William Bath Giles Sarum	M. Paris. 964.
1258 Sept. 22 Rome	Godfrey Ludham, or de Kineton, York, d. 1265. Jan. 12	P. Alexander IV.	M. Paris. 978. Stubbs 1726.
1258 Nov. 3 Canterbury	Richard Gravesend, Lincoln, d. 1279. Dec. 18	Boniface Walt. Worcester Walt. Exeter Sim. Norwich	P. R. C. M. Paris. 979.

DATE OF CONSECRATION.	NAME AND SEE.	CONSECRATORS.	AUTHORITIES, &c.
1260 Feb. 15 Southwark	Henry Wengham, London, d. 1262. July 13	Boniface Walt. Worcester Laur. Rochester Giles Sarum Roger Lichfield Walt. Exeter Sim. Norwich	P. R. C. Chron. Major. 44. Wikes 53. Polistoire MS. Cont. Gerv. MS.
1260 May 16 Rome	Aymer de Lesignan, Winchester, d. 1260. Dec. 4	P. Alexander IV.	Ann. Dunstaple. 346. Chron. Major. 49. Wikes 54.
1261 Feb. 13 Southwell	Robert de Stichill, Durham, d. 1274. Aug. 4	Godfrey York	Graystanes. vii.
1262 Sept. 10 Rome	John Gervais, Winchester, d. 1268. Jan. 20.	P. Alexander IV.	P. R. C. Wikes 56. Chron. Lewes. MS.
1262 Sept. 24 Canterbury	Stephen Berksted, or of Pageham, Chichester, d. 1287. Oct. 30	Boniface Will. Llandaff Walt. Exeter	P. R. C. Wikes 56. Cont. Gervas. MS.
1263 May 27 Canterbury	Henry Sandwich, London, d. 1273. Sept. 12 Walter de la Wyle, Sarum, d. 1271. Jan. 3	John Winchester Walt. Worcester Will. Llandaff Richard Lincoln Steph. Chichester	P. R. C. Wikes 56. Cont. Gervas. MS. Chr. Dover. MS.
1265 Jan. 4 Notre Dame, Paris	Walter Giffard, Bath. York 1266 d. 1279. Apr. 22	Pet. Hereford	P. R. C. Chr. Lewes. MS.
1266 Apr. 4 S. Paul's	Roger Skirving, Norwich, d. 1278. Jan. 22	Geoff. Rages	MS. Add. 5444. Chron. Maj. 216. Cont. Gerv. MS. Chron. Dover. MS. Wikes 76.
1266 Sept. 19 Canterbury	Nicolas Ely, Worcester, Winchester 1268, d. 1280. Feb. 12 William Bruce, Llandaff, d. 1287. Mar. 19	Boniface	MSS. Ad. 5444. Wikes 76. Ann.Wigorn.A.S.i.497. Ann.Wint. A. S. i. 312.

DATE OF CONSECRATION.	NAME AND SEE.	CONSECRATORS.	AUTHORITIES, &c.
1267 Farnham	William Button, Bath, d. 1274. Dec. 4	Nic. Worcester	Cont. Gerv. MS. Chron. Dover. MS. MS. Add. 5444.
1267 Canterbury	John, S. Asaph, d. 1267 or 8	Boniface Hugh Ely Will. Landaff	P. R. C.
1267 Canterbury	Anian, Bangor, d. 1305	Boniface Hugh Ely Will. Llandaff	P. R. C.
1268 Sept. 23 Canterbury	Godfrey Giffard, Worcester, d. 1302. Jan. 26	Boniface	P. R. C. MS. Add. 5444.
1268 Oct. 21 Southwark	Anian Schonaw, S. Asaph, d. 1293. Feb. 5	Boniface Walt. Exeter	P. R. C. Wharton. Ep.Asav.324.
1269 June 2 Waverley	John Breton, Hereford, d. 1275. May 12	Nic. Winchester	Wikes 87. Ann.Wint. A.S.i. 313. Waverley 224.
1273 Feb. 26 Canterbury	Robert Kilwardly, Canterbury, Cardinal Bishop of Portus 1278, d. 1279	William Bath Nic. Winchester Laur. Rochester Rich. S. David's Hugh Ely Roger Lichfield Walt. Exeter Rich. Lincoln Roger Norwich Will. Llandaff An. Bangor Godf. Worcester An. S. Asaph	Chron. Maj. 157. Wikes 99. Cont. Gervas. MS. Polistoire. MS. M. Westminster.
1274 Apr. 29 Lambeth	John Chishull, London, d. 1280. Feb. 8	Godf. Worcester An. S. Asaph	Chron. Major. 164. Letter in Reg. Cant. Wikes 100.Waverl.229.
1274 May 13 Lyons	Rob. Wickhampton, Sarum, d. 1284. Apr. 24	Robert Laur. Rochester	Letters in Reg. Cant.
1274 Oct. 21 Gillingham	Walter de Merton, Rochester, d. 1277. Oct. 27	Robert	P. R. C. and Letters. Wikes 101.Waverl.229. Cont. Gerv. Ann. Wig. A. S. i. 500.

Date of Consecration.	Name and See.	Consecrators.	Authorities, &c.
1274 Dec. 9 York	Rob. of Holy Island, Durham, d. 1283. June 7	Walter York	Graystanes xiv. Waverley 229.
1275 Apr. 7 Merton	Robert Burnell, Bath, d. 1292. Oct. 25	Robert	P. R. C. Wikes 102. Waverl. 230. Cont. Gerv. and Polistoire MSS.
1275 Sept. 8 Canterbury	Thomas Cantilupe, Hereford, d. 1282. Aug. 25	{ Robert, John London, Walt. Rochester	P. R. C. Wikes 103. Cont. Gerv. and Polistoire MSS. Add. MS. 5444.
1276 Merton	Gerard Grandeson, Verdun, d. 1278	Robert	Battely's Canterbury, pt. iii. c. 4. p. 106.
1278 May 29 Lambeth	William Middleton, Norwich, d. 1288. Sept. 1 John Bradfield, Rochester, d. 1283. Apr. 23	Robert	P. R. C. Wikes 106. Waverley 233. Ann. Dunstaple 449.
1279 Feb. 19 Rome	John Peckham, Canterbury, d. 1292. Dec. 8	P. Nicolas III.	Reg. Peckham
1279 Aug. 27 Waltham Abbey	John Darlington, Dublin, d. 1284. Mar. 28	{ John, Nic. Winchester, Robert Bath, Will. Norwich	John Oxenedes MS. Nero D. 2. Cont. Flor. Wig. ii. 222. Ware.
1279 Sept. 17 Viterbo	William Wikwan, York, d. 1285. Aug. 26	P. Nicolas III.	Constitut. E. Ebor. MS. Stubbs 1727. Trivet. 300. Wikes 108. Prynn iii. 226.
1280 Apr. 7 Rome	Ralph Ireton, Carlisle, d. 1292. Mar. 1	Odo Card. Tusc.	Rymer. Bull. Ap. 9.
1280 May 19 London	Oliver Sutton, Lincoln, d. 1299. Nov. 13	John	P. R. C. Ann. Lanercost. Chron. Hagnebie. MS. Chron. Peterborough. Reg. Peckham.
1280 Aug. 11 Coventry	Richard Gravesend, London, d. 1303. Dec. 9	{ John, Roger Lichfield	P. R. C. V. Wilk. Conc. ii. 85.

Date of Consecration.	Name and See.	Consecrators.	Authorities, &c.
1280 Oct. 6 Lincoln	Thomas Bek, S. David's, d. 1293. Apr. 20	John Will. Llandaff An. Bangor Godf. Worcester An. S. Asaph Robert Rath Will. Norwich Oliver Lincoln Geoff. Rages	P. R. C. Reg. Ant. Bek. MS. Wikes 110.
1280 Nov. 10 Canterbury	Peter Wyville, Exeter, d. 1291. Oct. 6	Rich. London	P. R. C. Wikes 109. Reg. Peckham.
1282 June 14 Cività Vecchia	John of Pontoise, Winchester, d. 1304. Dec. 4	Latinus C. Ostia	P. R. C. Reg. Pontoise. Trivet. 306. Prynn iii. 1255 & 1261.
1283 Mar. 7 Gloucester	Richard Swinfield, Hereford, d. 1317. Mar. 15	John	P. R. C. Waverley 240.
1283 Sept. 26 Canterbury	Thos. Ingaldsthorp, Rochester, d. 1291. May 12	John John Dublin Rich. London John Winchester	Cont. Flor. Wig. ii. 229. Cont. Gervas. MS. Chron. Dover. MS.
1284 Jan. 9 York	Anthony Bek, Durham, Patriarch of Jerusalem 1306. May 4, d. 1311. Mar. 3	Will. York Henry Whithern Robert Bath Will. Norwich Ralph Carlisle Oliver Lincoln John Winchester Thom. S. David's	Reg. York. Lansd. MS. 402. Stubbs 1727. Graystanes xviii. Trivet. 309. Hemingburgh ii. 15. Wikes 111.
1284 Oct. 22 Sunning	Walter Scammell, Sarum, d. 1286. Sept. 25	John	P. R. C. Wikes 112. Waverley 238. Dunstaple 510. Ann. Wig. A. S. i. 508.
1286 Feb. 10 Rome	John Romaine, York, d. 1296. Mar. 11	P. Honorius IV.	Stubbs 1727. Hemingburgh ii. 15. Trivet 311.
1286 Sept. 22 Canterbury	John Kirkby, Ely, d. 1290. Mar. 26	John	P. R. C. Polistoire MS. Cont. Gerv. MS. Chron. Dover. MS. Wikes 114. Galba E. 3

Date of Consecration.	Name and See.	Consecrators.	Authorities, &c.
1287 June 1 Canterbury	Henry Brandeston, Sarum, d. 1288. Feb. 11	John Godf. Worcester Oliver Lincoln Tho. Rochester	P. R. C. Wikes 114. Cont. Gerv. MS. Chron. Dover. MS.
1288 Sept. 5 Canterbury	Gilbert de S.Lèofard, Chichester, d. 1305. Feb. 12.	John	P. R. C. Cont. Gerv. MS.
1289 Mar. 20 Canterbury	Ralph Walpole, Norwich, Ely 1299, d. 1302. Mar. 20	John	P. R. C. Wikes 115. John Oxenedes. MS.
1289 May 8 Canterbury	William Corner, Sarum, d. 1291. Aug. 14	John	Polistoire. MS. Wikes 116. Cont. Gerv. MS.
1290 Oct. 1 Ely	William de Louth, Ely, d. 1298. Mar. 25	John Richard London Robert Bath Ralph Carlisle Oliver Lincoln	P. R. C. Wikes 132. Hist. Eli. A. S. i. 638. Ann. Wig. A. S. i. 511. Cont. Fl. Wig. ii. 243. Cont. Gerv. MS. Reg. Sutton. MSS. Hutton, and Records in Prynn. iii.
1292 Jan. 6 Chartham	Thom. of Wouldham, Rochester, d. 1317. Feb. 28	John	P. R. C. Ann. Roff. MS. Cont. Gerv. MS.
1292 Mar. 16 Canterbury	Thomas Button, Exeter, d. 1307. Sept. 26 Nicolas Longespée, Sarum, d. 1297. May 18	John	P. R. C. Polistoire MS. Cont. Gerv. MS. Wikes 124.
1292 Sept. 14 York	John de Halton, Carlisle, d. 1324. Nov. 1	Ant. Durham Hen. Whithern Robert Bath Will. Ely	Reg. Halton. Reg. Romaine. Rotuli Scot. 20 Edw. I.
1293 May 17 Canterbury	William March, Bath, d. 1302. June 11 Leoline Bromfield, S. Asaph, d. 1314	Richard London Will. Ely Thom. Rochester John Dublin	P. R. C. Reg. P. & C. Cant. Polistoire MS. Cont. Gerv. MS. Prynn iii. 567.

DATE OF CONSECRATION.	NAME AND SEE.	CONSECRATORS.	AUTHORITIES, &c.
1294 Sept. 12 Aquileia	Robert Winchelsey, Canterbury, d. 1313. May 11	Gerard C. Sabina	Rymer & Wilk. Conc. ii. p. 198. Polistoire MS.
1294 Oct. 10 Gedeling	Thomas Dalton, Whithern	{ John York John Carlisle Leol. S. Asaph	Reg. Romaine.
1296 Dec. Rome	David Martin, S. David's, d. 1328. Mar. 9	Hugh C. Ostia	P. R. C.
1296 Dec. 23 Cambray	Walter Langton, Lichfield, d. 1321. Nov. 9	Berard C. Albano	P. R. C. Cont. Gerv. MS. Cleop. D. 9. Reg. Langton.
1297 Feb. 10 Canterbury	John of Monmouth, Llandaff, d. 1323. Apr. 8	{ Robert Thom. Rochester David S. David's· Robert Clonfert	P. R. C. Reg. Winchelsey.
1297 Oct. 20 Canterbury	Simon of Ghent, Sarum, d. 1315. Mar. 31	Robert	P. R. C. Polistoire MS.
1297 Ghent	William Hotham, Dublin, d. 1298. Aug. 30	Ant. Durham	In the Autumn. V. Ware. And compare Records in Prynn.
1298 June 15 York	Henry Newark, York, d. 1299. Aug. 15	{ Ant. Durham Leol. S. Asaph Walter Lichfield Robert Cork	Reg. Newark. Stubbs 1728. Hemingburgh ii. 71.
1299 Nov. 15 Canterbury	John Salmon, of Ely, Norwich, d. 1325. July 6	Robert	P. R. C. Reg. Winchelsey.
1300 Feb. 28 Rome	Thomas Corbridge, York, d. 1303. Sept. 22	P. Boniface VIII.	Prynn iii. 860. Stubbs 1729. Hemingburgh ii. 187.
1300 June 12 Canterbury	John D'Alderby, Lincoln, d. 1320. Jan. 5	{ Robert Thomas Rochester Simon Sarum	P. R. C. Reg. Dalderby in MSS Hutton. Wilk. Conc. 2. 257. Reg. Cant. 17

Date of Consecration.	Name and See.	Consecrators.	Authorities, &c.
1302 Oct. 28 Rome	Wm. de Gainsborough, Worcester, d. 1307. Sept. 17 Robert Orford, Ely, d. 1310. Jan. 21	Leonard C. Albano	P. R. C. Prynn iii. 919. L. Wadding. Annals of the Minorites, vol. vi.
1302 Nov. 4 Canterbury	Walter Haselshaw, Bath, d. 1308. Dec. 11	Robert	Reg. Winchelsey. P. R. C. Reg. Cant. 17. Cont. Gerv. MS.
1305 May 30 Canterbury	Henry Woodlock, Winchester, d. 1316. June 28	Robert	P. R. C. Reg. Cant. 17. Reg. Gainsborough.
1305 Sept. 19 Canterbury	John Langton, Chichester, d. 1337. June 17	Robert	P. R. C. Reg. Cant. 17. MS. Add. 5444. Reg. Gainsborough.
1306 Jan. 30 Lyons	Ralph Baldock, London, d. 1313. July 24 William Greenfield, York, d. 1315. Dec. 6	Peter C. Sabina	P. R. C. Rymer. Stubbs 1729. Murimuth 7. Hemingburgh ii. 233.
1307 Mar. 26 Carlisle	Griffin ap Yorwerth, Bangor, d. 1309. May 27	Walter Lichfield	Reg. Greenfield.
1308 Oct. 13 Canterbury	Walter Reynolds, Worcester, Canterbury 1313 d. 1327. Nov. 16 Walter de Stapleton, Exeter, d. 1326. Oct. 15	Robert	P. R. C. Reg. Cant. 17.
1309 Nov. 9 Canterbury	John Drokensford, Bath, d. 1329. May 9 Anian Seys, Bangor, d. 1328. Jan. 26	Robert	P. R. C. Reg. Cant. 17.
1310 Sept. 6 Canterbury	John Keeton, Ely, d. 1316. May 14	Robert	P. R. C. Reg. Cant. 17. Reg. Baldock.

Date of Consecration.	Name and See.	Consecrators.	Authorities, &c.
1311 May 30 York	Richard Kellaw, Durham, d. 1316. Oct. 9	William York John Carlisle Thom. Whithern A. Argyle	Reg. Greenfield. Graystanes xxxii. Hemingburgh ii. 285. Ann. Lanercost.
1313 Oct. 7 Avignon	Walter Maidstone, Worcester, d. 1317		Reg. Maidstone. Murimuth 19.
1313 Nov. 25 Canterbury	Gilbert Segrave, London, d. 1316. Dec. 18	Henry Winchester	P. R. C. Reg. Eastry. P.& C. Cant. John of London MS.
1315 Jan. 12 Canterbury	David ap Blethyn, S. Asaph, d. 1352	Walter Simon Sarum	Reg. P. & C. Cant. P. R. C. Reg Sarum. MSS. Whar.
1315 Sept. 28 Canterbury	Roger Mortival, Sarum, d. 1330. Mar. 14	Walter Gilbert London Henry Winchester John Chichester	P. R. C. Reg. Mortival. MSS. Wharton.
1316 Oct. 3 Canterbury	John Hotham, Ely, d. 1337. Jan. 15	Walter Thomas Rochester John Bath	P. R. C.
1316 Oct. 31 Canterbury	John Sendale, Winchester, d. 1319	Walter	P. R. C. Reg. Sendale.
1317 May 15 Canterbury	Richard Newport, London, d. 1318. Aug. 24	Walter Walter Lichfield John Winchester Roger Sarum	P. R. C. Chandos MS. Lansd. 791.
1317 May 22 Avignon	Thomas Cobham, Worcester, d. 1327. Aug. 27 Adam Orlton, Hereford, Worcester 1327, Winchester 1333, d. 1345. July 18	Nic. C. Ostia	P. R. C. Reg. Orlton, &c. John of London MS. Leland. Itiner. 8. 38. (Id. Maii.)
1317 Sept. 25 Avignon	William de Melton, York, d. 1340. Apr. 4	P. John XXII.	Stubbs 1730. Murimuth 26 (Sep. 11).
1318 Mar. 26 Westminster	Lewis de Beaumont, Durham, d. 1333. Sept. 24	John Winchester	Rob Redding. MS. Graystanes xxxviii. MS. Chand. Lansd. 791.

DATE OF CONSECRATION.	NAME AND SEE.	CONSECRATORS.	AUTHORITIES, &c.
1319 Jan. 14 Canterbury	Stephen Gravesend, London, d. 1338. Apr. 8	Walter John Winchester John Chichester Walter Exeter John Bath Thomas Worcester	P. R. C. MS. Chandos.
1319 Aug. 26 Avignon	Haymo Heath, Rochester, d. 1352. May 4	Nic. C. Ostia	P. R. C. W. Dene. A. S. i. 360.
1320 July 20 Boulogne	Henry Burwash, Lincoln, d. 1340. Dec. 4	John Norwich Walter Exeter Ad. Hereford Ingelr. Terouanne	P. R. C.
1320 Nov. 16 S. Alban's	Rigaud Asser, Winchester, d. 1323. Apr. 12	Stephen London John Ely Haym. Rochester	P. R. C. Trokelow. 47.
13...	John of Egglescliffe, *Bethlehem*, Connor 1322, Llandaff 1323, d. 1347. Jan. 2		Gallia Christiana xii. 690. Hibernia Dominicana, c. 13.
1322 June 27 Hales Abbey	Roger Northburgh, Lichfield, d. 1359. Nov. 22	Thomas Worcester John Carlisle David S. Asaph Peter Corbavia John Glasgow Robert Clonfert	Reg. Cobham.
1323 June 26 Avignon	John Stratford, Winchester, Canterbury 1333, d. 1348. Aug. 23	Vitalis C. Albano	P. R. C. Birchington. A. S. i. 19. Ann. Southwark MS.
1325 Feb. 24 Avignon	John de Ross, Carlisle, d. 1332	P. John XXII.	Ann. Lanercost.
1325 Sept. 15 S. Germain des Prés Paris	William Ayermin, Norwich, d. 1336. Mar. 27	William Vienne William Mende Hugh Orange James Agram	P. R. C.
1327 Feb. 1 Westminster	Simon Wedehall, Whithern, d. 1355. Mar. 11	John Carlisle Roger Lichfield John Llandaff	Reg. Melton.

Date of Consecration.	Name and See.	Consecrators.	Authorities, &c.
1327 Mar. 22 Canterbury	James Berkeley, Exeter, d. 1327. June 24	Walter John Chichester Haym. Rochester	P. R. C. Murimuth. 53. W. Dene. A. S. i. 368.
1327 Oct. 18 Avignon	John Grandison, Exeter, d. 1369. July 16 Thomas Charlton, Hereford, d. 1344. Jan. 11	Peter C. Præneste	P. R. C. Murimuth. 58.
1328 June 5 Avignon	Simon Mepeham, Canterbury, d. 1333. Oct. 12	Peter C. Præneste	Rymer. Cont. Gerv. MS. Reg. Cant.
1328 June 12 Canterbury	Henry Gower, S. David's, d. 1347 Matthew Englefield, Bangor, d. 1357. Apr. 25	Stephen London John Bath H. Rochester	P. R. C. Reg. Drokensford MSS. Hutton.
1329 Sept. 3 Canterbury	Ralph of Shrewsbury, Bath, d. 1363. Aug. 14	Simon Hay. Rochester Matt. Bangor	P. R. C. Murimuth 64.
1330 July 15 Woodstock	Robert Wyville, Sarum, d. 1375. Sept. 4	Henry Lincoln Roger Lichfield John Llandaff	P. R. C. MS. Lansdowne 791.
1332 July 19 South Burton	John Kirkby, Carlisle, d. 1352	William York Lewis Durham Roland Armagh	Reg. Melton.
1333 Nov. 14 York	Robert Graystanes, Durham, dep. 1333	William York John Carlisle Roland Armagh	Reg. Melton. Graystanes. xlix.
1333 Dec. 19 Chertsey	Richard Aungervile de Bury, Durham, d. 1345. Apr. 14	John Cant. (elect) Henry Lincoln	Murimuth 74. Chambre i.
1334 May 8 Thame	Simon Montacute, Worcester, Ely 1337, d. 1345. June 20	Henry Lincoln Ralph Bath Robert Sarum	Reg. Montacute.

DATE OF CONSECRATION.	NAME AND SEE.	CONSECRATORS.	AUTHORITIES, &c.
1337 *Mar.* 30 Avignon	Antony Bek, Norwich, d. 1343. Dec. 19 Thomas Hemenhale, Worcester, d. 1338. Dec. 21	P. Benedict IX.	Cf. Reg. Bek & Hemenhale.
1337 Nov. 30 Canterbury	Robert Stratford, Chichester, d. 1362. Apr. 9	John Ad. Winchester Hay. Rochester Robert Sarum	P. R. C. W. Dene A. S. i. 374.
1338 July 12 Lambeth	Richard Bintworth, London, d. 1339. Dec. 8	Robert Chichester Ad. Winchester Hay. Rochester Roger Lichfield Robert Sarum	P. R. C. W. Dene A. S. i. 374. MS. Chandos.
1339 Mar. 21 Canterbury	Wulstan Bransford, Worcester, d. 1349. Aug. 6	Robert Chichester Hay. Rochester	P. R. C. Reg. Bransford. W. Dene A. S. i. 374.
1340 Mar. 12 Canterbury	Ralph Stratford, London, d. 1354. Apr. 7	John Robert Chichester Hay. Rochester Robert Sarum	P. R. C. W. Dene A. S. i. 374.
1342 July 7 Avignon	Thomas Bek, Lincoln, d. 1347. Feb. 2 William de la Zouch, York, d. 1352. July 19	P. Clement VI.	Reg. Bek. MSS. Hutton. Stubbs 1732. Const. Eccl. Ebor. Vitellius A. 2.
1344 May 23 Avignon	William Bateman, Norwich, d. 1355. Jan. 6	P. Clement VI.	P. R. C. Cf. Reg. Bateman.
1344 Aug. 29 Waverley	John Trilleck, Hereford, d. 1360. Nov. 30	Ralph London Ad. Winchester Robert Sarum Wulst. Worcester	P. R. C. Reg. Trilleck.
1345 July 10 *York*	Thomas Hatfield, Durham, d. 1381. May 8	*William York*	Chambre ii. & iii. He was confirmed June 1. Cawood. The king orders the Abbat of S. Mary's to receive his homage May 24.

Date of Consecration.	Name and See.	Consecrators.	Authorities, &c.
1345 July 24 Avignon	Thomas de Lisle, Ely, d. 1361. June 23		Reg. Lisle. MSS. Cole.
1346 May 14 Otford	William Edendon, Winchester, d. 1366. Oct. 7	John Ralph London Robert Sarum	Reg. Edendon. Birchington. MS.
1347 Avignon	John Pascal, Llandaff, d. 1361. Oct. 11		P. R. C.
1347 July 8 Exeter	Richard Fitz Ralph, Armagh, d. 1360. Nov. 14	John Exeter David S. Asaph Ralph Bath Robert Sarum	Reg. Grandison. MSS. Wharton.
1347 Sept. 23 Otford	John Thoresby, S. David's, Worcester 1350, York 1352, d. 1373. Nov. 6 John Gynwell, Lincoln, d. 1362. Aug. 5	John	W. Reade's Birchington. Cott. MS. Julius B. 3. & Reg. Gynwell. MSS. Hutton.
1349 July 19 Avignon	Thomas Bradwardin, Canterbury d. 1349. Aug. 26	Bertr.Card.S.Marc. (Abp. Embrun)	Birchington. A. S. i. 42.
1349 Dec. 20 S. Paul's	Simon Islip, Canterbury, d. 1366. Apr. 26	Ralph London Will. Winchester John S. David's	Reg. Islip. Birchington. A.S.i.43.
1350 Feb. 14 S. Mary's, Southwark	John de S. Paul, Dublin, d. 1362. Sept. 9	Will. Winchester John Worcester Cæs. B. M. de Rosis	Reg. Edendon.
1350	Roger Cradock, Waterford, Llandaff 1361, d. 1382		Provided Feb. 24. Ware and Wadding.
1350 May 2	William de S. Leger, Meath, d. 1352. Aug. 24	John Worcester	Ware.
1350 Sept. 26 Lambeth	Reginald Brian, S. David's, Worcester 1352, d. 1361. Dec. 10	John Worcester	Reg. Islip.

DATE OF CONSECRATION.	NAME AND SEE.	CONSECRATORS.	AUTHORITIES, &c.
1352 Avignon	John Trevor, S. Asaph, d. 1357		Reg. Islip. Profess. 1353. Mar. 24.
1352 Avignon	Thomas Fastolf, S. David's, d. 1361. June	} Will. C. Tusculum	P. R. C. & Reg. Islip. Provided Oct. 22.
1353 Mar. 10 S. Mary's, Southwark	John Sheppey, Rochester, d. 1360. Oct. 19	Will. Winchester John S. Asaph Cæs. B. M. de Rosis	Reg. Sheppey. Reg. Edendon.
1353 Apr. 21 Avignon	Gilbert de Welton, Carlisle, d. 1362	} P. Innocent VI.	Reg. Welton.
1355 July 12 S. Mary's, Southwark	Michael Northburgh, London, d. 1361. Sept. 9 Michael Malconhalgh, Whithern	Will. Winchester Cæs. B. M. de Rosis	Reg. Edendon.
1356 Jan. 3 Waverley	Thomas Percy, Norwich,. d. 1369. Aug. 8	Will. Winchester Robert Sarum Robert Chichester	Reg. Percy. Reg. Edendon.
1357 Avignon	Leoline ap Madoc, S. Asaph, d. 1375		Reg. Islip. Provided July 19.
1357 Avignon	Thomas Ringstead, Bangor, d. 1366. Jan. 8		Reg. Islip. He was the Pope's penitentiary. Provided 1357. Aug. 21.
1360 Sept. 27	Robert Stretton, Lichfield, d. 1385. Mar. 28	Michael London John Rochester	Birchington. A. S. i. 44. Reg. Islip.
1361 Oct. 3 *Avignon*	Lewis Charlton, Hereford, d. 1369. June 24		E Reg. Charlton.
1362 Jan. 2 S. Mary's, Southwark	Adam Houghton, S. David's, d. 1389. Feb. 13	Will. Winchester Rich. Nazareth Tho. Lycostomium	Reg. Edendon.
1362 Feb. 6 Otford	William Whittlesey, Rochester, Worcester 1364, Canterbury 1368, d. 1374. June 6	Simon Rich. Nazareth Thomas Lamberg	Reg. Whittlesey. Reg. Islip.

DATE OF CONSECRATION.	NAME AND SEE.	CONSECRATORS.	AUTHORITIES, &c.
1362 Mar. 20 S. Paul's	Simon Tybald, or Sudbury, London, Canterbury 1375, d. 1381. June 14 John Barnet, Worcester, Bath 1363, Ely 1366, d. 1373. June 7 Simon Langham, Ely, Canterbury 1366, Cardinal 1368, Bp. Præneste 1374, d. 1376. July 22	Will. Winchester Robert Sarum Ad. S. David's	Reg. Edendon.
1362 Avignon	William de Lynn, Chichester, Worcester 1368, d. 1373. Nov. 18		He was "Auditor causarum sacri palatii." Malvern. MS. Temp. Oct. 12. 1362. Profess. Aug. 18. 1363.
1363	John Swaffham, Cloyne, Bangor 1376, d. 1398. June 24		Ware.
1363 June 18 Avignon	Thomas Appleby, Carlisle, d. 1395. Dec. 5	P. Urban V.	Reg. Appleby.
1363 June 25 Wargrave	John Bokyngham, Lincoln, d. 1398. Mar. 10	Will. Winchester Robert Sarum John Ossory	Reg. Edendon. Birchington. MS.
1364 May 26 Avignon	Thomas Trilleck, Rochester, d. 1372	Guy Card. Portus	Reg. Trilleck.
1366 Avignon	Gervas de Castro, Bangor, d. 1370. Sept. 24		Reg. Langham. Provided Dec. 11. 1366.
1367 Mar. 7 Bourdeaux	John Harewell, Bath, d. 1386. July	Elias Bourdeaux	Reg. Harewell. MSS. Hutton.

I

DATE OF CONSECRATION.	NAME AND SEE.	CONSECRATORS.	AUTHORITIES, &c.
1367 Oct. 10 S. Paul's	William Longe, of Wykeham, Winchester, d. 1404. Sept. 27	Simon Simon London Robert Sarum	Birchington. MS. Reg. Wykeham.
1368 Avignon	William Reade, Chichester, d. 1385. Aug. 18		Provided 1368. Oct. 11.
1370 Mar. 17 London	William Courtenay, Hereford, London 1375, Canterbury 1381, d. 1396. July 31	S. London.	Cf. Reg. Courtenay.
1370 Apr. 21 Rome	Henry Spencer, Norwich, d. 1406. Aug. 23		Reg. Spencer.
1370 May 12 Stepney	Thomas Brentingham, Exeter, d. 1394. Dec. 23	Simon London Geoff. Damascus John "Ayubonens"	Reg. Brentingham. MSS. Wharton.
1371 Avignon	Howel ap Grono, Bangor, d. 1372. Feb.		Provided 1371. Apr. 21.
1372 Avignon	John Gilbert, Bangor, Hereford 1375, S. David's 1389, d. 1397. July 28		Provided 1372. Mar. 17. Profession 1372. Nov. 16.
1373 Feb. 6 Avignon	Thomas Brinton, Rochester, d. 1389		Pope's Penitentiary. Reg. Whittlesey.
1374 Apr. 9 Otford	Thomas Fitz Alan, of Arundel, Ely, York 1388, Canterbury 1396, d. 1414. Feb. 19	William Simon London Thomas Rochester	Reg. Whittlesey. Reg. Arundel. MSS. Cole.
1374 June 4 Westminster	Alexander Neville, York, d. 1392. May	Thomas Durham Will. Winchester Thomas Ely	Reg. Neville.
1374 Nov. 25 Avignon	John Duncan, Sodor and Man, d. 1380. (Keith ?)	Simon Præneste	MSS. Wharton.

DATE OF CONSECRATION.	NAME AND SEE.	CONSECRATORS.	AUTHORITIES, &c.
1375 Oct. 28 Hatfield	Henry Wakefield Worcester, d. 1395. Mar. 3	John Hereford Thom. Rochester Thomas Ely	Reg. Arundel. MSS. Cole Reg. Wakefield.
1375 Dec. 9 Bruges	Ralph Erghum, Sarum, Bath 1388, d. 1400. Apr. 10	Simon Will. Carpentras John Amiens	Reg. Erghum. MSS. Wharton. Reg. Sudbury.
1376 May 25 Lambeth	Will. Spridlington, S. Asaph, d. 1382. Apr. 9	Simon John Bath John Hereford	Reg. Sudbury.
13... Rome	William Bottlesham, (Pavada or Beth-lehem), Llandaff 1386, Rochester 1389 d. 1400		Cf. Rymer 7. 478. Wil-kins ad 1382 (Nava-tensis) : and Strype's Cranmer, p. 36.
1382 Jan. 5 Lambeth	Robert Braybrooke, London, d. 1404. Aug. 28 John Fordham, Durham, Ely 1388, d. 1425. Nov. 19	Thomas Exeter Thom. Rochester John Bangor	Reg. Courtenay. Reg. Braybrooke. Chambre IV.
1382 Rome	Laurence Child, S. Asaph, d. 1389. Dec. 27		Reg. Courtenay. Provided June 18. Profession Oct. 2.
1383 Mar. 8 S. Paul's	John Colton, Armagh, d. 1404. May 1	William Thomas Ely John Hereford	Reg. Courtenay.
1383 May 3 Blackfriars, London	Thomas Rushook, Llandaff, Chichester 1385, Kilmore 1388, d. 1388–9	William Will. Winchester Thomas Exeter Thomas Ely	Reg. Courtenay.
1385 July 9 Hadham	William, Tournay, (Suff. of London)	Robert London Simon Achonry Rob. Sebastopolis	Reg. Braybrooke.

DATE OF CONSECRATION.	NAME AND SEE.	CONSECRATORS:	AUTHORITIES, &c.
1386 Jan. 14 Westminster	Walter Skirlaw, Lichfield, Bath 1386, Durham 1388, d. 1405. Mar. 24	William Alex. York Robert London Will. Winchester Thomas Exeter Ralph Sarum Thomas Llandaff	Reg. Courtenay. Reg. Skirlaw. Malvern MS.
1386 Aug. 19 Genoa	Richard Scroope, Lichfield, York 1398, d. 1405. June 8	P. Urban VI.	Reg. Scroope.
1387	Robert Waldby, Aire in Gascony, Dublin 1391, Chichester 1396, York 1397, d. 1398. Jan. 6		Gallia Christiana I.1160. Ware.
1388 Sept. 20 Barnwell	John Waltham, Sarum, d. 1395. Sept.	William Robert London Will. Winchester	Reg. Waltham. MSS. Wharton.
1389 June 20 S. Gregory's Rome	Edmund Bromfield, Llandaff, d. 1393. June John Trevenant, Hereford, d.1404	Cosmo Bologna J. "Verens." Angelo Castello	Reg. Trevenant. Malvern MS.
1390 May 8 Westminster	Alexander Bache, S. Asaph, d. 1395 Richard Mitford, Chichester, Sarum 1395, d. 1407.	William	Malvern. MS. V. Reg. Courtenay. Provided Nov. 17. 1389. Temporals Mar. 10. 1390. Confirmed May 7 (1389 Indiction 13, Reg. Courtenay, wrongly) 1390 Indiction 13, and probably consecrated May 8.
1393	Tideman de Winchcomb, Llandaff, Worcester 1395, d. 1401. June 13		Royal Assent Aug. 19. 1393. Given in parliament Feb. 1394. Temporals restored July 3. 1394. Rymer.

DATE OF CONSECRATION.	NAME AND SEE.	CONSECRATORS.	AUTHORITIES, &c.
1394	Robert Reade, Waterford, Carlisle 1396, Chichester 1397, d. 1415. June		Provided 1394. Sept. 9. Hib. Dominic. c. 13. Ware and Cotton.
1395 June 20 Lambeth	Edmund Stafford, Exeter, d. 1419. Sept.	{ William Robert London John Sarum	Reg. Stafford. MSS. Wharton.
1395 Rome	Andrew Barrett, Llandaff, d. 1396		Clericus Cameræ Apostolicæ. MS. Donat. Temp. 1395. Aug. 25.
1395 *Rome*	John Trevor, S. Asaph, d. 1410 Apr. 10		Temp. July 6. 1395. He had licence to go to Rome in 1390. MS. Donat.
1396	John Burghill, Llandaff, Lichfield 1398, d. 1414. May		Temp. June 15. 1396. Abp. Courtenay's Register is imperfect from 1390.
1397	Thomas Merkes, Carlisle, deposed 1399, d. 1409		Temp. Mar. 18. 1397, Perhaps as he did not make profession until Oct. 19. 1399, he was consecrated at Rome.
1397	Thomas Peverell, Ossory, Llandaff 1398, Worcester 1407, d. 1419. Mar. 2		Ware.
1397 Nov. 11	Guy de Mohun, S. David's, d. 1407. Aug. 31		Reg. Mohun. MS. Tann.
1398 Feb. 3	Roger Walden, Canterbury, London 1405, d. 1406. Jan. 6	Robert London	Pall. Feb. 17, at HighClere, from W. Winchester. Reg. Wykeham. Successit circa Purificationem B. V. M. MS. Cotton. Tiberius, c. 9. Bodl. Digby 201, &c. Temporals restored Jan. 21. Rymer. Cf. Eulogium MS. &c. His preferment filled up Feb. 6.

Date of Consecration.	Name and See.	Consecrators.	Authorities, &c.
1398 July 14	Henry Beaufort, Lincoln, Winchester 1405 d. 1447. Apr. 11	Roger Cant.	Reg. Beaufort. MSS. Hutton.
1400 Rome	Richard Young, Bangor, Rochester 1404 d. 1418. Oct.		Temp. 1400. May 20, having been committed to him as Custos Oct. 21. 1399.
1400 July 4 Canterbury	John Bottlesham, Rochester, d. 1404. Apr. 17	Thomas	Reg. Arundel. Reg. Bottlesham.
1400 Aug. 15 Cawood	William Strickland, Carlisle, d. 1419. Aug. 30	Richard York Lewis Volterra Will. "Pharensis"	Reg. Scroope.
1401 Jan. 2	Roger Appleby, Ossory, d. 1404	Guy. S. David's William Tournay. Thom. Constantia.	Reg. Mohun. MS. Tann.
1401 Sept. 8 Bethlehem Hospital	John Greenlaw, Soltania, (Suffragan of Bath)	Thom. Chrysopolis John Surronensis Tho. Constantia.	Reg. Bowett. MSS. Hutton.
1401 Oct. 9 S. Paul's	Richard Clifford, Worcester, London 1407, d. 1421. Aug. 20	Thomas Robert London John Hereford Edm. Exeter Guy S. David's Lewis Volterra	Reg. Arundel. Reg. Clifford.
1401 Nov. 20 S. Paul's	Henry Bowett, Bath, York 1407, d. 1423. Oct. 20	Thomas Robert London John Hereford Edm. Exeter Richard Bangor Thom. Llandaff Rich. Worcester Lewis Volterra	Reg. Arundel.
1404 July 6 Rome	Robert Mascall, Hereford, d. 1416. Dec. 22		Reg. Mascall.
1405 Mar. 29 Canterbury	Philip Repingdon, Lincoln, res. 1419. Oct. 10	Thomas Rich. Worcester Lewis Volterra	Reg. Arundel.

DATE OF CONSECRATION.	NAME AND SEE.	CONSECRATORS.	AUTHORITIES, &c.
1406 Aug. 8 S. Paul's	Thomas Langley, Durham, d. 1437. Nov. 20	Thomas Hen. Winchester Rich. Worcester	Reg. Arundel.
1406 Sept. 26 Mortlake	Nicolas Bubwith, London, Sarum 1407, Bath 1407, d. 1424. Oct. 27	Thomas Hen. Winchester Rich. Worcester	Reg. Arundel. Reg. Bubwith.
1407 Sienna	Robert Hallam, Sarum, d. 1417. Sept. 4	P. Gregory XII.	Provided Oct. 7. Reg. Arundel.
1407 Oct. 23 Gloucester	Alexand. Tottington, Norwich, d. 1413. April	Thomas Thom. Durham Rich. Worcester Robert Hereford	Reg. Arundel. Reg. Tottington.
1408 June 17 Lucca	Henry Chicheley, S. David's, Canterbury 1414 d. 1443. Apr. 12	P. Gregory XII.	Reg. Chicheley. MS. Tanner.
1408 Aug. 12	John de la Zouch, Llandaff, d. 1423 Benedict Nicolls, Bangor, S. David's 1418, d. 1433. June 25	Thomas	Godwin. Reg. Arundel.
1411 June 28 Lincoln	Robert Lancaster, S. Asaph, d. 1433	Thomas Phil. Lincoln Will. "Soltoniens"	Reg. Arundel.
1413 Sept. 17 Windsor	Richard Courtenay, Norwich, d. 1415. Sept. 15	Thomas	Reg. Arundel. Reg. Courtenay.
1414 Apr. 29 Bologna	John Catterick, S. David's, Coventry 1415, Exeter 1419, d. 1419. Dec. 28	P. John XXIII.	Reg. Chicheley. Provided Apr. 27.
1415	Louis de Luxembourg, Terouanne, Rouen 1436, Ely 1438, d. 1443. Sept. 18	Reg. Rheims	Gallia Christiana X.1564.

Date of Consecration.	Name and See.	Consecrators.	Authorities, &c.
1415 June 9 Maidstone	Stephen Patrington, S. David's, Chichester 1417, d. 1417. Nov. 22	Henry Rich. London Rich. Norwich	Reg. Chicheley.
1416 May 31 S. Paul's	John Wakering, Norwich, d. 1425. Apr. 9	Henry Henry York Richard London John Ely Phil. Lincoln Steph. S. David's Rob. Hereford John Lichfield Thom. Worcester	Reg. Wakering. Reg. Chicheley.
1417 Apr. 18 Windsor	Edmund Lacy, Hereford, Exeter 1420, d. 1455. Sept. 18	Henry Steph. S. David's Thom. Worcester	Reg. Lacy. Reg. Chicheley.
1417 Dec. 12 S. Paul's	John Chandler, Sarum, d. 1426. July 16	Henry Thom. Durham John Llandaff Ben. Bangor Edm. Hereford	Reg. Chicheley.
1418 Constance	William Barrow, Bangor, Carlisle 1423, d. 1429. Sept. 4		Provided Feb. 14. Profession Apr. 16. Royal Letters May 15. Temp. June 5.
1418 July 17 Pont de l'Arche	Henry de la Ware, Chichester, d. 1420. June	J. C. Albano Reg. Rheims Will. Evreux	Reg. Chicheley, and comparison of various Records.
1419 Dec. 3 Rouen	Philip Morgan, Worcester, Ely 1426, d. 1435. Oct. 25		Reg. Morgan, and comparison of various Records.
	John Kemp, Rochester, Chichester 1421, London 1421, York 1426, Canterbury 1452, d. 1454. Mar. 22	Will. Ebronensis Mart. Arras	

DATE OF CONSECRATION.	NAME AND SEE.	CONSECRATORS.	AUTHORITIES, &c.
1420 London	Roger Whelpdale, Carlisle, d. 1423. Feb. 4.	} Hen. Winchester	Reg. Carlisle in MS. Lansd. 721.
1420 Apr. 28 Florence	Richard Fleming, Lincoln, d. 1431. Jan. 25		Reg. Chicheley. Reg. Fleming. MS. Hutton.
1420 *July* 21 Florence	Thomas Polton, Hereford, Chichester 1421, Worcester 1426, d. 1433. Aug. 23		Reg. Chicheley. Reg. Polton. Provided July 15.
1420 July 28 Fulham	William Heyworth, Lichfield, d. 1447. Mar. 13	} Richard London	Reg. Heyworth.
1422 May 24 Blackfriars, London	Thomas Spofford, Hereford, res. 1448	Hen. Winchester Thom. Durham Phil. Worcester John Norwich and Suffragans of London and Winchester.	Reg. Spofford.
1422 June 7 Canterbury	John Langdon, Rochester, d. 1434. Sept. 30	Henry Phil. Worcester John Dromore	Reg. Chicheley. Reg. Langdon.
1425 May 27 Blackfriars, London	John Stafford, Bath, Canterbury 1443, d. 1452. May 25	Hen. Winchester *John London* *Phil. Worcester* *Will. Lichfield* *John Rochester* *Ben. S. David's*	Reg. Stafford, and Comparison of various Records.
1425 Rome	John Wells, Llandaff, d. 1440. Nov.		Pope's Penitentiary. Reg. Chicheley. Provided July 9. 1425. Profess. Jan. 15. 1426.
1425 Rome	John Cliderow, Bangor, d. 1434		Clericus Cameræ Apostolicæ. Reg. Chich. Profess. Mar. 20. 1426.
1426 May 26 Leicester	William Gray, London, Lincoln 1431, d. 1436. Feb.	Henry	Reg. Chicheley. Reg. Gray.

K

Date of Consecration.	Name and See.	Consecrators.	Authorities, &c.
1426 June 30 Mortlake	John Rickingale, Chichester, d. 1429	} Henry	Reg. Chicheley.
1426 Aug. 18 Canterbury	William Alnwick, Norwick, Lincoln 1436, d. 1449. Dec. 5	} Henry	Reg. Chicheley. John Stone. MS.
1427 Oct. 26 Lambeth	Robert Neville, Sarum, Durham 1438, d. 1457. July 8	} Henry	Reg. Chicheley. Reg. Neville.
1430 Apr. 16 S. Thomas's, Eastbridge, Canterbury	Marmaduke Lumley, Carlisle, Lincoln 1450, d. 1450	John York John Rochester Will. Norwich	Reg. Kemp.
1431 Feb. 11	Simon Sydenham, Chichester, d. 1438	} Henry *Winchester*	Reg. Chicheley.
1431 Sept. 16 Foligno	Robert Fitzhugh, London, d. 1436. Jan. 15		Reg. Fitzhugh. "In Civitate Fulgensi."
1433 Nov. 1	John Low, S. Asaph, Rochester 1444, d. 1467	} Henry *Winchester*	Reg. Chicheley. Cf. Wharton. Ep. Asav.
1434 Jan. 31 Blackfriars, London	Thomas Rudborne, S. David's, d. 1442	} Henry *Winchester*	Reg. Rudborne. MS. Tanner.
1435 May 1 Canterbury	Thomas Brown, Rochester, Norwich 1436, d. 1445. Dec. 6	Henry Sim. Chichester Richard Ross	Reg. Chicheley. Reg. Brown.
1435 May 15 Blackfriars, London	Thomas Bouchier, Worcester, Ely 1443, Canterbury 1454, d. 1486. Mar. 30	Hen. Winchester John York } John Bath Robert Sarum John S. Asaph	Reg. Bouchier.
1436 Oct. 28 Carmelites, London	Robert Gilbert, London, d. 1448. June 22	} Henry Winchester	Reg. Gilbert.

DATE OF CONSECRATION.	NAME AND SEE.	CONSECRATORS.	AUTHORITIES, &c.
1436 Nov. 25 London	Thomas Cheriton, Bangor, d. 1447. Dec. 23	} *Henry Winchester*	Reg. Chicheley.
1437 Mar. 24 Durham House, Westminster	William Wells, Rochester, d. 1444. Feb.	Henry Thom. Norwich Marm. Carlisle Richard Ross	Reg. Wells.
1438 July 20 Windsor	William Aiscough, Sarum, d. 1450. June 29	Hen. Winchester John Bath Thom. Norwich Thom. S. David's	Reg. Aiscough. MSS. Wharton.
1438 July 27 Otford	Richard Praty, Chichester, d. 1445. Aug.	} Henry	Reg. Praty.
1441 *May* 21	Nicolas Ashby, Llandaff, d. 1458		V. Reg. Chicheley.
1442 S. Stephen's, Westminster	William Linwood, S. David's, d. 1446. Oct. 21		Linwood's Will. Reg. S. Stephen's MS. Between Aug. 26 and Oct. 2.
1442	James Blakedon, Achonry, Bangor 1453, d. 1464. Oct. 24		Provided 1442. Oct. 15. Hib. Dominic. c. 13. Ware and Cotton.
1443 Oct. 13 Eton Old College	Thomas Beckington, Bath, d. 1465. Jan. 14	Will. Lincoln Will. Sarum Nic. Llandaff	Reg. Beckington.
1444 Mar. 22 Eton	John Carpenter, Worcester, d. 1476	Will. Sarum Thom. Bath John S. Asaph	Reg. Carpenter.
1444 June 14 Croydon	Reginald Peacock, S. Asaph, Chichester 1450, dep. 1457. Dec. 4	John John Rochester Thom. Norwich Thom. Bath Richard Ross	Reg. Stafford.
1444 Nov. 1 Lambeth	" Ep. Lexoviensis," Pope's Collector in England.	John Robert London Thomas Ely	John Stone MS.
1446 Feb. 6 Lambeth	Adam Moleyns, Chichester 1450 d. 1450. Jan. 9	} John	V. Reg. Sarum. MSS. Wharton. and Reg. Stafford.

Date of Consecration.	Name and See.	Consecrators.	Authorities, &c.
1446 *Mar.* 27 Lambeth	Walter Lehart, Norwich, d. 1472. May 17	John	V. Reg. Lehart and Stafford.
1447 May 7 King's College, Cambridge	John Langton, S. David's, d. 1447. May 22	Will. Lincoln	Reg. Alnwick. MSS. Hutton.
1447 July 9 S. Paul's	William Booth, Lichfield, York 1452, d. 1464. Sept. 12	Robert London Thom. Bath Reg. S. Asaph Wal. Norwich	Reg. D. & C. S. Paul. MSS. Hutton. Reg. Booth.
1447 July 30 Eton	William Patten, of Wainfleet, Winchester, d. 1486. Aug. 11	John	Budden. V. Wainfl. ex Arch. Eton. Cf. MS. Rawlinson. B. 268. Bibl. Bodl. from Reg. Eton. 13. fol. 2.
1447 *Nov.* 19	John de la Bere, S. David's, res. 1460	John	Reg. Stafford. Profession Nov. 13.
1448 *June* 23	John Stanbery, Bangor, Hereford 1453, d. 1474. May 11	John	Reg. Stafford. Licence June 20.
1449 Feb. 9 Lambeth	Richard Beauchamp, Hereford, Sarum 1450, d. 1481	John John Rochester Thomas Bath John Worcester Reg. S. Asaph Ad. Chichester Walt. Norwich Marm. Carlisle	Reg. Beauchamp. Reg. Stafford.
1450 Feb. 8 York House, Westminster	Thomas Kemp, London, d. 1489. Mar. 28	John York Will. Winchester Thomas Ely Thomas Bath Walt. Norwich Rich. Hereford	Reg. Kemp. Lond.
1450 Mar. 15 York House	Nicolas Close, Carlisle, Lichfield 1452, d. 1452	John York Thom. London	Reg Kemp.

DATE OF CONSECRATION.	NAME AND SEE.	CONSECRATORS.	AUTHORITIES, &c.
1451	Thomas Knight, S. Asaph, d. 1471		Jan. 27. Browne Willis. Not improbably Feb. 14.
1451 Feb. 14	Reginald Boulers, Hereford, Lichfield 1453, d. 1459	John Rochester	Reg. Boulers.
1452 June 18	John Chadworth, Lincoln, d. 1471. Nov. 23		Reg. Chadworth. MSS. Hutton.
1452 *Nov.* 26 In the province of York	William Percy, Carlisle, d. 1462	Rob. Durham Thom. S. Asaph John Lincoln John The Isles John Philippopolis	Reg. Booth. Licence Nov. 16
1454 Sept. 8 Mortlake	William Gray, Ely, d. 1478. Aug. 4	Thomas John Worcester Richard Ross	Reg. Gray. MSS. Cole.
1457 Sept. 25 Sherburn	Laurence Booth, Durham, York 1476, d. 1480. May 19	*William York*	Chambre viii. Reg Booth.
1458	John Hunden, Llandaff, res. 1476		Temp. Aug. 25.
1458 Dec. 3	George Neville, Exeter, York 1464, d. 1476. June 8	*Thomas*	Cf. Reg. Neville. Licence Nov. 29.
1459 *June* 3	John Arundel, Chichester, d. 1477. Oct. 18	*Thomas*	Licence May 31.
1459 Nov. 25 Coventry	John Hales, Lichfield, d. 1490. Dec. 30	Thomas	Reg. Hales.
1460 *Aug.* 31	Robert Tully, S. David's, d. 1481	*Thomas*	Licence Aug. 28.
1462 Oct. 24 London	John Kingscote, Carlisle, d. 1463. Nov. 5		Reg. Booth.

Date of Consecration.	Name and See.	Consecrators.	Authorities, &c.
1464 June 24 York	Richard Scroope, Carlisle, d. 1468. May 10	George Exeter	Lansd. MS. 721.
1465 *Mar.* 10	Richard Edenham, Bangor, d. 1496	*Thomas*	Licence Mar. 8.
1465 July 7	John Booth, Exeter, d. 1478. Apr. 1	Thomas	Reg. Booth. MSS. Wharton.
1466 Mar. 16 York House, Westminster	Robert Stillington, Bath, d. 1491. May	George York	Reg. Stillington.
1468 Apr. 3	Thomas Scott, or Rotherham, Rochester, Lincoln 1472, York 1480, d. 1500. May 29	*Thomas*	Custumale Roffense. Licence Mar. 27.
1468 Oct. 16 Westminster	Edward Story, Carlisle, Chichester 1478, d. 1503. Jan. 29	George York	Lansd. MS. 721.
1471 *Oct.* 20	Richard Redman, S. Asaph, Exeter 1495–6, Ely 1501, d. 1505. Aug. 24	*Thomas*	Licence Oct. 13.
1472 Mar. 15	John Alcock, Rochester, Worcester 1476, Ely 1486, d. 1500. Oct. 1	*Thomas*	Custumale Roffense. Licence Mar. 13.
1472 Oct. 4 S. Blaise, Rome	James Goldwell, Norwich, d. 1499. Feb. 15	Simon Antibari	John Stone MS.
1474 Aug. 21 S. Mary's, Westminster	Thomas Milling, Hereford, d. 1492	Thom. London Rich. S. Asaph Will. Ardfert	Reg. Milling.
1476 *July* 21	John Smith, Llandaff, d. 1478. Jan. 29	*Thomas*	Licence July 17.

Date of Consecration.	Name and See.	Consecrators.	Authorities, &c.
1476 Sept. 22	John Russell, Rochester, Lincoln 1480, d. 1494. Dec. 30	*Thomas*	Custumale Roffense. Licence Sept. 20.
1476	William Dudley, Durham, d. 1483.	*Laurence York*	Betw. Sept. 1 & Oct. 30.
1478 Apr. 26 London	Richard Bell, Carlisle, d. 1495	Edw. Chichester	Lansd. MS. 721. Chambre ix.
1478 Nov. 8 S. Stephen's, Westminster	Peter Courtenay, Exeter, Winchester 1487, d. 1492. Sept. 22	Thom. London	Reg. Courtenay. MSS. Wharton.
1478	John Marshall, Llandaff, d. 1496		Temp. Sept. 18.
1479 Jan. 31 Lambeth	John Morton, Ely, Canterbury 1486, d. 1500. Sept. 15	Thomas	Ang. Sac. i. 674. Licence Jan. 15.
1480 Oct. 1	Edmund Audley, Rochester, Hereford 1492, Sarum 1502, d. 1524. Aug. 23	*Thomas*	Custumale Roffense. Licence Sept. 18.
1482 *Apr.* 21	Lionel Woodville, Sarum, d. 1484	*Thomas*	Licence Apr. 17.
1482 July 28	Richard Martin, S. David's, d. 1483	Thomas	Reg. Martin. MS. Tanner. Reg. Bouchier.
1483 Sept. 7	Thomas Langton, S. David's, Sarum 1485, Winchester 1493, d. 1501. Jan. 27	John Worcester	Licence Aug. 23. Commission Sept. 3. Reg. Bouchier.
1484 Rome	John Sherwood, Durham, d. 1494. Jan. 12		Reg. Rotherham. Before Oct. 14.

Date of Consecration.	Name and See.	Consecrators.	Authorities, &c.
1485 Oct. 9	Hugh Pavy, S. David's, d. 1496	*Thomas*	Reg. Pavy. MS. Tanner. Licence Sept. 22.
1487 *Jan. 28* *Canterbury*	Robert Morton, Worcester, d. 1497	John *John Ely* *Edm. Rochester* *Thomas Sarum*	Reg. R. Morton. Cf. MS. Cotton. Julius B. 12.
1487 Apr. 8 Norwich	Richard Fox, Exeter, Bath 1492, Durham 1494, Winchester 1501, d. 1528. Sept. 14	John *James Norwich* *Peter Winchester*	Reg. Morton. P. & C. Cant. and Julius B. 12.
1489 Nov. 15 Lambeth	Richard Hill, London, d. 1496. Feb. 20	John John Ely Edw. Chichester	Reg. Hill.
1493 Feb. 3 *S. Stephen's, Westminster*	Oliver King, Exeter, Bath 1495, d. 1503 Aug. 29	John	Cf. Reg. P. & C. Cant. Smith and King MSS. Wharton.
	William Smith, Lichfield, Lincoln 1496, d. 1514. Jan. 2		Cf. Churton's Life of Smith.
1493 Apr. 28 Lambeth	Thomas Savage, Rochester, London 1496, York 1501, d. 1507. Sept. 2	John Richard London Thomas Pavada	Reg. Savage.
1494 Feb. 23 Lambeth	John Blyth, Sarum, d. 1499. Aug. 23	John	Reg. Blyth.
1496 *Jan. 17*	Michael Deacon, S. Asaph, d. 1500	*John*	Licence Jan. 11.
1496	William Senhouse, Carlisle, Durham 1502, d. 1505		Temp. Dec. 11. 1495.

DATE OF CONSECRATION.	NAME AND SEE.	CONSECRATORS.	AUTHORITIES, &c.
1496 *Sept.* 11	John Ingleby, Llandaff, d. 1499	} John	Licence Sept. 6.
1496	Henry Dean, Bangor, Sarum 1500, Canterbury 1501, d. 1503. Feb. 15	} John	Temp. Oct. 6.
1496 *Nov.* 20	John Arundel, Lichfield, Exeter 1502, d. 1504. Mar. 15 John Morgan, S. David's, d. 1504	} John	Cf. Reg. Arundel, and P. and C. Cant. Licence Nov. 12.
1497 May 21 Lambeth	Richard Fitz James, Rochester, Chichester 1503, London 1506, d. 1522. Jan. 15	John John Llandaff, Henry Bangor,	Reg. Fitz James. Cf. Wood's Ath. Oxon. I. 564.
1497 Sept. 10 Rome	John de Gigliis, Worcester, d. 1498. Aug. 25		Reg. J. de Gigliis.
1498 Rome	Silvester de Gigliis, Worcester, d. 1521. Apr. 16		Prov. Dec. 24. 1498.
1499 *Oct.* 20	Thomas Jane, Norwich, d. 1500. Sept.	} John	Cf. Reg. P. & C. Cant. &c.
1500	Thomas Pigott, Bangor, d. 1504. Aug. 15		
1500 Apr. 26	Miles Salley, Llandaff, d. 1516–7 David ap Yorwerth, S. Asaph, d. 1503	} John	Reg. P. & C. Cant. Wharton Ep. Asav. 355. Licences Mar.13. Temp. May 12.
1501 Apr. 18	Richard Nykke, Norwich, d. 1536. Jan. 14	}	Cf. Reg. P. & C. Cant. Nykke, &c. Licence Apr. 17.

DATE OF CONSECRATION.	NAME AND SEE.	CONSECRATORS.	AUTHORITIES, &c.
1502 Sept. 25 Fulham	William Warham, London, Canterbury 1503 d. 1532. Aug. 23	Rich. Winchester John Exeter Rich. Rochester	Cf. Reg. Warham. Reg. Dean.
1503 *Sept.* 17	Roger Layburn, Carlisle, d. 1508	}	Lansd. MS. 721.
1503 Sept. 17	Geoffrey Blyth, Lichfield, d. 1533	} Rich. Winchester	Cf. Reg. Blyth, & P. & C. Cant.
1504 *Feb.* 4	David ap Owen, S. Asaph, d. 1513. Feb.	} William	Cf. Reg. P. & C. Cant. Licence Jan. 31.
1504 Oct. 27 Lambeth	Richard Mayew, Hereford, d. 1516. Apr. 18	{ William Will. Lincoln Geoff. Lichfield	Reg. Mayew.
1504 Nov. 24 Lambeth	William Barons, London, d. 1505. Oct. 10 John Fisher, Rochester, d. 1535. June 22	William Will. Lincoln Rich. Norwich	Reg. Barons, Fisher, &c. Cf. Churton's Life of Bp. Smith, 218. note.
1505 Jan. 5	Hugh Oldham, Exeter, d. 1519. June 25	} William	Cf. Reg. P. & C. Cant. Warham & Oldham. Licence Dec. 29.
1505 May 11	Robert Sherborn, S. David's, Chichester 1508, d. 1536. Aug. 21	} William	Cf. Reg. P. & C. Cant. Warham & Smith of Lincoln.
1505 *Aug.* 31	John Penny, Bangor, Carlisle 1509, d. 1520	} *William*	Warham's Register is mutilated at this point down to 1509. Licence Aug. 30.
1506 Nov. 8	James Stanley, Ely, d. 1515. Mar. 22	} *William*	V. Rymer. 1506.
1507 *Dec.* 12	Christ. Bainbridge, Durham, York 1508, d. 1514. July 14		Cf. Reg. D. & C. York.

Date of Consecration.	Name and See.	Consecrators.	Authorities, &c.
1509 June 17 Lambeth	Thomas Skirvington, Bangor, d. 1533	William Rich. London Rich. Norwich	Reg. Warham.
1509 June 24 York House	Thomas Ruthall, Durham, d. 1523. Feb. 4	Christ. York Rich. Norwich John Negropont	Reg. Bainbridge.
1509 July 22 Lambeth	Edward Vaughan, S. David's, d. 1522	Rich. London Rich. Norwich John ———	Reg. Warham.
1510 Jan. 20 S. Paul's	Nicolas Comyn, Ferns	R. London	Ware.
1512 Dec. 5	John, "Aviensis"	Miles Llandaff	Reg. Warham. Licence Dec. 4.
1513 Apr. 17	Roger Smith, Lydda, d. 1518	Miles Llandaff	Reg. Warham. Licence Apr. 11.
1513 May 29 Lambeth	Edmund Birkhead, S. Asaph, d. 1518. Apr.	William Thom. Durham John Chalcedon	Reg. Warham.
1513 July 3 S. Thomas of Acre, London	John Young, Gallipoli, d. 1526. Mar. 28 Richard, "Naturensis," Suff. of Durham	Rich. London	Reg. Fitz James.
1513	John Kite, Armagh, Thebes 1521, Carlisle 1521, d. 1537. June 19		Ware.
1514 Mar. 26 Lambeth	Thomas Wolsey, Lincoln, York 1514, d. 1530. Nov. 29	William Rich. London Rich. Winchester Rich. Norwich Hugh Exeter Edm. S. Asaph	Reg. Warham.
1514 Nov. 12 Lambeth	William Atwater, Lincoln, d. 1521. Feb. 4	William Rich. London Rich. Winchester Hugh Exeter M. Llandaff Edm. S. Asaph	Reg. Warham.

Date of Consecration.	Name and See.	Consecrators.	Authorities, &c.
1515 Oct. 7 Lambeth	Nicolas West, Ely, d. 1533. Apr. 28	William John Rochester Hugh Exeter	Reg. Warham.
1516 Nov. 30 Otford	Charles Booth, Hereford, d. 1535. May 5	William Rich. Winchester Rich. Norwich	Reg. Warham & Booth.
1517 Mar. 8 Blackfriars	George de Athequa, Llandaff, res. 1537	Charles Hereford John Gallipoli Fras. Castoriensis	Reg. Warham & Booth.
1518 July 11 Otford	Henry Standish, S. Asaph, d. 1535. July 9	William Rob. Chichester John Gallipoli	Reg. Warham.
1519 Nov. 6 Otford	John Voysey, Exeter, d. 1554. Oct. 23	William John Rochester Thom. Leighlin	Reg. Warham.
1521 May 5 Lambeth	John Longlands, Lincoln, d. 1547. May 7	William John Rochester Nicolas Ely John Exeter	Reg. Warham.
1522 Oct. 19 Lambeth	Cuthbert Tunstall, London, Durham 1530, d. 1559. Nov. 18	William Thom. Durham John Rochester	Reg. Warham & Tunstall.
1523 Apr. 26 Lambeth	Richard Rawlins, S. David's, d. 1536. Feb. 18	William John Rochester John Lincoln	Reg. Warham.
1523 Dec. 6 Rome	John Clerk, Bath, d. 1541. Jan. 3		Cotton. MS. Vitellius, B. 5.
1530 Nov. 27 B. London's Chapel	John Stokesley, London, d. 1539. Sept. 8	John Lincoln Hen. S. Asaph Rich. S. David's	Reg. Stokesley.
1531 Dec. 3	Stephen Gardiner, Winchester, d. 1555. Nov. 12		Reg. Gardiner.
1531 Dec. 10	Edward Lee, York, d. 1544. Sept. 13		Drake's Eboracum. MSS. Torre at York, &c.
1533 Mar. 30 S. Stephen's, Westminster	Thomas Cranmer, Canterbury, d. 1556. Mar. 21	John Lincoln John Exeter Hen. S. Asaph	Reg. Cranmer.

Date of Consecration.	Name and See.	Consecrators.	Authorities, &c.
1534 Apr. 19 Croydon	Thomas Goodrich, Ely, d. 1554. May 10 Rowland Lee, Lichfield, d. 1543. Jan. 24 John Salcot, or Capon, Bangor, Sarum 1539, d. 1557. Oct. 6	Thomas John Lincoln *Thom.* Sidon	Reg. Cranmer.
1535 Apr. 11 S. Stephen's, Westminster	Nicolas Shaxton, Sarum, res. 1539	Thomas John London Thom. Sidon	Reg. Cranmer.
1535 Sept. 26 Winchester	Edward Fox, Hereford, d. 1548. May 8 Hugh Latimer, Worcester, res. 1539. July 1 John Hilsey, Rochester, d. 1538	Thomas Steph. Winchester Nic. Sarum	Reg. Fox. Reg. Hilsey. Rymer.
1536 Mar. 19 Lambeth	George Brown, Dublin Thomas Manning, Ipswich John Salisbury, Thetford, Man 1571, d. 1573	Thomas Nic. Sarum John Rochester	Reg. Cranmer.
1536 June 11 Lambeth	Richard Sampson, Chichester, Coventry 1543, d. 1554. Sept. 25 William Barlow, S. David's, Bath 1549 Chichester 1559, d. 1569. Dec. 10 Wm. Rugg, or Repps, Norwich, res. 1550	Thomas John Exeter John Bath	Haddan on Bramhall, vol. iii. pp. 138–143, and Preface.

Date of Consecration.	Name and See.	Consecrators.	Authorities, &c.
1536 July 2 Lambeth	Robert Parfew, or Wharton, S. Asaph, Hereford 1554, d. 1558. Sept. 22	Thomas John Bangor Will. Norwich	Reg. Cranmer.
1536 Oct. 22 Lady Chapel, Blackfriars	William More, Colchester	John Rochester Rob. S. Asaph Thom. Sidon	Reg. Cranmer. Commission Oct. 20.
153–	Robert King, Rheon, Osney 1541, Oxford 1546, d. 1557. Dec. 4		Suffragan of Lincoln, as Bishop of Rheon in the province of Athens, in 1536.
1537 Mar. 25 Lady Chapel, Blackfriars	Robert Holgate, Llandaff, York 1545, d. 1556	John Rochester John Bangor Nic. Sarum	Reg. Cranmer.
1537 *June* 17	Thomas Sparke, Berwick, d. 1571	Edward York	Reg. Lee. Cf. Rymer.
1537 June 24 Lambeth	Lewis Thomas, Shrewsbury, John Bird, Penreth, Bangor 1539, Chester 1541, d. 1556	Thomas John Rochester Rob. S. Asaph	Reg. Cranmer.
1537 Aug. 19 Savoy Chapel	Robert Aldrich, Carlisle, d. 1556. Mar. 5	John London Rob. S. Asaph John Rochester	Reg. Lee.
1537 Nov. 4 Lambeth	Thomas Morley, Marlborough,	Thomas John Lincoln John Rochester	Reg. Cranmer.
1537 Dec. 9 S. Paul's	Richard Yngworth, Dover John Hodgkins, Bedford	John London John Rochester Rob. S. Asaph	Reg. Cranmer.
1538 Mar. 24 Rochester House, Lambeth	Henry Holbeach, Bristol, (Suff.) Rochester 1544, Lincoln 1547, d. 1551. Aug. 2	John Rochester Hugh Worcester Rob. S. Asaph	Reg. Cranmer.

DATE OF CONSECRATION.	NAME AND SEE.	CONSECRATORS.	AUTHORITIES, &c.
1538 Apr. 7 Lady Chapel, Blackfriars	William Finch, Taunton, d. 1559	John Rochester Rob. S. Asaph Will. Colchester	Reg. Cranmer.
1538 *Dec.* 29	Robert Pursglove, or Silvester, Hull, d. 1579. May 2	Edw. York	Cf. Rymer.
1539 Mar. 23 S. John's, Southampton	John Bradley, Shaftesbury	John Bangor John Hippo Tho. Marlborough	Reg. Cranmer.
1539 *Aug.* 17	John Bell, Worcester, d. 1556. Aug. 11	Thomas	Cf. Rymer.
1539 Nov. 23 Lambeth	John Skip, Hereford, d. 1552. Mar. 30	Thomas Rich. Dover Will. S. David's	Reg. Skip.
1540 Apr. 4 London House Chapel	Edmund Bonner, London, d. 1569. Sept. 5 Nicolas Heath, Rochester, Worcester 1543, York 1555, d. 1579	Steph. Winton Rich. Chichester John Hereford	Reg. Bonner. Reg. Cranmer.
1540 Dec. 19 Henry VII.'s Chapel	Thomas Thirlby, Westminster, Norwich 1550, Ely 1554, d. 1570. Aug. 26	Edm. London Nic. Rochester John Bedford	Reg. Thirlby.
1541 May 29 B. Bath's Chapel, in the Minories, London	William Knight, Bath, d. 1547. Sept. 29	Nic. Rochester Rich. Dover John Bedford	Reg. Cranmer.
1541 Sept. 25 Croydon	John Wakeman, Gloucester, d. 1549	Thomas Edm. London Tho. Westminster	Reg. Cranmer.
1541 Oct. 23 Peterborough	John Chamber, Peterborough, d. 1556. Feb.	Thomas Ely Rob. Down Tho. Philadelphia	Reg. Cranmer.

DATE OF CONSECRATION.	NAME AND SEE.	CONSECRATORS.	AUTHORITIES, &c.
1542 Feb. 19 D. of S. Paul's Chapel	Arthur Bulkeley, Bangor, d. 1553. Mar. 14	John Sarum Will. S. David's John Gloucester	Reg. Cranmer.
1542 June 25 Hampton	Paul Bush, Bristol, d. 1558. Oct. 11	Nic. Rochester Tho. Westminster John Bedford	Reg. Cranmer.
1543 May 6	George Day, Chichester, d. 1556. Aug. 11	Thomas	Cf. Rymer.
1545 May 3 Westminster Abbey	Antony Kitchin, Llandaff, d. 1563. Oct. 31	Tho. Westminster Thom. Sidon Lewis Shrewsbury	Reg. Cranmer.
1546 Feb. 14 S. Paul's	Henry Man, Sodor and Man, d. 1556. Oct. 19	Edm. London Thom. Sidon John Bedford	Reg. Bonner.
1547 Sept. 25 D. of S. Paul's Chapel	Nicolas Ridley, Rochester, London 1550, d. 1555. Oct. 16	Henry Lincoln John Bedford Thom. Sidon	Reg. Cranmer.
1548 Sept. 9 Chertsey	Robert Ferrar, S. David's, d. 1555. Mar. 30	Thomas Henry Lincoln Nic. Rochester	Reg. Cranmer.
1550 June 29 Lambeth	John Poynet, Rochester, Winchester 1551 d. 1556. Aug. 11	Thomas Nic. London Arth. Bangor	Reg. Cranmer.
1551 Mar. 8 Lambeth	John Hooper, Gloucester, d. 1555. Feb. 9	Thomas Nic. London John Rochester	Reg. Cranmer.
1551 Aug. 30 Croydon	Miles Coverdale, Exeter, d. 1565. May 20 John Scory, Rochester, Chichester 1552, Hereford 1559, d. 1585. June 26	Thomas Nic. London John Bedford	Reg. Cranmer.
1552 June 26 Croydon	John Taylor, Lincoln, d. 1554. Dec.	Thomas Nic. London John Rochester	Reg. Cranmer.

DATE OF CONSECRATION.	NAME AND SEE.	CONSECRATORS.	AUTHORITIES, &c.
1553 May 26 Croydon	John Harley, Hereford, d. 1554	Thomas Nic. London Rob. Carlisle	Reg. Cranmer.
1554 Apr. 1 S. Saviour's, Southwark	John White, Lincoln, Winchester 1556, d. 1560. Jan. 12 James Brooks, Gloucester, d. 1558. Sept. 7 Maurice Griffin, Rochester, d. 1558. Nov. 20 Gilbert Bourn, Bath, d. 1569. Sept. 10 Henry Morgan, S. David's, d. 1559. Dec. 23 George Coates, Chester, d. 1555	Edm. London Cuth. Durham Steph. Winchester	Reg. D. & C. Cant. sede vacante.
1554 Oct. 28 London House	John Hopton, Norwich, d. 1558	Edm. London Cuth. Durham Thom. Ely	Reg. D. & C. Cant.
1554 Nov. 18 London House	Ralph Bayne, Lichfield, dep. 1559 John Holyman, Bristol, d. 1558. Dec. 20	Edm. London John Norwich Gilb. Bath	Reg. D. & C. Cant. Machyn's Diary 75.
1554	Richard Pates, Worcester, dep. 1559		Temporals 1555. Mar. 5.
1555 Sept. 8 London House	William Glynne, Bangor, d. 1558. May 21 James Turberville, Exeter, dep. 1559 Hugh Curwen, Dublin, Oxford 1567 d. 1568. Oct.	Edm. London Thom. Ely Maur. Rochester	Reg. D. & C. Cant. Machyn's Diary 94.

M

Date of Consecration.	Name and See.	Consecrators.	Authorities, &c.
1555	Thomas Goldwell, S.Asaph, dep.1559		Temporals 1556. Jan. 22.
1556 Mar. 22 Greyfriars, Greenwich,	Reginald Pole, Canterbury, d. 1558. Nov. 19	Nic. York Edm. London Thom. Ely Rich. Worcester John Lincoln Maur. Rochester Thom. S̹ Asaph	Reg. Pole. Machyn's Diary 102.
1556	Cuthbert Scott, Chester, dep. 1559	Nic. York	Temporals 1556. Sept. 29.
1557 Aug. 15 Chiswick	Thomas Watson, Lincoln, dep. 1559 David Poole, Peterborough, dep. 1559 Owen Oglethorpe, Carlisle, dep. 1559	Nic. York Thom. Ely Will. Bangor	Reg. Pole.
1557 Nov. 21 London House	John Christopherson, Chichester, d. 1558	Edm. London Thom. Ely Maur. Rochester	Reg. Pole.
1559 Dec. 17 Lambeth	Matthew Parker, Canterbury, d. 1575. May 17	Will. Chichester John Hereford John Bedford Miles (ex) Exeter	Reg. Parker. Parker's Roll. MS. Machyn's Diary 220.
1559 Dec. 21 Lambeth	Edmund Grindal, London, York 1570, Canterbury 1576 d. 1583. July 6 Richard Cox, Ely, d. 1581. July 22 Rowland Meyrick, Bangor, d. 1566. Jan. 24 Edwin Sandys, Worcester, London 1570, York 1577, d. 1588. July 10	Matthew Will. Chichester John Hereford John Bedford	Reg. Parker. Le Neve. P. A. Wharton MS. 578. Ducarel's Abstract. Perceval. Apost. S. Parker Antiq. Mason de Minist. Angl. iii. 12.

DATE OF CONSECRATION.	NAME AND SEE.	CONSECRATORS.	AUTHORITIES, &c.
1560 Jan. 21 Lambeth	Nicolas Bullingham, Lincoln, Worcester 1571, d. 1576. Apr. 18 John Jewell, Sarum, d. 1571. Sept. 23 Thomas Young, S. David's, York 1561, d. 1568. June 26 Richard Davies, S. Asaph, S. David's 1561, d. 1581 Nov. 7	Matthew Edm. London Richard Ely John Bedford	Reg. Parker. Le Neve. P. A. Wharton MS. 578. Ducarel's Abstract. Perceval. Apost. S. Parker. Antiq. Mason. de Minist. Angl. iii. 12.
1560 Mar. 24 Lambeth	Edmund Gheast, Rochester, Sarum 1571, d. 1577. Feb. 28 Gilbert Berkeley, Bath, d. 1581. Nov. 2 Thomas Bentham, Coventry d. 1579. Feb. 21	Matthew Nic. Lincoln John Sarum	Ibid.
1560 July 14 Lambeth	William Alley, Exeter, d. 1570. Apr. 16	Matthew Edm. London Gilb. Bath	Ibid.
1560 Sept. 1 Lambeth	John Parkhurst, Norwich, d. 1575. Feb. 2	Matthew Gilb. Bath Will. Exeter	Ibid.
1561 Feb. 16 Lambeth	Robert Horne, Winchester, d. 1580. June 1 Edmund Scambler, Peterborough, Norwich 1585, d. 1594. May 7	Matthew Edm. London Thom. S. David's Thom. Lichfield	Ibid.

DATE OF CONSECRATION.	NAME AND SEE.	CONSECRATORS.	AUTHORITIES, &c.
1561 Mar. 2 London House	John Best, Carlisle, d. 1570. May 22 James Pilkington, Durham, d. 1576. Jan. 23	Thom. York	Parker. Antiq. Godwin. de Præs. Camden. Ann. Q. E. Machyn's Diary 252.
1561 May 4	William Downham, Chester, d. 1577. Dec. 3	Thom. York	Ibid.
1561 May 26 Croydon	Thomas Davis, S. Asaph, d. 1573	Matthew Rich. S. David's Edm. Rochester	Reg. Parker, &c.
1562 Apr. 19 Lambeth	Richard Cheyney, Gloucester, d. 1579. Apr. 25	Matthew Edm. London Edm. Rochester	Ibid.
1566 May 5 Lambeth	Hugh Jones, Llandaff, d. 1574. Nov.	Matthew Edm. London Edm. Rochester	Ibid.
1566 Oct. 20 Lambeth	Nicolas Robinson, Bangor, d. 1585. Feb. 13	Matthew Nic. Lincoln Edm. Rochester	Ibid.
1567 Mar. 9 York	Richard Barnes, Nottingham, Carlisle 1570, Durham 1577, d. 1587. Aug. 24	Thom. York James Durham Will. Chester	Reg. Young.
1569 May 15 Lambeth	Richard Rogers, Dover, d. 1597. May 19	Matthew Edm. London Edm. Rochester	Reg. Parker, &c.
1570 May 21 Canterbury	Richard Curteis, Chichester, d. 1582. Aug.	Matthew Edm. London Rob. Winchester Edm. Rochester	Ibid.
1571 Feb. 24 Lambeth	Thomas Cowper, Lincoln, Winchester 1584, d. 1594. Apr. 29	Matthew Rob. Winchester Nic. Worcester	Ibid.
1571 Mar. 18 Lambeth	William Bradbridge, Exeter, d. 1578. June 27	Matthew Rob. Winchester Nic. Worcester	Ibid.

DATE OF CONSECRATION.	NAME AND SEE.	CONSECRATORS.	AUTHORITIES, &c.
1572 Mar. 9 Lambeth	Edmund Freke, Rochester, Norwich 1575, Worcester 1584, d. 1591. Mar. 21	Matthew Rob. Winchester Edm. Sarum	Reg. Parker, &c.
1573 Dec. 13 Lambeth	William Hughes, S. Asaph, d. 1600. Nov. 18	Matthew Rob. Winchester Rich. Chichester	Ibid.
1575 Apr. 17 Lambeth	William Blethin, Llandaff, d. 1590. Oct. 15	Matthew Edw. London Edm. Rochester	Ibid.
1576 Apr. 15 Lambeth	John Piers, Rochester, Sarum 1577, York 1589, d. 1594. Sept. 28 John Meyrick, Sodor and Man, d. 1599	Edmund Edw. London Rob. Winchester	Reg. Grindal. Le Neve. P. A. Strype's Grindal. Wharton's MS. 578. Ducarel's Abstract. Perceval. A. S. Mason.
1577 Mar. 24 Lambeth	John Aylmer, London, d. 1594. June 3	Edmund Edw. York John Rochester	Ibid.
1577 Ap. 21 Lambeth	John Whitgift, Worcester, Canterbury 1583, d. 1604. Feb. 29	Edmund John London Rob. Winchester Rich. Chichester	Ibid.
1577 Sept. 29 Fulham	John May, Carlisle, d. 1598. Feb. 15	John London Will. Chester John Rochester Rich. Dover	Wharton's MS. 578. Godwin.
1578 Mar. 16 Lambeth	John Young, Rochester, d. 1605. Apr. 10	Edmund John London John Sarum	Reg. Grindal, &c.
1579	Marmad. Middleton, Waterford, S. David's 1582, dep. 1590, d. 1592. Nov. 30		Patent 1579. May 31. Cotton.
1579 Aug. 2 Croydon	John Wolton, Exeter, d. 1594. Mar. 13	Edmund John London John Rochester	Reg. Grindal, &c.

Date of Consecration.	Name and See.	Consecrators.	Authorities, &c.
1579 Nov. 8 S. Gregory's, by S. Paul's	William Chaderton, Chester, Lincoln 1595, d. 1608. Apr. 11	Edwin York John London John Rochester	Reg. Sandys. Wharton's MS. 578.
1580 Sept. 18 Croydon	John Watson, Winchester, d. 1584. Jan. 23 William Overton, Lichfield, d. 1609. Apr. 9	Edmund John London John Rochester	Reg. Grindal, &c.
1581 Sept. 3 Croydon	John Bullingham, Gloucester, d. 1598. May 20	Edmund John London John Rochester	Ibid.
1584 Sept. 13 Lambeth	Thomas Godwin, Bath, d. 1590. Nov. 19	John John London John Rochester	Reg. Whitgift. Le Neve. P. A. Wharton's MS. 578. Ducarel's Abstract. Perceval. A. S. Godwin. Mason.
1584 Dec. 6 Lambeth	William Wickham, Lincoln, Winchester 1595, d. 1595. June 11	John Edm. Worcester John Exeter M. S. David's	Ibid.
1585 Feb. 7 Lambeth	Richard Howland, Peterborough, d. 1600. June 23	John Thom. Winchester John Exeter Will. Lincoln	Ibid.
1586 Jan. 30 Lambeth	Herbert Westfaling, Hereford, d. 1602. Mar. 1 Hugh Bellott, Bangor, Chester 1595, d. 1596. June 13 Thomas Bickley, Chichester, d. 1596. Apr. 30	John John London John Sarum	Ibid.
1589 July 27 York	Matthew Hutton, Durham, York 1595, d. 1606. Jan. 15	John York John Carlisle Will. Chester	Reg. Piers. Le Neve. P. A., &c.

DATE OF CONSECRATION.	NAME AND SEE.	CONSECRATORS.	AUTHORITIES, &c.
1589 Dec. 14 Lambeth	Richard Fletcher, Bristol, Worcester 1593, London 1595, d. 1596. June 15 John Underhill, Oxford, d. 1592. May 12	John John London John Rochester John Gloucester	Reg. Whitgift, &c.
1591 Aug. 29 Croydon Church	Gervas Babington, Llandaff, Exeter 1595, Worcester 1597, d. 1610. May 17	John John London John Rochester	Ibid.
1591 Dec. 26 Lambeth	John Coldwell, Sarum, d. 1596. Oct. 14	John John London Thom. Winchester Rich. Bristol John Oxford	Ibid.
1592 Nov. 12 Fulham Church	John Sterne, Colchester,	John John London John Rochester Rich. Bristol	Ibid.
1593 Feb. 11 Lambeth	John Still, Bath, d. 1608. Feb. 26	John John London John Rochester Rich. Worcester	Ibid.
1593	John Thornborough, Limerick, Bristol 1603, Worcester 1616, d. 1641. July 3		Ware.
1594 June 9 Lambeth	Antony Rudd, S. David's, d. 1615. Mar. 7	John John Rochester Rich. Worcester	Reg. Whitgift, &c.
1595 Jan. 12 Lambeth	William Redman, Norwich, d. 1602. Sept. 25	John Rich. London John Rochester Will. Lincoln	Ibid.
1595 Apr. 13 London	Tobias Matthew, Durham, York 1606, d. 1628. Mar. 29	Matthew York	Surtees' Durham.

Date of Consecration.	Name and See.	Consecrators.	Authorities, &c.
1595 July 20 Croydon Church	William Morgan, Llandaff, S. Asaph 1601, d. 1604. Sept. 10	John Rich. London John Rochester Will. Norwich	Reg. Whitgift, &c.
1596 Jan. 25 Lambeth	William Day, Winchester, d. 1596. Sept. 20 Richard Vaughan, Bangor, Chester 1597, London 1604, d. 1607. Mar. 30	John Rich. London John Rochester	Ibid.
1596 June 13 Lambeth	Thomas Bilson, Worcester, Winchester 1597, d. 1616. June 18	John Rich. London Will. Winchester Rich. Bangor	Ibid.
1596 Aug. 15 Lambeth	Antony Watson, Chichester, d. 1605. Sept. 10	John John Rochester Rich. Bangor Tho. Worcester	Ibid.
1597 May 8 Lambeth	Richard Bancroft, London, Canterbury 1604 d. 1610. Nov. 2	John John Rochester Ant. S. David's Rich. Bangor Ant. Chichester	Ibid.
1598 July 23 London House	Henry Robinson, Carlisle, d. 1616. June 19	Rich. London John Rochester Ant. Chichester	Ibid.
1598 Nov. 12 Lambeth	Godfrey Goldsbrough, Gloucester, d. 1604. May 26 William Cotton, Exeter, d. 1621. Aug. 26 Henry Cotton, Sarum, d. 1615. May 7 Henry Rowlands, Bangor, d. 1616. July 6	John Rich. London Will. Lichfield Ant. Chichester	Ibid.

DATE OF CONSECRATION.	NAME AND SEE.	CONSECRATORS.	AUTHORITIES, &c.
1600 Feb. 3 Lambeth	Martin Heaton, Ely, d. 1609. July 12	John Rich. London Will. Lichfield Ant. Chichester	Reg. Whitgift, &c.
1600	George Lloyd, Sodor and Man, Chester 1605, d. 1615. Aug. 1		
1601 Apr. 26 Lambeth	Thomas Dove, Peterborough, d. 1630. Aug. 30	John Rich. London Tho. Winchester Ant. Chichester Mart. Ely	Ibid.
1601 Nov. 22 Henry VII.'s Chapel	Francis Godwin, Llandaff, Hereford 1617, d. 1633. Apr. 29	John Rich. London Will. Lincoln John Bath	Ibid.
1603 Feb. 20 Lambeth	Robert Bennett, Hereford, d. 1617. Oct. 25 John Jegon, Norwich, d. 1618. Mar. 13	John Rich. London John Rochester Ant. Chichester	Ibid.
1604 Feb. 12 Lambeth	John Bridges, Oxford, d. 1618. Mar. 26	John Rich. London Tobias Durham John Rochester Ant. Chichester	Ibid.
1604 Dec. 30 Lambeth	Richard Parry, S. Asaph, d. 1623. Sept. 26	Richard Rich. London Tob. Durham Mart. Ely	Reg. Bancroft. Le Neve P. A., &c.
1605 Feb. 10 London House	John Philips, Sodor and Man, d. 1633. Aug. 7	Rich. London Tob. Durham Ant. Chichester George Chester	Ibid.
1605 Mar. 17 Lambeth	Thomas Ravis, Gloucester, London 1607 d. 1609. Dec. 14	Richard Tob. Durham Ant. Chichester	Ibid.

Date of Consecration.	Name and See.	Consecrators.	Authorities, &c.
1605 June 30 Lambeth	William Barlow, Rochester, Lincoln 1608, d. 1613. Sept. 7	Richard Rich. London Ant. Chichester Thom. Gloucester	Reg. Bancroft. Le Neve P. A., &c.
1605 Nov. 3 Lambeth	Launcelot Andrewes, Chichester, Ely 1609, Winchester 1619, d. 1626. Sept. 25	Richard Rich. London John Norwich Thom. Gloucester Will. Rochester	Ibid.
1606 Sept. 7	William James, Durham, d. 1617. May 12	Tob. York Rich. London Will. Rochester Laun. Chichester	Mason. A. Wood. A. O. i. 356.
1607 July 12 Lambeth	Henry Parry, Gloucester, Worcester 1610, d. 1616. Dec. 12	Richard Thom. London Will. Rochester Launc. Chichester	Reg. Bancroft, &c.
1608 Apr. 17 Lambeth	James Montague, Bath, Winchester 1616, d. 1618. July 20	Richard Thom. London Hen. Sarum Will. Rochester Launc. Chichester Hen. Gloucester	Ibid.
1608 Oct. 9 Lambeth	Richard Neile, Rochester, Lichfield 1610, Lincoln 1614, Durham 1617, Winchester 1628, York 1632, d. 1640. Oct. 31	Richard Thom. London Launc. Chichester James Bath	Ibid.
1609 Dec. 3 Lambeth	George Abbot, Lichfield, London 1610, Canterbury 1611, d. 1633. Aug. 4 Samuel Harsnett, Chichester, Norwich 1619, York 1628, d. 1631. May 25	Richard Launc. Ely Rich. Rochester	Ibid.

DATE OF CONSECRATION.	NAME AND SEE.	CONSECRATORS.	AUTHORITIES, &c.
1610 Oct. 21 London House	John Spottiswoode, Glasgow Andrew Lamb, Brechin Gavin Hamilton, Galloway	George London Launc. Ely James Bath	Reg. Bancroft, &c. Perceval.
1611 June 9 Lambeth	Giles Thompson, Gloucester, d. 1612. June 14 John Buckridge, Rochester, Ely 1628, d. 1631. May 23	George John Oxford Launc. Ely James Bath Rich. Lichfield	Reg. Abbot. Wharton's MS. 578. Ducarel's Abstract. Le Neve. P. A. Perceval A. S. Mason.
1611 Sept. 8 Lambeth	John King, London, d. 1621. Mar. 30	George Rich. Lichfield Giles Gloucester John Rochester	Ibid.
1612 Sept. 20 Croydon	Miles Smith, Gloucester, d. 1624. Oct. 20	George John London Rich. Lichfield John Rochester	Ibid.
1614 Apr. 3 Lambeth	John Overall, Lichfield, Norwich 1618, d. 1619. May 12	George John London James Bath Rich. Lincoln John Rochester	Ibid. Lindsay, Preface to Mason.
1615 July 9 Lambeth	Richard Milbourne, S. David's, Carlisle 1621, d. 1624	George John London Launc. Ely John Rochester John Lichfield	Ibid.
1615 Dec. 3 Lambeth	Robert Abbot, Sarum, d. 1618. Mar. 2	George John London Launc. Ely Rich. Lincoln	Ibid.
1616 July 7 Lambeth	Thomas Morton, Chester, Lichfield 1619, Durham 1632, d. 1659. Sept. 22	George Chr. Armagh John London John Rochester John Lichfield John Caithness	Ibid.

Date of Consecration.	Name and See.	Consecrators.	Authorities, &c.
1616 Nov. 24 York	Robert Snowden, Carlisle, d. 1621. May 15	Tob. York Will. Durham Thom. Chester John Sodor & Man	Reg. Matthew, &c.
1616 Dec. 8 Lambeth	Arthur Lake, Bath, d. 1626. May 4 Lewis Bayly, Bangor, d. 1631. Oct. 26	George Launc. Ely Rich. Lincoln John Rochester John Lichfield	Reg. Abbøt, &c.
1617 Dec. 14 Lambeth	Nicolas Felton, Bristol, Ely 1619, d. 1626. Oct. 5 George Monteigne, Lincoln, London 1621, Durham 1628, York 1628, d. 1628. Nov. 6	George M. A. Spalato John London Launc. Ely John Rochester John Lichfield	Ibid.
1618 Apr. 19 Lambeth	Martin Fotherby, Sarum, d. 1620. Mar. 11	George John London John Lichfield Geo. Lincoln	Ibid.
1618 July 12 Lambeth	George Carleton, Llandaff, Chichester 1619, d. 1628. May	George John London John Rochester John Lichfield Geo. Lincoln	Ibid.
1619 May 9 Lambeth	John Bridgman, Chester, d. 1652 John Howson, Oxford, Durham 1628, d. 1632. Feb. 6 Rowland Searchfield, Bristol, d. 1622. Oct. 11	George John London John Rochester Thom. Lichfield Arthur Bath	Ibid.

Date of Consecration.	Name and See.	Consecrators.	Authorities, &c.
1619 Oct. 10 Lambeth	Theophilus Field, Llandaff, S. David's 1627, Hereford 1635, d. 1636. June 2	George John London John Rochester Rich. S. David's Geo. Derry	Reg. Abbot, &c.
1620 July 9 Lambeth	Robert Townson, Sarum, d. 1621. May 15	George John Rochester Thom. Lichfield Nic. Ely Geo. Lincoln	Ibid.
1621 Nov. 11 Westminster Abbey	John Williams, Lincoln, York 1641, d. 1650. Mar. 25	Geo. London John Worcester Nic. Ely John Oxford Theoph. Llandaff	Ibid.
1621 Nov. 18 London House	John Davenant, Sarum, d. 1641. Apr. 20 Valentine Carey, Exeter, d. 1626. June 10 William Laud, S. David's, Bath 1626, London 1628, Canterbury 1633, d. 1645. Jan. 10	Geo. London John Worcester Nic. Ely Geo. Chichester John Oxford Theoph. Llandaff	Ibid.
1621 Dec. 2 S. Peter's Drogheda	James Ussher, Meath, Armagh 1625, Carlisle 1642, d. 1656. Mar. 21	Chr. Armagh Thom. Kilmore Rob. Down & Con. Theoph. Dromore	Cotton.
1622 Dec. 18 S. Patrick's, Dublin	William Murray, Kilfenora, Llandaff 1627, d. 1640. Feb.	Lau. Dublin Jas. Meath Roland Clonfert	Cotton.
1623 Mar. 23 Lambeth	Robert Wright, Bristol, Lichfield 1632, d. 1643. Aug.	George Launc. Winchester John Lincoln Val. Exeter	Reg. Abbot, &c.

DATE OF CONSECRATION.	NAME AND SEE.	CONSECRATORS.	AUTHORITIES, &c.
1624 Feb. 15 Lambeth	John Hanmer, S. Asaph, d. 1629. July 23	George John Worcester Thom. Lichfield Theoph. Llandaff Will. S. David's	Reg. Abbot, &c.
1624 Sept. 26 York	Richard Senhouse, Carlisle, d. 1626. May 6	Tob. York Rich. Durham Thom. Lichfield John Chester	Reg. Matthew, &c.
1625 Mar. 6 Lambeth	Godfrey Goodman, Gloucester, dep. 1640, d. 1656. Jan. 19	George Geo. London John Rochester Theoph. Llandaff John Lincoln	Reg. Abbot, &c.
1626 Dec. 3 Durham House	Francis White, Carlisle, Norwich 1629, Ely 1631, d. 1638. Feb.	Rich. Durham John Rochester John Oxford Theoph. Llandaff Will. Kilfenora	Reg. Matthew, &c.
1627 Dec. 23 London House	Joseph Hall, Exeter, Norwich 1641, d. 1656. Sept. 8	Geo. London Rich. Durham John Rochester John Oxford Theo. S. David's Will. Kilfenora	Reg. Abbot, &c.
1628 Aug. 24 Croydon Chapel	Richard Montagu, Chichester, Norwich 1638, d. 1641. Apr. 13	George Will. London Rich. Winchester John Ely Fra. Carlisle	Ibid.
1628 Sept. 7 Croydon Chapel	Leonard Mawe, Bath, d. 1629. Sept. 2 Walter Curll, Rochester, Bath 1629, Winchester 1632, d. 1647	George Rich. Winchester John Ely Fra. Carlisle	Ibid.

Date of Consecration.	Name and See.	Consecrators.	Authorities, &c.
1628 Oct. 19 Lambeth	Richard Corbett, Oxford, Norwich 1632, d. 1635. July 28	George John Durham John Ely Fra. Carlisle Will. Llandaff	Reg. Abbot, &c.
1629 Mar. 15 Ely House	Barnabas Potter, Carlisle, d. 1642. Jan.	Sam. York	(Consecration Sermon). Wood. A. O. II. 6.
1629 Sept. 20	John Owen, S. Asaph, d. 1651. Oct. 15		Wood. A. O. I. 628.
1630 Feb. 7 Lambeth	John Bowle, Rochester, d. 1637. Oct. 9	George Sam. York Theo. S. David's Walter Rochester	Reg. Abbot, &c.
1630 Oct. 24 Croydon Chapel	William Piers, Peterborough, Bath 1632, d. 1670. Apr.	George Rich. Winchester Theo. S. David's Rich. Oxford Walter Rochester	Ibid.
1632 Mar. 4 Lambeth	David Dolben, Bangor, d. 1633. Nov. 27	George Will. London Theo. S. David's Fra. Ely	Ibid.
1632 June 10 Lambeth	John Bancroft, Oxford, d. 1641. Feb.	George Theo. S. David's Fra. Ely Will. Llandaff John Rochester	Ibid.
1633 Feb. 10 Lambeth	Augustine Lindsell, Peterborough, Hereford 1634, d. 1634. Nov. 6 George Coke, Bristol, Hereford 1636, d. 1646. Dec. 10	George Thom. Durham Theo. S. David's Rob. Lichfield Fra. Ely John Rochester John Oxford	Ibid.

Date of Consecration.	Name and See.	Consecrators.	Authorities, &c.
1633 Oct. 27 Lambeth	William Juxon, London, Canterbury 1660, d. 1663. June 4	William Rich. York Fra. Ely Will. Llandaff John Rochester John Oxford	Reg. Laud, &c.
1634 Feb. 16 Lambeth	Edmund Griffith, Bangor, d. 1637. May 26	William Will. London Fra. Ely Will. Llandaff John Oxford Aug. Peterborough	Reg. Laud, &c.
1634 Mar. 9 Winchester Ho. Southwark	William Forster, Sodor and Man, d. 1635	Rich. York Fra. Ely Aug. Peterborough	Reg. Neile.
1634 May 18 Lambeth	Francis Dee, Peterborough, d. 1638. Oct. 8	William Will. London Theo. S. David's Fra. Ely Will. Llandaff	Reg. Laud, &c.
1635 Mar. 8 Lambeth	Matthew Wren, Hereford, Norwich 1635, Ely 1638, d. 1667. Apr. 24	William Rich. York Walt. Winchester Fra. Ely Jos. Exeter Will. Llandaff	Ibid.
1635 June 10 Winchester Ho. Southwark	Richard Parr, Sodor and Man, d. 1643	Rich. York Fra. Ely Will. Llandaff	Reg. Neile.
1636 Feb. 28 Lambeth	Roger Mainwaring, S. David's, d. 1653. July 1	William Will. London Theo. Hereford Fra. Ely Will. Llandaff	Reg. Laud, &c.
1637 Jan. 15 Lambeth	Robert Skinner, Bristol, Oxford 1641, Worcester 1663, d. 1670. June 14	William Will. London Fra. Ely John Oxford Mat. Norwich	Ibid.

DATE OF CONSECRATION.	NAME AND SEE.	CONSECRATORS.	AUTHORITIES, &c.
1637 Sept. 3 Croydon Chapel	William Roberts, Bangor, d. 1665. Aug. 12	William Will. London Fra. Ely Will. Bath John Oxford	Reg. Laud, &c.
1638 Jan. 14 Lambeth	John Warner, Rochester, d. 1666. Oct. 14	William Will. London Walt. Winchester John Oxford Will. Bangor	Ibid.
1638 June 17 Lambeth	Brian Duppa, Chichester, Sarum 1641, Winchester 1660, d. 1662. Mar. 26	William Thom. Durham Rob. Lichfield John Oxford Matt. Ely	Ibid.
1639 Jan. 13 Lambeth	John Towers, Peterborough, d. 1649. Jan. 10	William Will. London Walt. Winchester Matt. Ely John Rochester	Ibid.
1640 Mar. 29 Lambeth	Morgan Owen, Llandaff, d. 1645. Mar. 4	William Will. London Walt. Winchester Matt. Ely John Rochester	Ibid.
1641 Dec. 19 Henry VII.'s Chapel	John Prideaux, Worcester, d. 1650. July 19	John York Will. London Walt. Winchester Rob. Lichfield	Ibid.
1642 Feb. 6 Fulham	Thomas Winniffe, Lincoln, d. 1654. Sept. 19 Henry King, Chichester, d. 1669. Sept. 30	Will. London Walt. Winchester John Rochester John Worcester	Ibid.
1642	Thomas Westfield, Bristol,d 1644.Jun.25		Cons. 1642. June 26. Hardy.
1642 May 15 Henry VII.'s Chapel	Ralph Brownrigg, Exeter, d. 1659. Dec. 7	John York Will. London Thom. Durham Hen. Chichester	Reg. Laud, &c.

Date of Consecration.	Name and See.	Consecrators.	Authorities, &c.
1644 Apr. Magdalene College, Oxford	Accepted Frewen, Lichfield, York 1660, d. 1664. Mar. 28	John York Rob. Oxford Br. Sarum John Peterborough John Worcester	Wood. A. O. II. 664. Le Neve gives Walt. Winchester instead of J. Worcester.
1644 Aug. Oxford	Thomas Howell, Bristol, d. 1646	James Armagh	Wood. A. O. II. 656.
1660 Oct. 28 Henry VII.'s Chapel	Gilbert Sheldon, London, Canterbury 1663, d. 1677. Nov. 9 Humfrey Henchman, Sarum, London 1663, d. 1675. Oct. 7 George Morley, Worcester, Winchester 1662, d. 1684. Oct. 29 Robert Sanderson, Lincoln, d. 1663. Jan. 29 George Griffith, S. Asaph, d. 1666. Nov. 28	Brian Winchester Acc. York Matt. Ely John Rochester Hen. Chichester	Reg. Juxon, &c. Kennett's Register, p. 296.
1660 Dec. 2 Henry VII.'s Chapel	William Lucy, S. David's, d. 1677. Oct. 4 Hugh Lloyd, Llandaff, d. 1667. June 7 John Gauden, Exeter, Worcester 1662, d. 1662. Sept. 20 Richard Sterne, Carlisle, York 1664, d. 1683. June 18	Acc. York Gilb. London John Rochester Humf. Sarum Geo. Worcester	Lucy, Lloyd, and Gauden, are said to have been consecrated on Nov. 18. Reg. Juxon, but wrongly, as may be seen by reference to Sancroft's Life, Wood. A. O., Le Neve, and Kennett, Reg. Frewen, &c. Kennett's Register, p. 323. The Bishops of Winchester and Lincoln are not given as

DATE OF CONSECRATION.	NAME AND SEE.	CONSECRATORS.	AUTHORITIES, &c.
	John Cosin, Durham, d. 1672. Jan. 15	*B. Winchester* *Rob. Lincoln*	Consecrators in the York Register, or by Kennett.
	Brian Walton, Chester, d. 1661. Nov. 29		
	Benjamin Laney, Peterborough, Lincoln 1663, Ely 1667, d. 1675. Jan. 24		
1661 Jan. 6 Henry VII.'s Chapel	Gilbert Ironside, Bristol, d. 1671. Sept. 19		Reg. Juxon gives Jan. 13 as the date of Consecration; but there is no doubt that the 6th, as given by Kennett and Le Neve, is the true date.
	Edward Reynolds, Norwich, d. 1676. July 28	Gilb. London Acc. York John Durham Hen. Chichester Rob. Lincoln Ben. Peterborough	
	Nicolas Monk, Hereford, d. 1661. Dec. 17		
	William Nicolson, Gloucester, d. 1672. Feb. 5		
1661 Mar. 24 Ely House	Samuel Rutter, Sodor and Man, d. 1663. May 30	John Durham Matt. Ely George Worcester Rich. Carlisle Brian Chester	Reg. Frewen, &c.
1661 Dec. 15 Westminster	John Sharpe, S. Andrews		Reg. Juxon, &c.
	Andrew Fairfowl, Glasgow	Gilb. London Geo. Worcester Rich. Carlisle Hugh Llandaff	
	Robert Leighton, Dumblane		
	James Hamilton, Galloway		
1661 Dec. 22 Lambeth	John Hackett, Lichfield, d. 1670 Oct. 28	Gilb. London Hen. Chichester Humf. Sarum George Worcester Will. Gloucester	Ibid.

DATE OF CONSECRATION.	NAME AND SEE.	CONSECRATORS.	AUTHORITIES, &c.
1662 Feb. 9 Lambeth	Herbert Croft, Hereford, d. 1691 May 18	Gilb. London Hen. Chichester Humf. Sarum George Worcester Will. Gloucester	Reg. Juxon, &c.
1662 Feb. 9 Ely House	Henry Fern, Sodor and Man, d. 1662 Mar. 16		Kennett's Register, p. 644.
1662 May 11 Ely House	George Hall, Chester, d. 1668 Aug. 23	Acc. York John Durham Matt. Ely Rob. Oxford Hen. Chichester Rich. Carlisle	Reg. Frewen.
1662 July 20 Lambeth	Seth Ward, Exeter, Sarum 1667, d. 1689 Jan. 6	Gilb. London Geo. Winchester Hen. Chichester Humf. Sarum Will. Gloucester	Reg. Juxon, &c.
1662 Nov. 30 Henry VII.'s Chapel	John Earle, Worcester, Sarum 1663, d. 1665 Nov. 17	Gilb. London Geo. Winchester Hen. Chichester Humf. Sarum Will. Gloucester	Ibid.
1663 May 10 Lambeth	Joseph Henshaw, Peterborough, d. 1679 Mar. 9	Gilb. London Geo. Winchester Hen. Chichester Humf. Sarum	Ibid.
1663 May 20 Chr. Ch., Dublin	William Fuller, Limerick, Lincoln 1667, d. 1675 Apr. 22	Mich. Dublin John Clogher Rob. Ferns Edw. Cork	Cotton.
1663 July 5 Henry VII.'s Chapel	Isaac Barrow, Sodor and Man, S. Asaph 1670, d. 1680 June 24	John Durham Humf. Sarum Rich. Carlisle Geo. Chester	Reg. Frewen, &c.
1663 Dec. 20 Lambeth	William Paul, Oxford, d. 1665 May 24	Acc. York Humf. London Geo. Winchester Hen. Chichester	Reg. Juxon, &c.

DATE OF CONSECRATION.	NAME AND SEE.	CONSECRATORS.	AUTHORITIES, &c.
1664 July 10 Henry VII.'s Chapel	Edward Rainbow, Carlisle, d. 1684 Mar. 26	} Gilbert	Wood. A. O. I. 861. Reg. Rainbow. Carlisle. MS. Wharton, 578.
1665 Dec. 3 New College, Oxford	Walter Blandford, Oxford, Worcester 1671, d. 1675 July 16	Humf. London Will. Gloucester Seth Exeter	Wood. A. O. II. 677.
1665 Dec. 31 New College, Oxford	Alexander Hyde, Sarum, d. 1667 Aug. 22	Gilbert Geo. Winchester Will. Gloucester Jos. Peterborough Walt. Oxford Will. Limerick	Wood. A. O. II. 668.
1666 July 1 Lambeth	Robert Morgan, Bangor, d. 1673 Sept. 1	Gilbert Humf. London Geo. Winchester Will. Limerick	Reg. Juxon, &c.
1666 Nov. 25 Lambeth	John Dolben, Rochester, York 1683, d. 1686 Apr. 11	Gilbert Rich. York Humf. London Geo. Winchester Benj. Lincoln John Lichfield	Reg. Sheldon, &c.
1667 Aug. 24 Lambeth	Francis Davies, Llandaff, d. 1675 Mar. 14	Gilbert Humf. London Benj. Ely John Rochester	Ibid.
1667 Oct. 13 Lambeth	Henry Glemham, S. Asaph, d. 1670 Jan. 17	Gilbert Geo. Winchester Benj. Ely Seth Sarum Will. Lincoln	Ibid.
1667 Nov. 3 Lambeth	Antony Sparrow, Exeter, Norwich 1676, d. 1685 May 19	Gilbert Geo. Winchester Benj. Ely Will. Gloucester Seth Sarum Rob. Bangor Will. Lincoln	Ibid.

Date of Consecration.	Name and See.	Consecrators.	Authorities, &c.
1668 Nov. 15 Ely House	John Wilkins, Chester, d. 1672 Nov. 19	John Durham Benj. Ely Seth Sarum	Wood. A. O. II. 371. Evelyn's Diary, 2.35, adds Canterbury & Rochester.
1670 Mar. 6 Lambeth	Peter Gunning, Chichester, Ely 1675, d. 1684 July 6	Gilbert Rich. York Humf. London Geo. Winchester Benj. Ely Seth Sarum John Rochester Ant. Exeter	Reg. Sheldon, &c.
1670 June 19 Lambeth	Robert Creighton, Bath, d. 1672 Nov. 21	Humf. London Geo. Winchester Benj. Ely John Rochester Will. Lincoln	Ibid.
1671 July 2 Lambeth	Thomas Wood, Lichfield, d. 1692 Apr. 18 Nathanael Crewe, Oxford, Durham 1674, d. 1721 Sept. 18	Gilbert Humf. London Benj. Ely Walt. Worcester John Rochester Will. Lincoln	Ibid.
1671 Oct. 1 Chester	Henry Bridgman, Sodor and Man, d. 1682 May 15	John Chester Isaac S. Asaph Rob. Bangor Rob. Clogher	Wood. A. O. II. 682. London Gazette, 615.
1672 Feb. 11 Henry VII.'s Chapel	Guy Carleton, Bristol, Chichester 1679, d. 1685 July 6	Rich. York Walt. Worcester John Rochester Will. Lincoln Nath. Oxford	Reg. Sheldon, &c.
1672 Nov. 3 Lambeth	John Pritchett, Gloucester, d. 1681 Jan. 1	Gilbert Humf. London Benj. Ely John Rochester John Chester	Ibid.

DATE OF CONSECRATION.	NAME AND SEE.	CONSECRATORS.	AUTHORITIES, &c.
1673 Feb. 9 Lambeth	John Pearson, Chester, d. 1686 July 16 Peter Mews, Bath, Winchester 1684 d. 1706. Nov. 9	Gilbert Humf. London John Rochester Ant. Exeter Isaac S. Asaph Peter Chichester Nath. Oxford John Gloucester	Reg. Sheldon, &c. Wood. A. O. II. 675.
1673 Nov. 16 London House	Humfrey Lloyd, Bangor, d. 1689. Jan. 18	Humf. London Geo. Winchester Seth Sarum John Rochester Ant. Exeter Fra. Llandaff	Reg. Sheldon, &c.
1674 Dec. 6 Lambeth	Henry Compton, Oxford, London 1675, d. 1713. July 7	Gilbert Geo. Winchester Seth Sarum John Rochester Jos. Peterborough Peter Chichester	Ibid.
1675 Apr. 18 Lambeth	Ralph Brideoake, Chichester, d. 1678. Oct. 5 William Lloyd, Llandaff, Peterborough 1679, Norwich 1685, dep. 1691. Feb. 1 d. 1710. Jan. 1	Gilbert Geo. Winchester Seth Sarum Ant. Exeter Peter Bath Guy Bristol John Gloucester	Ibid.
1675 June 27 Ely House	Thomas Barlow, Lincoln, d. 1691. Oct. 8	Geo. Winchester Seth Sarum Peter Ely Peter Bath Guy Bristol	Ibid.
1675 Aug. 29 S. Peter le Poor, London	James Fleetwood, Worcester, d. 1683. July 17	John Rochester Peter Ely Ralph Chichester Thom. Lincoln	Ibid.

Date of Consecration.	Name and See.	Consecrators.	Authorities, &c.
1676 Feb. 6 Winchester House, Chelsea	John Fell, Oxford, d. 1686. July 10	Hen. London Geo. Winchester John Rochester Peter Ely Ralph Chichester	Reg. Sheldon, &c.
1676 Nov. 12 Lambeth	Thomas Lamplugh, Exeter, York 1688, d. 1691. May 5	Hen. London Seth Sarum John Rochester Ant. Norwich	Ibid.
1678 Jan. 27 Westminster	William Sancroft, Canterbury, dep. 1691. Feb. 1, d. 1693. Nov. 24 William Thomas, S. David's, Worcester 1683, d. 1689. June 25	Hen. London Seth Sarum Jos. Peterborough John Rochester Peter Ely Guy Bristol Thom. Lincoln Thom. Exeter	Reg. Sancroft. Le Neve, P. A. Wharton's MS. Ducarel's Abstract. Lindsay.
1679 Feb. 9 Lambeth	William Gulston, Bristol, d. 1684. Apr. 4	William Hen. London Seth Sarum John Rochester Guy Chichester	Ibid.
1679 June 22 Lambeth	William Beaw, Llandaff, d. 1706. Feb. 10	William Hen. London Edw: Carlisle Will. Peterborough	Ibid.
1680 Oct. 3 Lambeth	William Lloyd, S. Asaph, Lichfield 1692, Worcester 1699, d. 1717. Aug. 30	William Hen. London John Rochester Peter Ely John Oxford	Ibid.
1681 Mar. 27 All Souls', Oxford	Robert Frampton, Gloucester, dep. 1691. Feb. 1, d. 1708. May 25	William Hen. London John Rochester Peter Ely Thom. Lincoln Thom. Exeter	Reg. Sancroft, &c

Date of Consecration.	Name and See.	Consecrators.	Authorities, &c.
1683 *Jan.* 7 London	John Lake, Sodor and Man, Bristol 1684, Chichester 1685, d. 1689. Aug. 30		Conf. Jan. 6. Reg. Sterne. Licence Jan. 2. Reg. Sancroft.
1683 Mar. 11 Cashel	Edward Jones, Cloyne, S. Asaph 1692, d. 1703. May 10	Thom. Cashel Hugh Waterford John Killaloe Simon Limerick	Cotton.
1683 Nov. 11 Lambeth	Francis Turner, Rochester, Ely 1684, dep. 1691. Feb. 1, d. 1700. Nov. 2 Laurence Womock, S. David's, d. 1686. Mar. 12	William Hen. London Nath. Durham Seth Sarum Will. Peterborough	Reg. Sancroft, &c.
1684 June 19 York	Thomas Smith, Carlisle, d. 1702. Apr. 12	John York Nath. Durham John Sodor & Man	Reg. Dolben, &c.
1684 Nov. 2 Lambeth	Thomas Spratt, Rochester, d. 1713. May 20	William Hen. London Seth Sarum Will. Peterborough Fran. Ely Ezekiel Derry	Reg. Sancroft, &c.
1685 Jan. 25 Lambeth	Thomas Ken, Bath, dep. 1691. Feb. 1, d. 1711. Mar. 19	William Hen. London Nath. Durham Will. Peterborough Fran. Ely Thom. Rochester	Ibid.
1685 Mar. 15 Lambeth	Baptist Levinz, Sodor and Man, d. 1693. Jan. 31	William Hen. London Will. S. Asaph Fran. Ely Alex. Glasgow	Wharton MS. 578.

Date of Consecration.	Name and See.	Consecrators.	Authorities, &c.
1685 Oct. 25 Lambeth	Thomas White, Peterborough, dep. 1691. Feb. 1 d. 1698. May 30	William Hen. London Will. S. Asaph John Chichester Fran. Ely Thom. Rochester James Dunkeld	Reg. Sancroft, &c.
1685 Nov. 8 Lambeth	Jonathan Trelawney, Bristol, Exeter 1689, Winchester 1707, d. 1721. July 19	William John York Hen. London Nath. Durham Peter Winchester Thom. Exeter Fran. Ely Thom. Rochester	Ibid.
1686 Oct. 17 Lambeth	John Lloyd, S. David's, d. 1687. Feb. 13 Samuel Parker, Oxford, d. 1688. Mar. 20 Thomas Cartwright, Chester, d. 1689. Apr. 15	William Nath. Durham Will. Norwich Fran. Ely Thom. Rochester	Ibid.
1687 June 26 Lambeth	Thomas Watson, S. David's, dep. 1699, d. 1717. June 3	William Thom. Rochester Thom. Chester	Ibid.
1688 Oct. 7 Lambeth	Timothy Hall, Oxford, d. 1690. Apr. 10	William John Chichester Thom. Chester	Ibid.
1689 Mar. 31 Fulham	Gilbert Burnett, Sarum, d. 1715. Mar. 17	Hen. London Peter Winchester William Llandaff William S. Asaph	Ibid. Le Neve adds Lincoln and Carlisle.
1689 June 30 Fulham	Humfrey Humphries, Bangor, Hereford 1701, d. 1712. Nov. 20	Hen. London Thom. Carlisle Gilb. Sarum	Reg. D. & C. Cant., &c. Le Neve adds S. Asaph.

DATE OF CONSECRATION.	NAME AND SEE.	CONSECRATORS.	AUTHORITIES, &c.
1689 Sept. 15 Fulham	Nicolas Stratford, Chester, d. 1707. Feb. 12	} Hen. London	Wharton MS., &c. Wood. A. O. II. 631.
1689 Oct. 13 Fulham	Edward Stillingfleet, Worcester, d. 1699. Mar. 27 Simon Patrick, Chichester, Ely 1691, d. 1707. May 31 Gilbert Ironside, Bristol, Hereford 1691, d. 1701. Aug. 27	Hen. London Will. S. Asaph Tho. Rochester	Reg. D. & C. Cant., &c.
1690 May 11 Fulham	John Hough, Oxford, Lichfield 1699, Worcester 1717, d. 1743. May 8	Hen. London Peter Winchester Will. Llandaff Will. S. Asaph Gilbert Sarum Edw. Worcester	Ibid.
1691 May 31 Bow Church	John Tillotson, Canterbury, d. 1694. Nov. 22	Peter Winchester Will. S. Asaph Gilb. Sarum Edw. Worcester Gilb. Bristol John Oxford	Reg. Tillotson, &c.
1691 July 5 Bow Church	John Moore, Norwich, Ely 1707, d. 1714. July 31 Richard Cumberland, Peterborough, d. 1718. Oct. 9 Edward Fowler, Gloucester, d. 1714. Aug. 26 John Sharpe, York, d. 1714. Feb. 2	John Peter Winchester Gilb. Sarum Edw. Worcester Gilb. Bristol Simon Ely	Ibid.

Date of Consecration.	Name and See.	Consecrators.	Authorities, &c.
1691 Aug. 30 Bow Church	Robert Grove, Chichester, d. 1696. Sept. 25 Richard Kidder, Bath, d. 1703. Nov. 26 John Hall, Bristol, d. 1710. Feb. 4	John Gilb. Sarum Edw. Worcester John Norwich Edw. Gloucester	Reg. Tillotson, &c.
1692 Jan. 10 Lambeth	Thomas Tenison, Lincoln, Canterbury 1695, d. 1715. Dec. 14	John Hen. London Gilb. Sarum Edw. Worcester Simon Ely	Ibid.
1695 Mar. 10 Lambeth	James Gardiner, Lincoln, d. 1705. Mar. 1	Thomas Hen. London Peter Winchester Will. Lichfield Thom. Rochester	Reg. Tenison, &c.
1696 Dec. 13 Lambeth	John Williams, Chichester, d. 1709. Apr. 24	Thomas Hen. London Peter Winchester Will. Lichfield Thom Rochester Gilb. Sarum	Ibid.
1698 Jan. 16 Savoy Chapel	Thomas Wilson, Sodor and Man, d. 1755. Mar. 7	John York Nic. Chester John Norwich	Reg. Sharpe, &c.
1699 Sept. 24 Lambeth	William Talbot, Oxford, Sarum 1715, Durham 1721, d. 1730. Oct. 10	Thomas Hen. London Thom. Rochester John Norwich	Reg. Tenison, &c.
1702 Jan. 4 Lambeth	John Evans, Bangor, Meath 1715 d. 1724. Mar. 2	Thomas Hen. London Will. Worcester Gilb. Sarum Humf. Hereford John Norwich	Ibid.

DATE OF CONSECRATION.	NAME AND SEE.	CONSECRATORS.	AUTHORITIES, &c.
1702 June 14 Lambeth	William Nicholson, Carlisle, Derry 1718, Cashel 1727 d. 1727. Feb. 15	Thomas Hen. London John Norwich Edw. Gloucester John Bangor,	Reg. Tenison, &c.
1703 Oct. 31 Lambeth	George Hooper, S. Asaph, Bath 1704, d. 1727. Sept. 6	Thomas Hen. London Thom. Rochester Simon Ely John Lichfield	Ibid.
1704 July 16 Lambeth	William Beveridge, S. Asaph, d. 1708. Mar. 5	Thomas Thom. Rochester George Bath	Ibid.
1705 Apr. 29 Lambeth	George Bull, S. David's, d. 1710. Feb. 17	Thomas Simon Ely John Norwich John Chichester	Ibid.
1705 Oct. 21 Lambeth	William Wake, Lincoln, Canterbury 1716, d. 1737. Jan. 24	Thomas Hen. London Gilb. Sarum John Norwich John Chichester	Ibid.
1706 June 30 Lambeth	John Tyler, Llandaff, d. 1724. July 6	Thomas Hen. London Thom. Rochester John Bangor	Ibid.
1708 Feb. 8 Lambeth	Offspring Blackall, Exeter, d. 1716. Nov. 29 Charles Trimnell, Norwich, Winchester 1721, d. 1723. Aug. 15	Hen. London Gilb. Sarum John Lichfield John Ely Will. Oxford	Ibid.
1708 Feb. 8 Henry VII.'s Chapel	William Dawes, Chester, York 1714, d. 1724. Apr. 30	John York Jonath. Winchester Thom. Rochester Will. Carlisle	Perceval MS. from the Chester Register. London Gazette, No. 4410.
1708 June 6 Lambeth	William Fleetwood, S. Asaph, Ely 1714, d. 1723. Aug. 4	Thomas John Chichester Will. Oxford John Bangor	Reg. Tenison, &c.

Date of Consecration.	Name and See.	Consecrators.	Authorities, &c.
1709 Nov. 13 Lambeth	Thomas Manningham, Chichester, d. 1722. Aug. 25	Thomas Hen. London John Lichfield John Ely Charles Norwich	Reg. Tenison, &c.
1710 Nov. 19 Lambeth	John Robinson, Bristol, London 1714, d. 1723. Apr. 11 Philip Bisse, S. David's, Hereford 1713, d. 1721. Sept. 6	Thomas Hen. London John Lichfield John Bangor	Ibid.
1713 Mar. 15 Lambeth	Adam Ottley, S. David's, d. 1723. Oct. 3	Hen. London John Lichfield John Llandaff Off. Exeter Thom. Chichester Phil. Hereford	Ibid.
1713 July 5 Lambeth	Francis Atterbury, Rochester, dep. 1723, d. 1733. Feb. 15	Jonath. Winchester John Ely Charles Norwich Ad. S. David's	Ibid.
1714 Apr. 4 Lambeth	George Smalridge, Bristol, d. 1719. Sept. 27	John London Jon. Winchester John Lichfield George Bath	Ibid.
1714 Apr. 4 Somerset House	Francis Gastrell, Chester, d. 1725. Nov. 14	Will. York Phil. Hereford Ad. S. David's	Reg. Dawes.
1715 Jan. 16 Lambeth	Richard Willis, Gloucester, Sarum 1721, Winchester 1723, d. 1734. Aug. 10	Gilb. Sarum John Lichfield John Bangor	Reg. Tenison, &c.
1715 Feb. 6 Lambeth	John Wynne, S. Asaph, Bath 1727, d. 1743. July 15	Gilb. Sarum John Lichfield John Bangor Rich. Gloucester	Ibid.

DATE OF CONSECRATION.	NAME AND SEE.	CONSECRATORS.	AUTHORITIES, &c.
1715 May 15 Lambeth	John Potter, Oxford, Canterbury 1737, d. 1747. Oct. 10	Jon. Winchester John Bangor Will. Lincoln Rich. Gloucester	Reg. Tenison, &c.
1716 Feb. 12 Somerset House	Edmund Gibson, Lincoln, London 1723, d. 1748. Aug. 4	William John London Jon. Winchester Chas. Norwich Rich. Gloucester	Reg. Wake. Ducarel's Abstract. Perceval. A. S.
1716 Mar. 18 Ely House	Benjamin Hoadly Bangor, Hereford 1721, Sarum 1723, Winchester 1734, d. 1761. Apr. 17	William Jon. Winchester Chas. Norwich William Ely Edm. Lincoln	Ibid.
1717 Feb. 24 Ely House	Launcelot Blackburn, Exeter, York 1724, d. 1743. Mar. 23	William Jon. Winchester Will. Sarum Chas. Norwich Will. Ely	Ibid.
1717 Nov. 17 Lambeth	Edward Chandler, Lichfield, Durham 1730, d. 1750. July 20	William John Worcester Will. Sarum Edm. Lincoln	Ibid.
1718 June 1 Lambeth	Samuel Bradford, Carlisle, Rochester 1723, d. 1731. May 17	William John London Fran. Rochester Rich. Gloucester	Ibid.
1718 Nov. 9 Lambeth	White Kennett, Peterborough, d. 1728. Dec. 19	William John Worcester Will. Sarum Chas. Norwich Rich. Gloucester	Ibid.
1719 Nov. 15 Lambeth	Hugh Boulter, Bristol, Armagh 1724 d. 1742. Sept. 27	William John Worcester Will. Sarum Will. Ely Rich. Gloucester	Ibid.

Date of Consecration.	Name and See.	Consecrators.	Authorities, &c.
1721 Oct. 8 Lambeth	Thomas Greene, Norwich, Ely 1723, d. 1738. May 18	William John London Chas. Winchester Will. Sarum Edm. Lincoln	Reg. Wake. Ducarel's Abstract. Perceval. A. S.
1721 Dec. 3 Lambeth	Richard Reynolds, Bangor, Lincoln 1723, d. 1744. Jan. 15 Joseph Wilcocks, Gloucester, Rochester 1731, d. 1756. Feb. 28	William Rich. Sarum Edm. Lincoln Wh. Peterborough	Ibid.
1722 Oct. 7 Lambeth	Thomas Bowers, Chichester, d. 1724. Aug. 22	William Chas. Winchester Rich. Sarum Edm. Lincoln Thom. Norwich	Ibid.
1723 Aug. 11 Croydon	William Baker, Bangor, Norwich 1727, d. 1732. Dec. 4	William Edm. London John S. Asaph Benj. Hereford Rich. Lincoln	Ibid.
1723 Oct. 13 Lambeth	John Waugh, Carlisle, d. 1734. Oct. 29	William Edm. London Rich. Winchester Sam. Rochester Thom. Ely	Ibid.
1723 Nov. 3 Lambeth	John Leng, Norwich, d. 1727. Oct. 26	William Edm. London Rich. Winchester Launc. Exeter Sam. Rochester	Ibid.
1724 Feb. 2 Lambeth	Henry Egerton, Hereford, d. 1746. Apr. 1 Richard Smallbrooke, S. David's, Lichfield 1731, d. 1749. Dec. 22	William Edm. London Rich. Winchester Launc. Exeter Sam. Rochester	Ibid.

DATE OF CONSECRATION.	NAME AND SEE.	CONSECRATORS.	AUTHORITIES, &c.
1724 Oct. 11 Lambeth	Edward Waddington, Chichester, d. 1731. Sept. 8	William Edm. London Rich. Winchester Sam. Rochester Thom. Ely	Reg. Wake. Ducarel's Abstract. Perceval. A. S.
1724 Oct. 18 Lambeth	William Bradshaw, Bristol, d. 1732. Dec. 16	William Edm. London Rich. Winchester Sam. Rochester Thom. Ely	Ibid.
1724 Dec. 28 Lambeth	Stephen Weston, Exeter, d. 1742. Jan. 8	William Edm. London Rich. Winchester John S. Asaph Rich. Lincoln	Ibid.
1725 Jan. 2 Lambeth	Robert Clavering, Llandaff, Peterborough 1729, d. 1747. July 21	William Edm. London Rich. Winchester John S. Asaph John Oxford	Ibid.
1726 Apr. 12 S. Margaret's, Westminster	Samuel Peploe, Chester, d. 1752. Feb. 21	Launc. York Will. Durham John S. Asaph John Carlisle	Ibid.
1727 Dec. 17 Lambeth	Francis Hare, S. Asaph, Chichester 1731, d. 1740. Apr. 26	William John Bath Edw. Lichfield Sam. Rochester Thom. Ely	Ibid.
1728 Feb. 4 Lambeth	Thomas Sherlock, Bangor, Sarum 1734, London 1748, d. 1761. July 18	William John Bath John Oxford Edw. Lichfield Rich. Lincoln	Ibid.
1729 Oct. 19 Lambeth	John Harris, Llandaff, d. 1738. Aug. 28	William Edm. London Rich. Winchester Edw. Chichester Fra. S. Asaph	Ibid.

Date of Consecration.	Name and See.	Consecrators.	Authorities, &c.
1731 Apr. 11 Ely House	Elias Sydall, S. David's, Gloucester 1731, d. 1733. Dec. 24	Edm. London Rich. Winchester John Bath John Oxford Thom. Ely	Reg Wake. Ducarel's Abstract. Perceval. A. S.
1732 Jan. 23 Lambeth	Nicolas Claggett, S. David's, Exeter 1742, d. 1746. Dec. 8 Thomas Tanner, S. Asaph, d. 1735. Dec. 4	William Edm. London Thom. Ely Rich. Lincoln Jos. Rochester	Ibid.
1733 Feb. 25 Bow Church	Robert Butts, Norwich, Ely 1738, d. 1748. Jan. 26 Charles Cecil, Bristol, Bangor 1734, d. 1737. May 29	Edm. London Rich. Winchester Thom. S. Asaph Nic. S. David's	Ibid.
1735 Jan. 19 Lambeth	Martin Benson, Gloucester, d. 1752. Aug. 30 Thomas Secker, Bristol, Oxford 1737, Canterbury 1758, d. 1768. Aug. 3 George Fleming, Carlisle, d. 1747. July 2	Edm. London John Oxford Jos. Rochester	Ibid.
1736 July 14 Lambeth	Isaac Maddox, S. Asaph, Worcester 1743, d. 1759. Sept. 27	Edm. London Jos. Rochester Hen. Hereford Nic. S. David's	Ibid.
1737 June 12 Lambeth	Thomas Gooch, Bristol, Norwich 1738, Ely 1748, d. 1754. Feb. 14	John John Bath Jos. Rochester Fra. Chichester	Reg. Potter. Ducarel's Abstract. Perceval. A. S.

DATE OF CONSECRATION.	NAME AND SEE.	CONSECRATORS.	AUTHORITIES, &c.
1738 Jan. 15 Lambeth	Thomas Herring, Bangor, York 1743, Canterbury 1747, d. 1757. Mar. 13	John Nic. S. David's Rob. Norwich Thom. Oxford	Reg. Potter. Ducarel's Abstract. Perceval. A. S.
1738 Dec. 3 Lambeth	Joseph Butler, Bristol, Durham 1750, d. 1752. June 16	John Jos. Rochester Nic. S. David's Rob. Ely	Ibid.
1739 Feb. 18 Lambeth	Matthias Mawson, Llandaff, Chichester 1740, Ely 1754, d. 1770. Nov. 23	John Rich. Lincoln Jos. Rochester Rich. Lichfield	Ibid.
1740 Dec. 28 Lambeth	John Gilbert, Llandaff, Sarum 1749, York 1757, d. 1761. Aug. 9	John Jos. Rochester Nic. S. David's Isaac S. Asaph	Ibid.
1743 Jan. 2 Lambeth	Edward Willes, S. David's, Bath 1743, d. 1773. Nov. 24	John Rich. Lincoln Jos. Rochester Thom. Norwich	Ibid.
1743 Nov. 13 Lambeth	Matthew Hutton, Bangor, York 1747, Canterbury 1757, d. 1758. Mar. 19	Jos. Rochester Nic. Exeter Isaac Worcester Jos. Bristol	Ibid.
1744 Apr. 1 Lambeth	John Thomas, Lincoln, Sarum 1761, d. 1766. July 20 Samuel Lisle, S. Asaph, Norwich 1748, d. 1749. Oct. 3 Richard Trevor, S. David's, Durham 1752, d. 1771. June 9	John Jos. Rochester Nic. Exeter Mart. Gloucester Thom. Norwich	Ibid.

DATE OF CONSECRATION.	NAME AND SEE.	CONSECRATORS.	AUTHORITIES, &c.
1746 May 11 Lambeth	James Beauclerk, Hereford, d. 1787. Oct. 20	John Mart. Gloucester Isaac Worcester Rich. S. David's	Reg. Potter. Ducarel's Abstract. Perceval. A. S.
1747 Feb. 8 Lambeth	George Lavington, Exeter, d. 1762. Sept. 13	John Mart. Gloucester Jos. Bristol Rich. S. David's	Ibid.
1747 Oct. 4 Lambeth	John Thomas, Peterborough, Sarum 1757, Winchester 1761, d. 1781. May 1 Richard Osbaldeston, Carlisle, London 1762, d. 1764. May 13	Jos. Rochester Jos. Bristol Sam. S. Asaph	Ibid.
1748 Feb. 21 Kensington Church	Zachary Pearce, Bangor, Rochester 1756, d. 1774. June 29	Thomas Jos. Rochester Mart. Gloucester Jos. Bristol	Reg. Herring. Ducarel's Abstract. Perceval A. S.
1748 Apr. 24 Kensington Church	Rob. Hay Drummond, S. Asaph, Sarum 1761, York 1761, d. 1776. Dec. 10	Thomas Jos. Rochester Mart. Gloucester John Llandaff	Ibid.
1749 Feb. 12 Kensington Church	Edward Cressett, Llandaff, d. 1755. Feb. 13	Thomas Rich. Lichfield James Hereford John Peterborough	Ibid.
1749 Dec. 3 Lambeth	Thomas Hayter, Norwich, London 1761, d. 1762. Jan. 9	Thomas Jos. Rochester Jos. Bristol Rich. S. David's	Ibid.
1750 Feb. 19 Lambeth	Frederick Cornwallis, Lichfield, Canterbury 1768, d. 1783. Mar. 19	Thomas Jos. Rochester Mart. Gloucester Thom. Norwich	Ibid.

DATE OF CONSECRATION.	NAME AND SEE.	CONSECRATORS.	AUTHORITIES, &c.
1750 Dec. 23 Lambeth	John Conybeare, Bristol, d. 1755. July 13	Thomas Jos. Rochester Thom. Oxford Thom. Norwich	Reg. Herring. Ducarel's Abstract. Perceval. A. S.
1752 Mar. 22 Ely House	Edmund Keene, Chester, Ely 1771, d. 1781. July 6	Thomas Jos. Durham Rich. Carlisle Fred. Lichfield	Ibid.
1752 Dec. 10 Lambeth	James Johnson, Gloucester, Worcester 1759, d. 1774. Nov. 26	Thomas Jos. Rochester Matt. Chichester Zach. Bangor	Ibid.
1753 Jan. 28 Lambeth	Antony Ellis, S. David's, d. 1761. Jan. 16	Thomas Jos. Rochester Isaac Worcester Zach. Bangor	Ibid.
1754 Mar. 31 Lambeth	Will. Ashburnham, Chichester, d. 1797. Sept. 4	Jos. Rochester Matt. Ely Fred. Lichfield	Ibid.
1755 Apr. 13 Lambeth	Richard Newcome, Llandaff, S. Asaph 1761, d. 1769. June 4	Thomas Thom. Oxford George Exeter Zach. Bangor	Ibid.
1755 Apr. 27 Whitehall	Mark Hildersley, Sodor and Man, d. 1772. Dec. 7	Matt. York Rich. Durham Rich. Carlisle Edm. Chester	Ibid.
1756 July 4 Lambeth	John Hume, Bristol, Oxford 1758, Sarum 1766, d. 1782. June 26 John Egerton, Bangor, Lichfield 1768, Durham 1771, d. 1787. Jan. 18	Thom. Norwich Zach. Rochester Edm. Chester James Gloucester	Ibid.
1757 July 3 Lambeth	Richard Terrick, Peterborough, London 1764, d. 1777. Mar. 29	Matthew John Sarum Thom. Norwich John Bristol	Reg. Hutton. Perceval. A. S.

DATE OF CONSECRATION.	NAME AND SEE.	CONSECRATORS.	AUTHORITIES, &c.
1758 June 29 Bow Church	Philip Young, Bristol, Norwich 1764, d. 1783 Apr. 23	Thomas Zach. Rochester John Oxford Rich. Peterborough	Reg. Secker. Perceval. A. S.
1760 Jan. 20 Lambeth	William Warburton, Gloucester, d. 1779 June 11	Thomas Rich. Durham James Worcester Phil. Bristol	Ibid.
1761 May 24 Lambeth	Samuel Squire, S. David's, d. 1766 May 7	Thomas John Winchester Matt. Ely Zach. Rochester Rob. S. Asaph	Ibid.
1761 Sept. 13 Lambeth	John Ewer, Llandaff, Bangor 1769, d. 1774 Oct. 28	Thomas Zach. Rochester Rob. Sarum Thom. Norwich	Ibid.
1761 Dec. 28 Lambeth	John Green, Lincoln, d. 1779 Apr. 25 Thomas Newton, Bristol, d. 1782 Feb.14	Thom. London John Winchester John Sarum Zach. Rochester	Ibid.
1762 Mar. 21 Whitehall	Charles Lyttelton, Carlisle, d. 1768 Dec. 22	Robert York Rich. Durham James Hereford Edm. Chester	Ibid.
1762 Nov. 7 Lambeth	Frederick Keppel, Exeter, d. 1777 Dec. 27	Thomas John Winchester John Oxford Rich. Peterborough John Llandaff	Ibid.
1764 July 8 Lambeth	Robert Lambe, Peterborough, d. 1769 Nov. 3	Thomas Rich. London John Winchester Matt. Ely Zach. Rochester	Ibid.
1766 June 15 Lambeth	Robert Lowth, S. David's, Oxford 1766, London 1777, d. 1787 Nov. 3	Thomas Rich. London Edw. Bath Zach. Rochester	Ibid.

DATE OF CONSECRATION.	NAME AND SEE.	CONSECRATORS.	AUTHORITIES, &c.
1766 Nov. 30 Lambeth	Charles Moss, S. David's, Bath 1774, d. 1802 Apr. 13	Rich. London John Winchester Edw. Bath Zach. Rochester	Reg. Secker. Perceval. A. S.
1769 Feb. 12 Lambeth	Jonathan Shipley, Llandaff, S. Asaph 1769, d. 1788 Dec. 9	Frederick Rich. London John Winchester Rob. Oxford	Reg. Cornwallis. Perceval. A. S.
1769 Feb. 24 Whitehall	Edmund Law, Carlisle, d. 1787 Aug. 14	Rob. York Rich. Durham Edm. Chester Phil. Norwich	Ibid.
1769 Oct. 1 Lambeth	Shute Barrington, Llandaff, Sarum 1782, Durham 1791. d. 1826 Mar. 25	Frederick Rich. London Zach. Rochester	Ibid.
1769 Dec. 17 Lambeth	John Hinchcliffe, Peterborough, d. 1794 Jan. 11	Frederick Rich. London John Winchester Phil. Norwich	Ibid.
1771 Feb. 17 Whitehall	William Markham, Chester, York 1777, d. 1807 Nov. 3	Rob. York Rich. Durham James Worcester Edm. Carlisle	Ibid.
1771 Sept. 8 Lambeth	Brownlow North, Lichfield, Worcester 1774, Winchester 1781, d. 1820 July 12	Frederick Rich. London Zach. Rochester Will. Chester	Ibid.
1773 Feb. 14 Whitehall	Richard Richmond, Sodor and Man, d. 1780 Feb. 4	Rob. York John Durham Edm. Ely Will. Chester	Ibid.
1774 June 26 Lambeth	James Yorke, S. David's, Gloucester 1779, Ely 1781, d. 1808 Aug. 26	Frederick Rich. London John Lincoln Thom. Bristol Br. Lichfield	Ibid.

Date of Consecration.	Name and See.	Consecrators.	Authorities, &c.
1774 Nov. 13 Lambeth	John Thomas, Rochester, d. 1793 Aug. 22	Frederick Rich. London Phil. Norwich Shute Llandaff	Reg. Cornwallis. Perceval. A. S.
1775 Feb. 12 Lambeth	Richard Hurd, Lichfield, Worcester 1781, d. 1808 May 28 John Moore, Bangor, Canterbury 1783, d. 1805 Jan. 18	Frederick Edm. Ely Rob. Oxford John Rochester	Ibid.
1777 Feb. 9 Whitehall	Beilby Porteus, Chester, London 1787, d. 1809 May 14	Will. York John Durham Edm. Carlisle Shute Llandaff	Ibid.
1777 May 25 Lambeth	John Butler, Oxford, Hereford 1788, d. 1802 Dec. 10	Frederick Rob. London Will. Chichester Phil. Norwich	Ibid.
1778 Jan. 25 Lambeth	John Ross, Exeter, d. 1792 Aug. 14	Frederick Rob. London Will. Chichester John Oxford	Ibid.
1779 May 30 Lambeth	Thomas Thurlow, Lincoln, Durham 1787, d. 1791 May 27	Frederick Edm. Ely Phil. Norwich Charles Bath	Ibid.
1779 Sept. 19 Lambeth	John Warren, S. David's, Bangor 1783, d. 1800 Jan. 27	Frederick Rob. London John Rochester Rich. Lichfield	Ibid.
1780 Mar. 5 Whitehall	George Mason, Sodor and Man, d. 1783 Dec. 8	William York John Bangor Beilby Chester John Exeter	Ibid.
1781 Sept. 16 Lambeth	James Cornwallis, Lichfield, d. 1824 Jan. 20	Frederick Rob. London James Ely John Rochester	Ibid.

DATE OF CONSECRATION.	NAME AND SEE.	CONSECRATORS.	AUTHORITIES, &c.
1781 Oct. 28 Lambeth	Samuel Hallifax, Gloucester, S. Asaph 1789, d. 1790 Mar. 5	Frederick Phil. Norwich John Rochester James Lichfield	Reg. Cornwallis. Perceval. A. S.
1782 Apr. 7 Lambeth	Lewis Bagot, Bristol, Norwich 1783, S. Asaph 1790, d. 1802 June 4	Frederick Br. Winchester Charles Bath Shute Llandaff	Ibid.
1782 Oct. 20 Lambeth	Richard Watson, Llandaff, d. 1816. July 4	Frederick Phil. Norwich John Rochester	Ibid.
1783 July 6 Lambeth	Edward Smallwell, S. David's, Oxford 1788, d. 1799 June 26 Christopher Wilson, Bristol, d. 1792 Apr. 18	John Br. Winchester Tho. Lincoln John Bangor	Ibid.
1784 Apr. 4 Whitehall	Claudius Crigan, Sodor and Man, d. 1813 Apr. 26	Will. York John Rochester John Oxford John Exeter	Ibid.
1787 Feb. 4 Lambeth	William White, Pennsylvania, d. 1836 Samuel Provoost, New York, d. 1815	John Will. York Charles Bath John Peterborough	Ibid.
1787 Mar. 11 Lambeth	George Pretyman, Lincoln, Winchester 1820, d. 1827 Nov. 14	John Will. Chichester Shute Sarum Beilby Chester	Ibid.
1787 Aug. 12 Lambeth	Charles Inglis, Nova Scotia	John John Rochester B. Chester	Ibid.
1787 Nov. 18 Whitehall	John Douglas, Carlisle, Sarum 1791, d. 1807 May 18	Will. York B. Chester John Oxford Geo. Lincoln	Ibid.

R

Date of Consecration.	Name and See.	Consecrators.	Authorities, &c.
1787 Dec. 9 Lambeth	John Harley, Hereford, d. 1788 Jan. 9	John B. London John Oxford John Bangor	Reg. Cornwallis. Perceval. A. S.
1788 Jan. 20 Whitehall	William Cleaver, Chester, Bangor 1800, S. Asaph 1806, d. 1815 May 15	William York Thom. Durham John Rochester John Carlisle	Ibid.
1788 May 11 Lambeth	Samuel Horsley, S. David's, Rochester 1793, S. Asaph 1802, d. 1806 Oct. 4	John B. London Sam. Gloucester Edw. Oxford	Ibid.
1789 June 7 Lambeth	Richard Beadon, Gloucester, Bath 1802, d. 1824 Apr. 21	John B. London John Peterborough Sam. S. Asaph	Ibid.
1790 June 6 Lambeth	George Horne, Norwich, d. 1792 Jan. 17	John B. London James Lichfield Sam. S. David's	Ibid.
1790 Sept. 19 Lambeth	James Madison, Virginia, d. 1812	John B. London John Rochester	Ibid.
1791 Nov. 6 Whitehall	Edw. Venables Vernon (Harcourt,) Carlisle, York 1808, d. 1847 Nov. 12	William York B. London John Sarum	Ibid.
1792 Apr. 8 Lambeth	Chas. Manners Sutton, Norwich, Canterbury 1805, d. 1828 July 21	John John Peterborough James Lichfield Rich. Gloucester	Ibid.
1792 June 3 Lambeth	Spencer Madan, Bristol, Peterborough 1792 d. 1813 Oct. 8	John B. London John Peterborough John Sarum	Ibid.
1792 Dec. 2 Lambeth	William Buller, Exeter, d. 1796 Dec. 12	John John Hereford Sam. S. David's Rich. Gloucester	Ibid.

Date of Consecration.	Name and See.	Consecrators.	Authorities, &c.
1793 July 7 Lambeth	Jacob Mountain, Quebec d. 1825 June 16	John B. London John Bangor Sam. S. David's	Reg. Cornwallis. Perceval. A. S.
1794 Jan. 12 Lambeth	William Stuart, S. David's, Armagh 1800, d. 1822 May 6	John Rich. Llandaff Rich. Gloucester	Ibid.
1794 May 11 Lambeth	Hen. Reg. Courtenay, Bristol, Exeter 1797, d. 1803 June 9	John B. London Sam. Rochester Charles Norwich	Ibid.
1797 Apr. 9 Lambeth	Ffolliott Herbert Walker Cornewall, Bristol, Hereford 1803, Worcester 1808, d. 1831 Sept. 5	John B. London James Lichfield Charles Norwich	Reg. Moore. Perceval. A. S.
1798 Mar. 4 Lambeth	John Buckner, Chichester, d. 1824 May 2	John B. London Sam. Rochester Edw. Carlisle	Ibid.
1799 Sept. 1 Lambeth	John Randolph, Oxford, Bangor 1807, London 1809, d. 1813 July 28	John Br. Winchester Sam. Rochester	Ibid.
1800 June 15 Whitehall	Hen. Wm. Majendie, Chester, Bangor 1809, d. 1830 July 9	William York B. London Will. S. David's John Oxford	Ibid.
1801 Feb. 11 Lambeth	George Murray, S. David's, d. 1803 June 3	John B. London Rich. Gloucester H. W. Chester	Ibid.
1802 June 27 Lambeth	Geo. I. Huntingford, Gloucester, Hereford 1815, d. 1832 Apr. 29	John B. London Sam. Rochester Rich. Bath	Ibid.

DATE OF CONSECRATION.	NAME AND SEE.	CONSECRATORS.	AUTHORITIES, &c.
1802 Aug. 22 Lambeth	Thomas Dampier, Rochester, Ely 1808, d. 1812 May 13	John B. London Br. Winchester Rich. Bath	Reg. Moore. Perceval. A. S.
1803 Mar. 27 Lambeth	George Pelham, Bristol, Exeter 1807, Lincoln 1820, d. 1827 Feb. 7	John B. London Br. Winchester Sam. S. Asaph	Reg. Moore.
1803 July 17 Lambeth	Thomas Burgess, S. David's, Sarum 1825, d. 1837 Feb. 19 John Fisher, Exeter, Sarum 1807, d. 1825 May 8	John B. London Br. Winchester Sam. S. Asaph	Ibid.
1805 Apr. 28 Lambeth	Henry Bathurst, Norwich, d. 1837 Apr. 5	Charles B. London John Oxford Thom. Rochester	Reg. Sutton.
1807 Feb. 1 Lambeth	Charles Moss, Oxford, d. 1811 Dec. 16	Charles John Bangor H. W. Chester John Exeter	Ibid.
1807 Oct. 4 Lambeth	John Luxmoore, Bristol, Hereford 1808, S. Asaph 1815, d. 1830 Jan. 21	Charles James Ely G. I. Gloucester	Ibid.
1808 Mar. 13 Whitehall	Samuel Goodenough, Carlisle, d. 1827 Aug. 12	Edw. York John Bangor H. W. Chester John Sarum	Ibid.
1808 Oct. 30 Lambeth	Wm. Lort Mansell, Bristol, d. 1820 June 27	Charles Br. Winchester John Sarum Charles Oxford	Ibid.
1809 Feb. 12 Lambeth	Walker King, Rochester, d. 1827 Feb. 22	Charles John Bangor Thom. S. David's Sam. Carlisle	Ibid.

DATE OF CONSECRATION.	NAME AND SEE.	CONSECRATORS.	AUTHORITIES, &c.
1810 Jan. 21 Whitehall	Bowyer Ed. Sparke, Chester, Ely 1812, d. 1836 Apr. 4	Edw. York Rich. Bath H. W. Bangor John Hereford	Reg. Sutton.
1812 Feb. 23 Lambeth	William Jackson, Oxford, d. 1815 Dec. 2	Charles John London Will. S. Asaph	Ibid.
1812 July 5 Whitehall	George Henry Law, Carlisle, Bath 1824, d. 1845 Sept. 22	Edw. York John London B. E. Ely Will. Oxford	Ibid.
1813 Oct. 3 Lambeth	William Howley, London, Canterbury 1828, d. 1848 Feb. 11	Charles G. I. Gloucester John Sarum Will. Oxford	Ibid.
1813 Dec. 12 Lambeth	John Parsons, Peterborough, d. 1819 Mar. 12	Charles Will. London John Sarum G. H. Chester	Ibid.
1814 Mar. 6 Whitehall	George Murray, Sodor and Man, Rochester 1827	Edw. York Geo. Exeter G. H. Chester	Ibid.
1814 May 8 Lambeth	Thomas Fanshawe Middleton, Calcutta d. 1822 July 8	Charles Will. London Geo. Lincoln John Sarum	Ibid.
1815 July 30 Lambeth	Henry Ryder, Gloucester, Lichfield 1824, d. 1836 Mar. 31	Charles Will. London W. Rochester	Ibid.
1816 Mar. 24 Lambeth	Edward Legge, Oxford, d. 1827 Jan. 27	Charles Will. London H. W. Bangor Hen. Norwich	Ibid.
1816 May 19 Lambeth	Robert Stanser, Nova Scotia	Charles Will. London Geo. Exeter Edw. Oxford	Ibid.
1816 Aug. 25 Lambeth	Herbert Marsh, Llandaff, Peterborough 1819 d. 1839 May 1	Charles Will. London Edw. Oxford	Ibid.

DATE OF CONSECRATION.	NAME AND SEE.	CONSECRATORS.	AUTHORITIES, &c.
1819 May 31 Lambeth	Wm. Van Mildert, Llandaff, Durham 1826, d. 1836 Feb. 21	Charles Will. London John S. Asaph Herb.Peterborough	Reg. Sutton.
1820 July 30 Lambeth	John Kaye, Bristol, Lincoln 1827, d. 1853 Feb. 19	Charles Will. London Geo. Exeter Will. Llandaff	Ibid.
1820 Nov. 12 Lambeth	William Carey, Exeter, S. Asaph 1830, d. 1846 Sept. 13	Charles Will. London G. H. Chester Will. Llandaff	Ibid.
1823 June 1 Lambeth	Reginald Heber, Calcutta, d. 1826 Apr. 3	Charles Will. London John S. Asaph Will. Llandaff	Ibid.
1824 Apr. 11 Lambeth	Christopher Bethell, Gloucester, Exeter 1830, Bangor 1830	Charles Will. London John S. Asaph B. E. Ely	Ibid.
1824 June 6 Lambeth	Robert James Carr, Chichester, Worcester 1831, d. 1841 Apr. 24	Charles Will. London Geo. Lincoln Chr. Gloucester	Ibid.
1824 June 20 Whitehall	Chas. Jas. Blomfield, Chester, London 1828, resigned 1856 d. 1857 Aug. 5	Edw. York Will. London Will. Exeter	Ibid.
1824 July 25 Lambeth	Wm. Hart Coleridge, Barbadoes, res. 1841, d. 1850 Dec. 21 Christoph. Lipscomb, Jamaica, d. 1843 Apr. 4	Charles Will. London Geo. Lincoln Will. Llandaff	Ibid.
1825 Mar. 27 Lambeth	John Inglis, Nova Scotia, d. 1850 Oct. 27	Charles Will. London Geo. Lincoln Will. Llandaff	Ibid.

DATE OF CONSECRATION.	NAME AND SEE.	CONSECRATORS.	AUTHORITIES, &c.
1825 July 24 Lambeth	John B. Jenkinson, S. David's, d. 1840 July 7	Will. London, Edw. Oxford, J. Bristol, R. J. Chichester	Reg. Sutton.
1826 Jan. 1 Lambeth	Chas. James Stewart, Quebec d. 1837 July 13	Charles Will. London Will. Llandaff C. J. Chester	Ibid.
1826 May 21 Lambeth	Chas. Rich. Sumner, Llandaff, Winchester 1827	Charles Will. London R. J. Chichester J. B. S. David's	Ibid.
1827 Mar. 4 Lambeth	Charles Lloyd, Oxford, d. 1829 May 31	Charles Will. London Will. Durham C. J. Chester	Ibid.
1827 Mar. 25 Lambeth	Robert Gray, Bristol, d. 1834 Sept. 28	Charles Will. London Will. Durham J. B. S. David's	Ibid.
1827 June 3 Lambeth	John Thomas James, Calcutta, d. 1828 Aug. 22	Charles Will. London Will. Durham J. B. S. David's	Ibid.
1827 July 15 Lambeth	Hugh Percy, Rochester, Carlisle 1827, d. 1856 Feb. 5	Charles Will. London B. E. Ely R. J. Chichester	Ibid.
1828 Jan. 13 Lambeth	Edward Copleston, Llandaff, d. 1849 Oct. 14	Charles Will. London C. R. Winchester Hugh Carlisle	Ibid.
1828 Mar. 9 Whitehall	William Ward, Sodor and Man, d. 1838 Jan. 26	Edw. York Will. London Geo. Rochester	Ibid.
1828 Sept. 14 York	John Bird Sumner, Chester, Canterbury 1848	Edw. York C. R. Winchester Chr. Gloucester	Reg. Howley.
1829 May 17 Lambeth	John Matt. Turner, Calcutta d. 1831 July 7	William C. J. London Geo. Rochester J. B. Chester	Ibid.

DATE OF CONSECRATION.	NAME AND SEE.	CONSECRATORS.	AUTHORITIES, &c.
1829 Aug. 23 Lambeth	Richard Bagot, Oxford, Bath 1845, d. 1845 May 15	William C. J. London C. R. Winchester Geo. Rochester	Reg. Howley.
1830 July 11 Lambeth	James Henry Monk, Gloucester, Bristol 1836, d. 1856 June 6	William C. J. London Hugh Carlisle Geo. Rochester	Ibid.
1831 Jan. 2 Lambeth	Henry Phillpotts, Exeter	William C. J. London Rob. Bristol	Ibid.
1831 Oct. 2 Lambeth	Edward Maltby, Chichester, Durham 1836, resigned 1856	William G. H. Bath Rob. Bristol	Ibid.
1832 Apr. 29 Lambeth	Daniel Wilson, Calcutta	William C. J. London Rob. Bristol J. H. Gloucester	Ibid.
1832 May 20 Lambeth	Edward Grey, Hereford, d. 1837 June 24	William C. J. London J. B. S. David's Rob. Bristol	Ibid.
1834 Dec. 7 Lambeth	Joseph Allen, Bristol, Ely 1836, d. 1845 Mar. 20	William C. J. London R. J. Worcester Edw. Chichester	Ibid.
1835 June 14 Lambeth	Daniel Corrie, Madras, d. 1837 Feb. 5	William Hen. Lichfield Chr. Bangor Hugh Carlisle	Ibid.
1836 Feb. 14 Lambeth	Geo. Jehos. Mountain, Montreal, Quebec 1850 Wm. G. Broughton, Australia, Sydney 1847 d. 1853 Feb. 20	William C. J. London C. R. Winchester J. H. Gloucester	Ibid.
1836 July 3 Lambeth	Samuel Butler, Lichfield, d. 1839 Dec. 4	William Edw. Durham John Lincoln Jos. Bristol	Ibid.

DATE OF CONSECRATION.	NAME AND SEE.	CONSECRATORS.	AUTHORITIES, &c.
1836 Oct. 2 Lambeth	William Otter, Chichester, d. 1840 Aug. 20	William C. J. London Geo. Rochester	Reg. Howley.
1836 Nov. 6 York	Chas. Thom. Longley, Ripon, Durham 1856	Edw. York *John Lincoln* Hugh Carlisle J. B. Chester	Perceval. A. S. British Magazine for December.
1837 Apr. 16 Lambeth	Edward Denison, Sarum, d. 1854 Mar. 6	William C. J. London Edw. Durham C. T. Ripon	Reg. Howley.
1837 June 11 Lambeth	Edward Stanley, Norwich, d. 1849 Sept. 6	William C. J. London John Lincoln J. B. Chester	Ibid.
1837 Oct. 1 Lambeth	Thomas Musgrave, Hereford, York 1847.	William C. J. London Jos. Ely Will. Chichester	Ibid.
1837 Nov. 19 Lambeth	Thomas Carr, Bombay, res. 1851 Geo. John T. Spencer, Madras, res. 1849	William Sam. Lichfield Edw. Sarum	Ibid.
1838 July 22 Lambeth	James Bowstead, Sodor and Man, Lichfield 1840, d. 1843 Oct. 11	William John Lincoln Jos. Ely Thom. Hereford	Ibid.
1839 June 16 Lambeth	George Davys, Peterborough	William C. J. London John Lincoln J. B. Chester	Ibid.
1839 Aug. 4 Lambeth	Aubrey Geo. Spencer, Newfoundland, Jamaica 1843 John Strachan, Toronto	William C. J. London Will. Chichester John Nova Scotia	Ibid.
1840 Mar. 1 Whitehall	Henry Pepys, Sodor and Man, Worcester 1841,	Edw. York Geo. Rochester James Lichfield	Ibid.

Date of Consecration.	Name and See.	Consecrators.	Authorities, &c.
1840 Aug. 9 Lambeth	Connop Thirlwall, S. David's,	William Jos. Ely Thom. Hereford James Lichfield	Reg. Howley.
1840 Sept. 20 Lambeth	P. N. Shuttleworth, Chichester, d. 1842 Jan. 7	William Geo. Rochester Geo. Peterborough	Ibid.
1841 May 30 Whitehall	Thom. Vowler Short, Sodor and Man, S. Asaph 1846	Edw. York C. J. London C. T. Ripon	Ibid.
1841 Oct. 17 Lambeth	Geo. August. Selwyn, New Zealand	William C. J. London John Lincoln W. H. Barbadoes	Ibid.
1841 Nov. 7 Lambeth	Mich. Sol. Alexander, Jerusalem d. 1845 Nov. 23	William C. J. London Geo. Rochester G. A. New Zealand	Ibid.
1842 Feb. 27 Lambeth	Ash. Turner Gilbert, Chichester	William John Lincoln Edw. Llandaff	Ibid.
1843 Aug. 24 Westminster	Thomas Parry, Barbadoes George Tomlinson, Gibraltar Fran. Russell Nixon, Tasmania Daniel G. Davis, Antigua, d. 1857 Oct. 25 Wm. Piercy Austin, Guiana	C. J. London C. R. Winchester Geo. Rochester A. T. Chichester W. H. Coleridge	Ibid.
1843 Dec. 3 Lambeth	John Lonsdale, Lichfield	William C. J. London C. R. Winchester A. T. Chichester	Ibid.
1844 Apr. 28 Lambeth	Edward Feild, Newfoundland	William C. J. London Chr. Bangor Hen. Worcester	Ibid.

Date of Consecration.	Name and See.	Consecrators.	Authorities, &c.
1845 May 4 Lambeth	Thomas Turton, Ely John Medley, Fredericton John Chapman, Colombo	William C. J. London John Lincoln Geo. Rochester Thom. Hereford John Lichfield *W. H. Coleridge*	Reg. Howley.
1845 Nov. 30 Lambeth	Samuel Wilberforce, Oxford	William C. J. London C. R. Winchester Edw. Sarum	Ibid.
1846 July 5 Lambeth	Samuel Gobat, Jerusalem	William C. J. London John Lichfield Dan. Calcutta	Ibid.
1847 Jan. 10 Whitehall	Walt. Aug. Shirley, Sodor and Man, d. 1847 Apr. 21	Hugh Carlisle John Lichfield T. V. S. Asaph	Ibid.
1847 May 23 Whitehall	Robert John Eden, Sodor and Man, Bath 1854	Hugh Carlisle C. T. Ripon Sam. Oxford	Ibid.
1847 June 29 Westminster	Robert Gray, Capetown Augustus Short, Adelaide Charles Perry, Melbourne William Tyrrell, Newcastle	William C. J. London C. R. Winchester J. H. Gloucester A. T. Chichester John Lichfield *Sam. Oxford* *T. V. S. Asaph* *Dan. Calcutta*	Ibid.
1848 Jan. 23 Whitehall	James Prince Lee, Manchester	Thom. York J. B. Chester Hen. Worcester	Ibid.
1848 Mar. 26 Lambeth	Renn Dick. Hampden, Hereford	John B. Cant. Edw. Llandaff Edw. Norwich Hen. Worcester	Reg. Sumner.
1848 May 14 Whitehall	John Graham, Chester	Thom. York Edw. Durham John Lincoln	Ibid.

DATE OF CONSECRATION.	NAME AND SEE.	CONSECRATORS.	AUTHORITIES, &c.
1849 May 29 Canterbury	George Smith, Victoria David Anderson, Rupert's Land	John B. Cant. C. J. London C. R. Winchester T. V. S. Asaph Sam: Oxford W. H. Coleridge	Reg. Sumner.
1849 Dec. 2 Lambeth	Samuel Hinds, Norwich, resigned 1857 Alfred Olivant, Llandaff Thomas Dealtry, Madras	John B. Cant. C. J. London John Lincoln Hugh Carlisle J. P. Manchester R. D. Hereford	Ibid.
1850 July 25 Westminster	Francis Fulford, Montreal	John B. Cant. Edw. Sarum A. T. Chichester Sam. Oxford Sam. Norwich John Toronto	Ibid.
1851 Mar. 25 Lambeth	Hibbert Binney, Nova Scotia	John B. Cant. C. J. London A. T. Chichester Sam. Oxford	Ibid.
1851 Aug. 10 Lambeth	John Harding, Bombay	John B. Cant. C. J. London Thomas Carr	Ibid.
1852 May 30 Lambeth	Owen Emeric Vidal Sierra Leone d. 1854 Dec. 23	John B. Cant. C. J. London A. T. Chichester Sam. Oxford Rob. Capetown	Ibid.
1853 May 5 Lambeth Church	John Jackson, Lincoln	John B. Cant. C. J. London C. R. Winchester John Lichfield Sam. Oxford G. J. Quebec C. P. Ohio	Ibid.

DATE OF CONSECRATION.	NAME AND SEE.	CONSECRATORS.	AUTHORITIES, &c.
1853 Nov. 30 Lambeth Church	John Armstrong, Grahamstown, d. 1856 May 16 John Wm. Colenso, Natal	John B. Cant. C. J. London Sam. Oxford John Lincoln Rob. Capetown W. P. Guiana Aug. Adelaide	Reg. Sumner.
1854 May 14 Lambeth	Walt. Kerr Hamilton, Sarum	John B. Cant. C. R. Winchester A. T. Chichester Sam. Oxford G. A. New Zealand	Ibid.
1854 July 25 York	Horace Powys, Sodor and Man,	Thom. York Hugh Carlisle C. T. Ripon J. P. Manchester	
1854 Nov. 30 Lambeth	Francis Barker, Sydney Vincent Wm. Ryan, Mauritius	John B. Cant. John Lichfield John Chester Geo. Gibraltar	Ibid.
1855 May 17 Lambeth Church	John Wills Weeks, Sierra Leone, d. 1857 Mar. 25	John B. Cant. C. J. London C. R. Winchester Sam. Oxford	Ibid.
1855 Oct. 18 Calcutta	Fran.T. Mac Dougall, Labuan	Dan. Calcutta Geo. Victoria Thom. Madras	
1856 Mar. 24 Lambeth	Reginald Courtenay, Kingston, Jamaica	John B. Cant. Hen. Worcester Sam. Oxford A. G. Jamaica	Ihid.
1856 Apr. 13 Whitehall	Henry M. Villiers, Carlisle	Thom. York C. T. Ripon J. P. Manchester John Chester	Ibid.
1856 Aug. 10 Lambeth	Charles Baring, Gloucester and Bristol Henry J. C. Harper, Christ Church, New Zealand	John B. Cant. C. R. Winchester A. T. Chichester Sam. Oxford	Ibid.

DATE OF CONSECRATION.	NAME AND SEE.	CONSECRATORS.	AUTHORITIES, &c.
1856 Nov. 23 Whitehall	Archib. Campb. Tait, London Henry Cotterill, Grahamstown	John B. Cant. A. T. Chichester John Lincoln H. M. Carlisle A. G. Jamaica D. Rupert's Land	Reg. Sumner.
1857 Jan. 18 Bishopthorpe Church	Robert Bickersteth, Ripon	Thom. York C. T. Durham J. P. Manchester H. M. Carlisle	
1857 June 11 Marylebone Church	John Thom. Pelham, Norwich	John B. Cant. A. C. London J. P. Manchester C. Gloucester Rob. Ripon	
1857 July 25 Lambeth	Matt. Blagden Hale, Perth, Australia	John B. Cant. A. C. London Rob. Ripon	
1857 Sept. 21 Lambeth	John Bowen, Sierra Leone	John B. Cant. Geo. Peterborough Geo. Victoria	
1857 Oct. 28 Lambeth	Benjamin Cronyn, Huron, Canada	John B. Cant. C. R. Winchester H. Nova Scotia J. Sierra Leone	

APPENDICES.

I.—TABLE OF SAXON KINGDOMS AND MARRIAGES.

II.—TABLE OF SAXON AND ENGLISH SEES.

III.—LIST OF PALLS.

IV.—DATES OF LEGATIONS.

V.—SUFFRAGAN BISHOPS.

VI.—MANX BISHOPS.

VII.—WELSH BISHOPS, &c.

VIII.—INDEX LISTS OF ENGLISH BISHOPS.

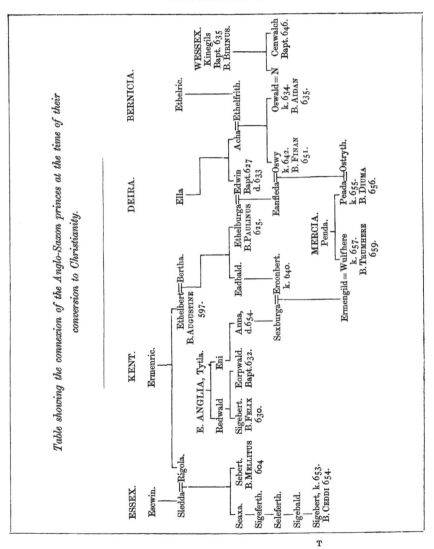

Table showing the connexion of the Anglo-Saxon princes at the time of their conversion to Christianity.

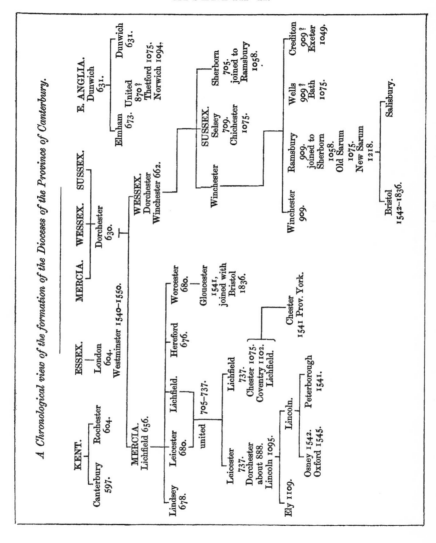

A Chronological view of the formation of the Dioceses of the Province of Canterbury.

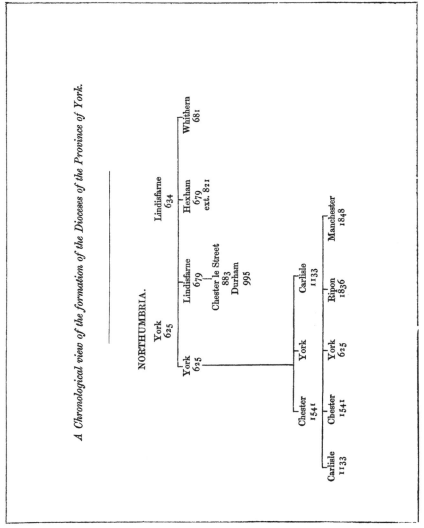

A Chronological view of the formation of the Dioceses of the Province of York.

NORTHUMBRIA.

York
625

York
625

Lindisfarne
679

Chester le Street
883
Durham
995

Lindisfarne
634

Hexham
679
ext. 821

Whithern
681

York
625

York
625

Carlisle
1133

Ripon
1836

Manchester
1848

Chester
1541

Chester
1541

Carlisle
1133

APPENDIX III.

*Dates of the Reception of the Pall by the Archbishops of Canterbury,
from Lanfranc to Pole.*

Recipient.	Bishops presenting the Pall.	Recipient.	Bishops presenting the Pall.
Lanfranc, 1070, at Rome.		Robert Winchelsey, 1294, (At Rome).	
Anselm, 1094 June 10, Canterbury.	Walter C. Albano.	Walter Reynolds, 1314 Feb. 13, Chartham.	Walter Worcester.
Ralph, 1115 June 28, Canterbury.	Anselm the Legate.	Simon Mepeham, 1328 June 9, Avignon.	P. John XXII.
William de Corbeuil, 1123, at Rome.		John Stratford, 1334 April 23, Rue in Ponthieu.	Haymo Rochester.
Theobald, 1139, at Rome.		Thomas Bradwardin, Died before the ceremony.	
Thomas à Becket, 1162 Aug. 10, Canterbury.		Simon Islip, 1350 Mar. 25, Esher.	William Winchester.
Richard, 1174 April 10, Anagni.	P. Alexander III.	Simon Langham, 1366 Nov. 4, S. Stephen's, Westm.	John Bath.
Baldwin. 1185 May 19, Canterbury.		William Whittlesey, 1369 April 19, Lambeth.	William Winchester.
Hubert Fitz Walter, 1193 Nov. 7, Canterbury.	Gilbert Rochester.	Simon Sudbury. Inthroned 1376 Apr.6	} Thomas Rochester.
Stephen Langton, (At Rome).		William Courtenay, 1382 May 6, Croydon.	Robert London.
Richard Grant, 1229 Nov. 23,	Henry Rochester.	Thomas Arundel, 1397 Feb. 2, Westminster.	William Winchester. Richard Sarum. Robert Chichester.
Edmund Rich, 1234 Apr. 2, Canterbury.	Roger London.	Roger Walden, 1398 Feb. 17, High Clere.	William Winchester.
Boniface, (Before consecration)	Peter Hereford.	Henry Chicheley, 1414 July 29, Sutton Regis.	Henry Winchester. Thomas Norwich.
Robert Kilwardby, 1273 May 8, Tenham.	} Nic. Winchester. Walter Exeter.	John Stafford, 1443 Aug. 23,	William Rochester.
John Peckham, 1279, (At Rome).			

RECIPIENT.	BISHOPS PRESENTING THE PALL.	RECIPIENT.	BISHOPS PRESENTING THE PALL.
John Kemp, 1452 Sept. 24, Fulham.	Thomas London. William Winchester.	Henry Dean, 1501 July 20, S. Stephen's, Westm.	John Lichfield.
* Thomas Bouchier, *Inthr.* 1455 *Jan.* 25	*Thomas London* *William Winchester* *John Rochester* *Richard Ross.*	William Warham, 1504 Feb. 2, Lambeth.	Oliver Bath. William Lincoln.
John Morton, *Inthr.* 1487 *Jan.* 28	*John Ely* *Edmund Rochester* *Thomas Sarum* *Robert Worcester.*	Thomas Cranmer, 1533 Mar. 3. Reginald Pole, 1556 Mar. 25, Bow Church.	Richard Worcester. Thomas Ely.

APPENDIX IV.

Legates.

NAMES OF LEGATES.	DATE OF LEGATION.
Archbishop William	1127 January 25.
Henry of Winchester	1139 March 1.
Archbishop Theobald	1150
Archbp. Roger of York	1164 February 27.
Archbp. Thomas à Becket	1166 April 24.
Archbishop Richard	1174 April.
Archbishop Baldwin	1186 January 12.
William Longchamp	1190 June 5.
Archbishop Hubert	1195 March 18.

After this time the Archbishops of Canterbury were, with a few exceptions, considered Legati nati—ex officio Legates.

---

* The corresponding dates for Archbishops Sudbury, Bouchier and Morton I have not been able to discover: for the Archbishops of York only in a few instances ; these are

John Thoresby, 1353 Mar. 29, from W. Winchester at Esher.
Thomas Arundel, 1388 Sept. 14.
William Booth, 1452 Sept. 24, from Thom. London at Fulham.
George Neville, 1465 Sept. 6, from John Lincoln at York.
Thomas Rotherham, 1480, Sept 3, at York House.

These dates are of importance, as marking the time at which the plenary power of Metropolitan was assumed by the Archbishops. Between their election and reception of the pall they (usually at least) were restrained from taking even a subordinate part in the consecration of Bishops. Other Bishops however could consecrate without the pall and to the exclusion of the Archbishop ; Bishops Edendon and Beaufort are the most eminent instances.

APPENDIX V.

Suffragans and Bishops in Partibus.

Under the common designation of Suffragan Bishops are comprehended (besides the proper provincial Bishops in their relation to their Metropolitan) all Bishops bearing foreign titles, who have been employed on occasional duties in England, and several who at different periods have been consecrated for the special relief of aged Bishops and overgrown dioceses. They may be classed as,

1. Suffragans of the Saxon Archbishops consecrated with or without promise of succession. Without prospect of succession were the Bishops of S. Martin's, who are said to have been the predecessors of the Archdeacons of Canterbury, of whom only two, Eadsige, afterwards Archbishop, and Godwin, (d. 1061), have left their names : with prospect of succession were Siward of Upsal, abbat of Abingdon, and perhaps S. Dunstan.

2. Danish Bishops introduced by Canute and his successors, some of whom survived till the conquest.

3. Foreign Refugee Bishops, employed as vicars by the diocesans.

4. Bishops in partibus, consecrated either for the help of the diocesans, or for the service of the exempt monasteries.

5. Irish Bishops employed in the same way. See the Note at the end of this Appendix.

6. French and Scotch Bishops consecrated during the wars of Edward III. and the schism of the papacy.

7. Suffragans appointed under the Act 26 Hen. VIII. c. 14. These will be found above.

The following lists are not by any means complete, nor are they intended as more than an illustration of the ecclesiastical state of England during the periods when the diocesan Bishops were employed principally as statesmen and warriors. The lists are taken from Henry Wharton's laborious collection, with a few additional names and particulars.

I. Saxon and Danish Bishops.

Siegfried, a Norwegian Bishop of the time of Edgar. V. Ang. S. i. p. 603. (Sigidwold natione Græcus) p. ult. : buried at Glastonbury. (W. Malmsb. 1722 Ed. Migne), perhaps the same who is called Bishop of Lindsey.

Siward, Abbat of Abingdon, consecrated as coadjutor to Abp. Eadsige 1044.

Ralph, a cousin of Edward the Confessor, a Norwegian Bishop, Abbat of Abingdon 1050–1052.—Hist. Abingd. A. S. i. p. 167.

Osmund, consecrated in Poland, went about acting as a Bishop, saying that he had been consecrated at Rome.—Adam of Bremen (Pertz. 7. 340).

Christiern, came to England with Sweyn in 1070. V. Chr. Sax. 1070.

II. Foreign refugee, resigned, and In partibus.

1266. Geoffrey or William, Archbishop of Edessa, alias Rages in Media. " Anglicus et tunc temporis in Anglia moram continuans, circumspectus et eloquentia commendabilis." Rishanger, p. 54, and note è Chron. Barnwell, p. 150. Consecrated the Bishop of Norwich in 1266. Consecrated the Prior's Chapel at Bury in 1275. Cont. Flor. Wig. ii. 215. Was present at the translation of S. Hugh in 1280. Harl. MS. 3720. In 1286 he was

Suffragan or Commissary of the Bishop of Norwich, and consecrated the cemetery of the Carmelites "Lincæ."—Bale. Harl. 1819.

1287. Gilbert "Hammensis." Buried at the Carmelites, Norwich, d. 1287 Oct. 9. Granted forty days' indulgence to all who should attend the preaching of the Carmelites, 1273, 1274, and 1276. He was probably the Bishop "Hamarensis" in Norway, cons. 1263.

Geoffrey Grandefelde, perhaps Bishop of Ferns, 1347 and 1348. An Austin friar of Northampton; chaplain to the Bishop of Tusculum; suffragan of Lincoln.

1316. David Recreensis, suffragan of York, 1316 Feb. 20; receives for salary five marks, 1316 Apr. 9, and in 1317, 10 marks.

1310. Augustine Nottingham, Bishop of Laodicea, (Bale); a Franciscan; suffragan of York. "Licentia Domino Hugoni (or Augustino) de Nottingham clerico Regio ad construendam unam alam ex parte Australi Ecclesiæ B. Nicolai apud Nottingham et in ea unum altare in honorem S. Annæ, Oct. 5, 1300." Reg. Corbridge. The Franciscans of Nottingham have licence to get their church consecrated by any Catholic Bishop, 1310 Nov. 23. Reg. Greenfield.

1322. Peter, Bishop of Corbavia in Dalmatia, (Farlati 4. 95), d. on S. Wulstan's day, 1332. Assisted at a consecration in 1322. Consecrated S. Mary's bell at S. Paul's, Feb. 2, 1331. (Lansd. 791). Buried at the Franciscans' church, London. Suffragan of London, Canterbury, and Winchester 1322-1327.

1340. Benedict "Cardicensis" (Sardis or Sardica). Prior of the Austin Friars of Norwich; suffragan of Norwich, and Winchester 1333-1346.

1340. John Pascal, Bishop of Llandaff, is said to have been Bishop of Scutari, and suffragan of Norwich, 1340. He is sometimes called Thomas, and there is some doubt whether the Bishops of Scutari and Llandaff were the same person.

1344. Hugh, Archbishop of Damascus; suffragan of York 1344-1351. Consecrated a cemetery at Thorp, 1349 Aug. 15. Had a commission to bless the Abbat of Rufford 1352. Reg. Zouch. "1347 Aug. 8. Johannes Episcopus convenit coram Archiepiscopum Cantuariensem Archiepiscopum Damascenum ordinis Heremitarum S. Augustini, qui a Cantabrigia usque ad civitatem Exon: iter faciens episcopalia officia in diocesi Exon: peregerat sine licentia Episcopi, eumque ad confessionem delicti et veniam petendam adegit." Reg. Grandison. 1351 Aug. 2, he accused the Abbat of Byland of breaking into his park at Newstead, and stealing a horse. Rymer v. 20. This seems to point to some connexion with the abbey at Jerveaulx. One Hugh was Abbat there about this time.

1348. Richard, Archbishop of Nazareth, elected Oct. 10, 1348; consecrated at Avignon by Bertrand, Bishop of Sabina, shortly before the issue of the Bull of Provision, 6 Id. Dec.; d. 1366. Ughelli 7. 773. Assisted at two consecrations in 1362; suffragan for Canterbury 1349, Worcester 1350, London 1361, and Ely 1361.

1349. Cæsarius "Episcopus Beatæ Mariæ de Rosis." Assisted at consecrations 1353 and 1355. Suffragan of Canterbury and Winchester, St. Alban's 1349.

1350. Robert Worksop, suffragan of York.

1353. Thomas "Magnatiensis," a Monk of Miraval, had licence to be consecrated by any Catholic Bishop in S. Mary's Southwark, 1353 July 26. Reg. Edendon. Suffragan of York 1365, Lichfield, S. V. 1360, Llandaff, S. V. 1361 Dec. 5, Hereford, S. V. 1361 Apr. 10.

1353. Thomas Waleys, Bishop of Lycostomium, a Dominican, has like licence. He assisted at a consecration in 1362, and was perhaps the doctor whose dispute with Pope John XXII, on the Beatific Vision of the Patriarchs, is mentioned by W. Thorne 2067 and Bale, Catalogue I. 406.

1354. Thomas Salkeld, Bishop of Chrysopolis; suffragan of York 1349-1358. Had a salary of forty marks per annum for consecrating altars and churches and confirming. Reg. Zouch. Commission renewed 1354 July 11. Reg. Thoresby. The king acquits the Bishop of Durham on several charges brought against him by the Bishop of Chrysopolis, 1358 Mar. 2. Rymer 6. 79. His salary in 1349 was 40 marks, and in 1354 £20.

1354. John Ware " Comanageniensis," consecrated 1354. Suffragan of Exeter 1355 Dec. 12 to 1386 ; of Hereford 1371.

1360. Robert " Prissinensis." Suffragan of Hereford 1360, Worcester 1373–1375, Chichester S. V. 1362 May 12.

1361. Geoffrey " Miliensis," suffragan of York 1361–1364.

1362. John Langebrugge " Buduensis," appointed suffragan of Wells in consequence of the number of unauthorized Bishops who were acting as suffragans in England, 1362 July 16. Commission renewed S. V. 1363 Sept. 3.

1362. Thomas " Lambergensis," assisted at a consecration in 1362.· Suffragan of London 1362.

1366. Robert " Lambrensis," suffragan of York 1366, S. Alban's 1384, Bangor 1371.

1367. John " Lambergensis," perhaps the same as John Langebrugge ; has a commission to examine the election of the Abbess of Burnham. Reg. Lincoln.

1370. Geoffrey, Archbishop of Damascus, assisted at a consecration in 1370.

1370. John Ayobanensis, or Ayubonensis, assisted at a consecration in 1370 ; suffragan of Canterbury 1369 Mar. 30. William Ayoboniensis had a commission to consecrate an altar in any church in the Arches Deanery, 1366 Nov. 28.

1370. Richard " Serviensis," suffragan of York 1370–1397.

1379. Robert Derling, Bishop of Dunkeld ; consecrated 1379 Oct. 30, at S. Benedict's, Rome, by Peter, Bishop of Æmonia, or Citta Nuova ; suffragan of York 1380–1384.

   ₊ After him appears as Bishop of Dunkeld, Nicolas, Abbat of Pershore, R. of Beoly 1396 Dec. 18, Belbroughton 1411 Mar. 28 ; suffragan of Worcester 1392–1421 and Hereford 1404. Nicolas was succeeded by William Gunwardby, B. of Dunkeld, R. of Houghton Conquest 1452 Mar. 16, Great Hallingbury 1440 May 28. Suffragan of Lincoln 1431, and Ely 1448–1454 ; d. 1457. These are omitted in Keith, not having been recognised in Scotland, as neither were John B. of Glasgow, suffragan of London 1393–1394, Sarum 1396, and Robert " Archiliensis," suff. of Hereford 1386.

1382. William Bottlesham, Bishop of Pavada " Navatensis ;" of Bethlehem 1385. Translated to Llandaff 1386.

1384. Nicolas, Bishop of Christopolis, suffragan of Wells 1385–1403. Commission renewed 1403 Nov. 30. Sarum 1395 Feb. 1 to 1406, Llandaff 1382.

1385. Robert Hyntlesham, or Hyrtlesham, Bishop of Sevastopolis, suffragan of Norwich, Sarum 1388–9 ; assisted at a consecration in 1385.

1385. William " Tornacensis," appointed to Tournay during the schism of the Papacy ; consecrated 1385 ; assisted at a consecration in 1401 ; ordained in London diocese 1399-1406.

1390. William Egmund " Prissinensis," an Austin friar of Stamford ; suffragan of Lincoln ; Had a commission to examine the election of the Abbat of S. Mary's, Northampton, 1394 July 31. See Bale.

1390. Oswald, Bishop of Whithern, consecrated 1380. Suffragan of York 1391–1397.

1390. William Northbrugge " Pharensis," consecrated at Rome. He was rector of Trinity Goodramgate, York, 1400 ; Nafferton 1398 ; warden of the hospital of S. Mary Magdalene at Kynewaldsgrave 1399 ; suffragan of York 1390 ; commission renewed 1408 Dec. 29 ; suffragan of Lichfield 1385–1387, and Worcester in 1395.

1394. William " Basiliensis," suffragan of London 1394–1399.

1396. Thomas Edwardston, Archbishop, perhaps of Nazareth ; suffragan of Norwich ; buried at Clare in Suffolk ; d. 1396. Blomfield (Hist. Norfolk) speaks of Thomas Bedingfield, Archbishop of Nazareth.

1395. Thomas Botyler, Bishop of Chrysopolis ; assisted at a consecration in 1401 ; subcollector for the crusade against Bajazet in 1399. Rymer 8. 82. Suffragan of Winchester 1401, Worcester 1420.

1397. John Sewale " Surronensis," appointed by bull 1397 July 20 ; has general licence of nonresidence, &c. from the pope, 1399 Oct. 28. Reg. Arundel. Assisted at a consecration in 1401 ; suffragan of Winchester 1417-1418, London 1417-1423, S. Edmund's 1414, Sarum 1420-1426, S. David's 1405. The name is spelled Surrenensis and Cironensis ; he was perhaps Bishop of Cyrene.

1400. John Leicester, Archbishop of Smyrna, a Carmelite. Rector of Threxton, Norfolk, 1400 Apr. 6 ; suffragan of Norwich 1413 ; commission renewed 1416 June 1. till 1423 : of S. Edmund's 1418 ; d. 1424 Nov. 6. Weaver.

1400. Thomas Merks, alias Sumestre, was translated from Carlisle " ad Ecclesiam Samastenam, in quâ clerus seu populus Christianus non habetur," and thence to some unknown see in 1402. He was Rector of Todenham 1404 Aug. 13 ; Suffragan of Winchester 1403-1404 ; d. 1409.

1400. Thomas Bishop of Constantia in Media, or of Coutances, assisted at a consecration.

1401. John Greenlaw " Soltaniensis in Mediâ," provided Sept. 20, 1401. (Wadding), but consecrated Sept. 8. (Reg. Bowet). Suffragan of Wells 1401 Dec. to 1408 ; York 1421 ; Lincoln 1422 ; Sarum 1409.

1402. John " Ancoradensis," had a commission to purify the cemetery of S. Peter's, Cambridge, 1402 Sept. 7. Reg. Fordham. Suffragan of Lincoln 1420-1432 ; Ely 1402 ; Canterbury 1424.

1407. John Bishop of Gallipoli. Suffragan of Sarum 1407 ; ordains 1408 Mar. 17.

1410. Matthew Bishop of Hebron. Suffragan of Hereford 1410.

1409. William " Solubriensis" (Selymbria). Suffragan of Sarum 1409 Jan. 20 to 1417 ; Exeter 1415 and 1416 ; Winchester 1407-1417.

1411. William Bellers " Soltoniensis ;" perhaps the same as the last ; suffragan of Canterbury ; assisted at a consecration in 1411 ; suffragan of Lincoln 1418 ; consecrated Borstall chapel 1418 Nov. 2.

1414. Richard " Katensis ;" suffragan of Sarum 1414 Feb. 23. Ordains 1420-1437; Bath 1414-1418 ; Exeter 1420 Nov. 1 ; ordains 1417-1433.

1423. John " Stephaniensis ;" suffragan of Lincoln 1423-1431. Commission renewed 1431 Sept. 1 ; Ely 1424-1443.

1426. Robert " Gradensis ;" Norwich 1426 Dec. 22 to 1446.

1436. John (Bloxwych?) " Olensis" (Hollensis Islandiæ prov. 1427). Vicar of East Ham 1444 Sept. 17 ; died before 12 June 1446. Suffragan of Bath 1437 Mar. 10 to 1443 ; Canterbury 1443 Oct. 5 ; Exeter 1442. In 1436 May 28 he was allowed to send John May, captain of the ship Catherine of London, to Iceland, to report the condition of his diocese which he had not visited. He seems to have resigned it soon after, and is styled "nuper Olensis."

1441. John Bishop of Philippopolis ; provided 1441 July 25, (Wadding) ; suffragan of York 1446-1458.

1454. Roderic " Arlatensis ;" Rector of Buckland Fyllegh ; suffragan of Exeter 1454 Nov. 8 to 1457.

1458. William Westkarre Bishop of Sidon ; Black Canon ; Prior of Mottisfont ; consecrated the Chrism at Canterbury 1463 April 14 ; suffragan of Winchester 1457-1486 ; Canterbury 1480 ; Worcester 1480 ; Wells 1459. He was Rector of S. Martin's, Ludgate, 1465-1468 ; Romney Marsh, S. Mary's, 1468-1473.

1459. John "Tinensis," (Tenos); Canon regular of S. Austin; Vicar of Devizes; died 1480; suffragan of Wells 1459 Oct. 17 to 1479; Exeter 1461 and 1462.

1471. Henry Bishop of Joppa; Prior of Combwell; suffragan of Canterbury 1471. Rector of Lydd 1471 Feb. 7; Charryng 1471 Oct. 24; Lambeth 1471 Apr. 3. In his will, dated 1474 April 24, and proved 1474 May 25, he left all he had to Combwell Priory.

1480. Richard Wycherley "Olenensis;" a black friar of Warwick; died 1502 Sept.; suffragan of Worcester 1482-1501; Hereford 1480. He was Rector of Powick 1493 Dec. 5 to 1501; Salwarp 1486 Oct. 14 to 1502. He is called John in the London Registers of 1497. Vid. Wood, A. O. I. 551, and "Notes and Queries," August 1856.

1480. Thomas Cornish "Tinensis;" Master of S. John's Hospital, Wells 1483 August; Provost of Oriel College, Oxford, 1493; Vicar of S. Cuthbert's, Wells, 1497 July 29; Chancellor of Wells 1499 Apr. 21; Precentor 1502 Sept. 4; Vicar of Chewe 1505 Oct. 8, Axbridge 1489 Apr. 3, Wokey and Banwell; Warden of Ottery 1489 Dec. 1 to 1511. Suffragan of Wells 1486-1513; Exeter 1487 June 3 to 1505; d. 1513 June 3. Wood, A. O. I. 555. (Oliver.)

1492. Thomas Bishop of Pavada. Assisted at a consecration in 1494; suffragan of London 1492-1502; Rector of Thorley 1493; Thorp, 1495.

1493. Augustine Church, Bishop of Lydda; Rector of Washingburgh 1509; Malden 1504; East Borscombe 1498-1499; suffragan of Sarum 1494 Feb. 27, 1499; Exeter 1493; Lincoln 1501-1511.

1498. Richard Martin, Bishop of the Catholic Church and suffragan of Canterbury; died 1498 Nov. 19; Prior of the Minorites at Canterbury; Rector of Lydd 1474, and Ickham 1492.

1502. Edmund Bishop of Chalcedon; Norwich.

1503. Edward Bishop of Gallipoli; suffragan of London 1503; Worcester 1503.

1503. Ralph Heylesden, Bishop of Ascalon; provided 1503 March 8, (Wadding); has a pension of 150 golden ducats from the revenues of Worcester, being still elect, (MS. C. C. C. 170); suffragan of Worcester 1503-1523, Hereford 1510.

1505. John Underwood, Bishop of Chalcedon; Rector of North Creek and Eccles; suffragan of Norwich 1531.

1505. Thomas Wells, Bishop of Sidon; Prior of S. Gregory's Canterbury; d. 1526 Sept. 17 (Hasted); suffragan of Canterbury 1505-1511; Incumbent of Holy Cross, Westgate, Canterbury, 1507 Feb. 8; Rector of Woodchurch 1519 May 15; Adisham 1523 Dec. 7.

1506. John Hatton, Bishop of Negropont; Prebendary of Givendale 1503, Ulleskelf 1504; Archdeacon of Nottingham 1506 Sept. to 1516; d. 1516 Apr. 25; suffragan of York. Wood, A. O. I. 560.

1506. —— Sebastiensis; suffragan of Exeter 1506.

1506. John Thornden, Bishop of Sirmium or Cyrene. Commissary at Oxford 1506-1514; Prior of Dover; suffragan of Canterbury 1508-1514. He held Highardys 1505 Dec. 23; Harbledown 1507 Aug. 30; Newington 1506 Aug. 6; Aldington 1512 July 31; Monks Illegh 1513 Feb. 25; Folkstone Priory 1514 Mar. 4; and died 1516. Wood, A. O. I. 559.

1508. William Barton "Saloniensis." Prebendary of Roscombe 1509 Sept. 7, Beaminster Nov. 18, Grimston 1515 May 3. Suffragan of Sarum 1509-1517.

1508. Thomas Chard "Solubriensis," consecrated 1508. Vicar of Torrington Parva, 1508 Sept. 26; S. Gluvias; Holbeton; Wellington 1512 June; Warden of Ottery 1513 Oct. 9; resigned 1518; Prior of Montacute 1515-1525; Prior of Carswell 1535; Abbat of Forde 1521; Vicar of Thorncombe 1529 Apr. 15; Rector of Nothill 1532 Apr. 10; Vicar of Tintenhull 1521; Minister of Ottery 1540 Mar. 22; resigned 1543 Oct. 20. (Oliver.)

1512. John "Aviensis;" cons. 1512. Reg. Warham.

1512. John Tinmouth, Bishop of Argos; a Grey friar of Lynn. Rector of Ludgarshall; resigned

1511 ; Prebendary of Sarum 1510 ; Vicar of Boston, Lincolnshire ; d. 1524. Suffragan of Sarum 1510-1524. Wood, A. O. I. 566.

1513. Thomas Wolf, Bishop of Lacedæmon ; prohibited by Bp. Fitz James from officiating in the diocese of London, (about 1510) ; Vicar of East Ham 1514 May 2 ; d. before 1518 Nov. 6. Suffragan of Wells 1513 Sept. 30.

1513. John Young, Bishop of Gallipoli ; cons. July 3, 1513 ; d. 1526 Mar. 28. Rector of S. Martin's, Oxford ; Warden of New College 1521 ; Master of S. Thomas's Hospital 1510 Sept. 16 ; Rector of S. Magnus the Martyr 1514 Mar. 20 ; S. Christopher Stocks 1514 Jan. 23 ; Preb. of Holborn 1511 Nov. 28 ; Newington 1513 Feb. 10 ; Archdeacon of London 1514 Mar. 28 ; Dean of Chichester 1517. Suffragan of London 1513-1526. Wood, A. O. I. 567.

1513. Richard "Naturensis," (in the province of Heraclea), Suffragan of Durham ; cons. 1513.

1513. Roger Smith, Bishop of Lydda ; cons. 1513 ; d. 1518. Prior of Ronton ; Abbat of Dorchester ; Suffragan of Sarum 1517-1518.

1515. William Grant, Bishop of Pavada in the province of Constantinople ; Vicar of Redgwell 1522 Aug. 30 to 1524 Mar. 23 ; Suffragan of Ely 1516 Jan. 20, and 1525 July 21.

1515. Richard Wilson, Bishop of Negropont ; Prior of Drax. Buried at Bingley, Yorkshire. Suffragan of York 1515-1518. Wood, A. O. I. 561.

1515. William Bachelor, a Carmelite of Burnham, Prior of the London Carmelites, Bishop "Carvahagonensis in Grecia ;" Suffragan of Chichester. Buried at Rome, at S. Thomas of Canterbury's, July 30, 1515. Bale, Harl. 1819, and Br. Willis.

1518. John Pinnock, Bishop of Syene ; Vicar of Inglesham ; Prebendary of Dornford 1519, Chardstock 1523 ; Suffragan of Sarum 1518-1535.

1518. Thomas Vivian, Bishop of Megara ; Suffragan of Exeter 1518-1532 ; Prior of Black Canons at Bodmin. Wood, A. O. I. 554. Rector of Withiel ; Vicar of Egloshel ; Prebendary of Endellient ; d. 1533 June 1.

1520. Thomas Bele, Bishop of Lydda ; Prior of S. Mary's, Oxford, 1508 ; of S. Mary's Hospital, Bishopsgate ; Vicar of Witham 1528 Jan. 28 ; Suffragan of London 1521-1528. Master of S. John's Hospital, Ely, 1528 April 10. Wood, A. O. I. 569.

1526. William How "Aurensis." Wood, A. O. I. 567.

1526. Andrew Whitmay, Bishop of Chrysopolis ; d. 1546. Suffragan of Worcester 1526-1541 ; Hereford 1540. Wood, A. O. I. 577.

1526. John Smart, Bishop of Pavada ; Abbat of Wigmore ; Suffragan of Hereford 1526-1535 ; Worcester 1526-1531.

1529. Thomas Hallam, Bishop of Philadelphia. Nominated 1529 May 13, and consecrated before July 21. Prior of Newstead by Stamford ; subscribed the Royal Supremacy 1534 as Prior, and died or resigned before 1555. Suffragan of Lincoln.

Thomas Swillington, Bishop of Philadelphia ; probably the same person ; Preb. of Stow in Lindsey 1544 Apr. 12 ; d. 1546. Suffragan of Lincoln 1533 July 15 ; London 1534 March 21. V. Memoir on the Winkburne Seal, Archæologia, Vol. 7.

1530. John Holt, Bishop of Lydda, d. 1540 Aug. 12. Buried at S. Mary's, Bury. Wood, A. O. I. 569.

1530. Thomas Chetham, Bishop of Sidon ; d. 1558. Rector of Wrotham 1557 ; Penitentiary of S. Paul's ; Suffragan of London and Canterbury 1535-1553. Commission renewed 1558 Mar. 8.

    *** I have placed Bishop Chetham in this year on the authority of Wharton, although I have not found his name in records earlier than 1535. Christopher, Bishop of Sidon, is said to have assisted at the consecration of Goodrich, Lee and Capon in 1534 ; but as the name occurs no where else, it may be a clerical error for Chetham. From the

Valor Ecclesiasticus (I. 75 and 98) we learn that the Bishop of Sidon in 1535 had a pension of £40 from the Priory of Leeds, which he had resigned ; but in the Lists of Priors, Richard, and not Thomas, is the Christian name of Chetham, and no Christopher appears at all, though one Christopher Matteras was a monk of Leeds about this time. One Richard Bishop of Sidon ordains in Winchester in 1492. Altogether the question is unsettled, though I have suggested the reading "Thomas" for "Christopher" at p. 77.

1532. William Fawell, Bishop of Hippo ; Archdeacon of Totness ; d. 1557 July 25. Buried at Exeter. Bp. Voysey gave him the advowson of Boseham D. Chichester 1540 Feb. 15. Suffragan of Exeter 1532–1544. He was V. Probus 1537 Aug. 26 ; resigned 1550 Jan. He ordained for the last time 1554 Sept. 22. (Oliver.)

1535. William Bishop of Ascalon. Suffragan of York 1535.

1535. Matthew Mackarell, Bishop of Chalcedon, Suffragan of Lincoln, Abbat of Berling, was hanged in 1537 for his share in the pilgrimage of Grace.

1535. Robert King, Bishop of Rheon in the province of Athens ; Suffragan of Lincoln 1535 Apr. 15 ; Abbat of Thame and afterwards of Osney ; Bishop of Osney 1542 Sept. 1 ; Bishop of Oxford 1545 June 9. Wood, A. O. I. 585.

1535. John Stanywell "Poletensis." Abbat of Pershore ; Prior of Gloucester College, Oxford ; d. 1553. Buried at Longdon in Staffordshire. Wood, A. O. I. 579.

1539. John Draper, Bishop of Neapolis ; Prior of Christ Church, Twynham, elected 1520 Jan. 31 ; Prebendary of Winchester 1541 ; Suffragan of Winchester.

1545. Richard Thornden or Le Stede, Bishop of Dover. Bishop Yngworth died in 1545 ; his will is in the Prerogative Court. Thornden must have been consecrated soon after, but no record of the fact is preserved. Hence he has been confounded with his predecessor. He was Warden of Canterbury Hall, Oxford, in 1528. Rector of Wrotham 1546 April 3 ; and one of the first Prebendaries of Canterbury ; d. 1557. Wood, A. O. I. 586.

NOTE REFERRED TO AT PAGE 142.

The following are the names of the principal Irish Bishops who had permanent duty as Suffragans in England.

Armagh.
Roland de Jorz, cons. 1311 Nov. at Vienne by Berenger Bishop of Tusculum. Suffragan of Canterbury 1323, York 1332.
Edmund Conisburgh, 1477 Suffragan of Ely.
Meath.
William Andrew. Suffragan of Canterbury 1380.
Clogher.
Florence Wolley " Glowhoriensis." Suffragan of Norwich 1478–1486.
Down and Connor.
Richard Wolsey. Suff. of Lichfield 1452, Worcester 1465–1479. Cf. Wood, A. O. I. 551.
Thomas. Rector of Eastham 1459 ; S. Botolph's, Bishopsgate, 1461.
Robert Blyth. Suffragan of Ely 1539–1541.
Connor.
Adam. 1242–1244.
Simon. Suff. of Sarum 1459–1481 ; Exeter 1463.

Derry.
John Dongan. Suffragan of London 1392.
Raphoe.
Carbric. Suffragan of Canterbury 1273.
Triburna.
John Stokes. Suff. Lichfield 1407 ; Worcester 1416.
Ardagh.
Henry Nony. Suffragan of Exeter 1396.
James. Suffragan of Sarum 1466 ; Exeter 1478.
Dromore.
Nicolas Warter. Suffragan of York 1420–1445.
John. Suffragan of Canterbury 1420, and London 1419–1426 ; d. 1433. He was Rector of Stisted and S. Mary, Somerset.
David Chirbury. Suffragan of S. David's. Archdeacon of Brecon 1437.
Richard Mesin. Suffragan of York 1460.
Thomas Bradley. Suffragan of Norwich 1450–1477.

Dromore (continued).

Thomas Radcliffe. Suffragan of Durham 1441–1487.
William Egremont. Suffragan of York 1463–1501.
George Brann. Suff. London 1497, Worcester 1497.

Kildare.

Geoffrey. Hereford 1449; R. S. Mary's, Lothbury, 1454.
Richard. Suff. of Winchester 1488; Chichester 1480.
James Wale 1475–1494; R. Great Horkesley 1488; Laindon 1483; S. Christopher's, Threadneedle St., 1485; Suffragan of London 1491.
William. Suff. Winchester 1520–1525; York 1530.

Leighlin.

Ralph. Suff. York has 10 marks salary 1344 Jan. 20.
Thomas Halsey. Suffragan 1519.

Cashel.

Ralph Kelly. Suffragan of Winchester 1346.

Emly.

Robert Windel. 1423. Suffragan of Norwich 1424, Sarum 1435–1441, Worcester 1433, S. Edmund's 1430.
Robert. Cons. 1444. Suffragan of Winchester 1456.
Donatus ô Brien. Suffragan of Worcester 1500.

Limerick.

John Donnowe, 1486. Suffragan of Exeter 1489.

Waterford.

Richard. Suffragan of Exeter 1338.
John Geese, 1409–1425. Suffragan of London 1424.

Cloyne.

Thomas Hartperry. Suffragan of Hereford 1490.

Ross.

Stephen Brown, 1402. Suffragan of S. David's 1408, Wells 1410, Worcester 1420.
Richard. Suffragan of Canterbury 1439–1465, London 1434–1441, Sarum 1454. He was Dean of Shoreham 1453, R. Saltwood 1455, d. 1465.
John. Suff. Wells 1479–1481, R. Broxbourne 1475, and S. Andrew Undershaft 1478.

Killaloe.

Robert Mulfield; resigned 1418. Suff. of Lichfield.

Ardfert.

John; d. 1245. Suffragan of Canterbury.
John. R. of S. Christopher's, Threadneedle Street, 1462–1483.

Tuam.

John Baterley. Suffragan of Sarum 1425.
Philip Pinson. Suffragan of Hereford 1503.

Elphin.

Robert Forster, 1418. Suffragan of Durham 1426.

Clonfert.

Robert, 1296–1307. Suffragan of Canterbury.
Robert le Petit, 1319–1325. Suff. of Worcester 1322.
John Heyne, cons. 1438. Rector of West Thurrock 1457. Suffragan of London 1443–1448, Worcester 1443, Exeter 1447.

Killalla.

Thomas Orwell, cons. 1389. Suffragan of Ely 1389–1406. He had a commission for the Isle of Wight from W. of Wykeham.
Thomas Clark, 1497. Rector of Chedsey 1505–1508. Wood, A. O. I. 553.

Mayo.

John Bell, provided 1493 Nov. 4. Suffragan of London 1499, Sarum 1501, Exeter 1501, Lichfield 1503, Wells 1519, Canterbury 1503.
William Gilbert. Abbat of Bruton. Suffragan of Wells 1519–1526. Wood, A. O. I. 568.

Achonry.

Simon, a Cistertian of Quarr. Suffragan of Canterbury 1386, London 1385, Lichfield 1387, Winchester 1387–1395. He died in 1398.
Richard. Suffragan of Worcester 1426–1433, Hereford 1430.
James Blakedon. V. page 67. Suffragan of Wells 1443–1451, Sarum 1443–1449, Worcester 1443.
Thomas Fort, provided 1492 Oct. 5. Suffragan of Lincoln 1496–1504; Rector of Southwick 1504; Prior of S. Mary's, Huntingdon, 1496.

Enaghdun.

Gilbert. Suffragan of Winchester 1313, Worcester 1313.
Robert le Petit. Suffragan of Sarum 1326.
Henry Twillowe. Suffragan of Exeter 1395–1398, Sarum 1397, Winchester 1399–1401.
John Britt, provided 1402 Jan. 25. Suffragan of Winchester 1402, York 1417–1420.
John Camere or Bonere, provided 1421 June 9. Suffragan of Sarum 1421, Exeter 1438; Provost of S. Elizabeth's, Winchester, and Rector of Cheddington.
Thomas. Suffragan of Lincoln 1449, Exeter 1458; Rector of Willoughby, Lincolnshire.
Thomas Barrett. Suffragan of Wells 1482–1485.

*** Thomas Ingilby "Rathlurensis," provided 1471 Apr. 3, d. 1499. He was Vicar of South Weald 1498 Oct. 8; Suffragan of Lincoln 1484, London 1489. His see is supposed by Ware to have been in the present diocese of Derry, but it may have been Raphoe.

APPENDIX VI.

A List of the Bishops of Sodor and Man, from the Conquest to the union of the See with the Province of York.

[A perfect List of the Bishops of Sodor and Man is a desideratum. The common Lists contain many names which ought not to be there, e. g. Hildebert, Bishop of Le Mans, Robert Waldby, Adurensis, (Aire in Gascony,) and others which perhaps belong to Iceland or to the Scotch see of the Isles. The following is founded on the List at the end of the Manx Chronicle down to 1374.

Rolwer, Buried at Kilmachow.

William.

1113. Wimund or Aumund Mac Anlay, a monk of Savigny and Furness, to which latter Abbey the election of the Bishop belonged, was consecrated by Thomas II, Archbishop of York, 1109 × 1114, and was deposed or died in 1151. W. Newburgh, Lib. 1. c. 14 ; Wendover ; Stubbs, 1713.

1151. John, a monk of Seez, was consecrated 1151 × 1153 by Henry Murdac, Archbishop of York.—Chron. Norman. (Duchesne), p. 986 ; Hist. Ebor. MS. Cotton. Cleopatra, C. 4.

1160. Gamaliel, consecrated by Roger Archbishop of York 1154 × 1161. Buried at Peterborough.—Cleopatra, c. 4.

Ronald, or Reginald, a Norwegian.

Christian of Argyle ; possibly the Bishop of Whithern of that name 1154–1186. Buried at Benchor.

Michael, or Manxman. Buried at Fountains 1203.

1210. Nicolas of Meaux, Abbat of Furness, "consecratus ad Ebudas ubi tunc per 40 annos episcopus non fuerat ex quo Nemarus episcopus in vivis erat." (Chron. Island. Langebek.) He was probably consecrated by the Archbishop of Drontheim ; died 1217 ; and buried at Benchor. Compare Monasticon, Vol. 6, p. 1186. Appendix 46.

1217. Reginald, or Ronald, of the blood royal ; d. 1225, and was buried at Rushen. He was probably appointed by the King of Man, and consecrated in Norway : for we find

1219. A Bishop of Man, elected by the Monks of Furness and consecrated by the Archbishop of Dublin, unable to get possession of his see, owing to the hostility of the King. This was probably John Mac Ivar or Harfare. 1219 Nov. 9 Honorius III. charges Pandulf and the Bishop of Carlisle to see him righted ; and 1224 May 15 the same Pope allows him to resign, retaining the episcopal insignia. Vatican Papers. John Bishop of Man is found as late as 1230 attesting a deed of Abp. Walter Grey. (Le Neve.) He was buried at Jerveaux or Jarrow.

1226. Simon of Argyle, consecrated at Bergen by the Archbishop Peter of Drontheim ; his Statutes, aº. 1229, are in the Monasticon. He was Bishop 18 years, and died Feb. 28, 1247, (Chron. Manniæ,) or more probably 1243, as we find in

1244. Feb. 15, Innocent IV, at the request of the Monks at Furness, allows the Archbishop of York, with permission from the Archbishop of Drontheim, to consecrate the Bishop of Man. However the see was vacant 6 years after the death of Simon, during which time Laurence Archdeacon of Man was elected, and sent to Norway for the royal assent and consecration. The latter being delayed from the informality of his election, he returned to be reelected, and was lost at sea with King Harald and his court, 1249. In the Paisley Cartulary, A. D. 1253, is a Charter of Stephen B. of Sodor, and administrator of Lesmore (Argyle), perhaps a Scotch nominee.

1252. Richard, an Englishman, consecrated at Rome by the Archbishop of Drontheim. Consecrated S. Mary's, Rushen, in the fifth year of his pontificate, 1257; ruled 23 years; d. 1274, and was buried at Furness.

1275. Mark of Galloway; consecrated in Norway by John Archbishop of Drontheim; ruled 24 years; then exiled for 3, during which time the Isles were under interdict; afterwards he returned, and died about 1303; buried at S. German's.

1305. Allan, consecrated by Jorund of Drontheim; d. 1321 Feb. 13; buried at Rothsay.

1321. Gilbert Mac Lellan; consecrated by Eilulf of Drontheim; subscribes 1327; according to the Chron. Manniæ he ruled only 2½ years.

1328. Bernard de Linton, elected 1328; Bishop 1329; consecrated in Norway; ruled 4 years, and d. 1333; buried at Kilwinin.

1334. Thomas; consecrated in Norway; ruled 18 years, and d. 1348 Sept. 20; buried at Scone.

1348. William Russell; consecrated at Avignon by P. Clement VI; d. 1374 April 21, and buried at Furness.

1374. John Donkan; consecrated at Avignon 1374 Nov. 25 by Simon Langham, Bishop of Præneste; he is said to have died in 1380, and the see of the Isles to have been separated from Sodor and Man. The date of his death is questionable.

1390. John "Sodorensis Episcopus" has a suffragan's commission from the Bishop of Salisbury 1390 Jan. 14. This may have been Donkan, or Sprotton, who is stated by Train in his List to have been Bishop in 1396. He ordains in London 1391 and 1392, and in 1388 July 14 was sent by Richard II. to treat with the sons of the Lord of the Isles. (Rymer.)

1425. John Burgherlin, a Franciscan; provided 1425 July 20. Wadding. Ann. Minor. Whether he ever had possession is doubtful.

1429. Richard Pulley. His Statutes are printed in the Monasticon.

1449. John Green. He held the living of Dunchurch in Warwickshire 1414 Nov. 22, and had leave to hold it in commendam 1449 Feb. 9; he exchanged it for Little Billing 1452 Feb. 6, and the living of Gumchester for Stow Nine Churches 1459 Mar. 21. In 1462 he resigned Stow, and 1464 Dec. 13 was collated to Merseham in Kent. He acted as suffragan in Lichfield in 1452, ordaining Dec. 23, and soon after must have resigned his see.

1455. Thomas Burton, a Franciscan; provided 1455 Sept. 25, (Wadding); made his will 1458 Feb. 18.

1458. Thomas of Kirkham, Abbat of Vale Royal; provided 1458 June 21; was alive in 1472, and d. 1480, (Hardy); d. before 1475 (Monasticon).

1480. Richard Oldham, Abbat of Chester (royal assent 1453 June 2); d. 1485 Oct. 13, and was buried at Chester. He was Bishop in 1483; elected about 1475, (Monasticon.)

1487. Huan Hesketh, or Blackleach; fl. 1487–1521; died probably in 1528 or 9.

1530. Thomas Stanley, consecrated in 1530, when his preferment of Thorngate P. in Lincoln was vacated. He was consecrated, according to a note of Kennett which I have not been able to discover, corrected by Br. Willis, 1530 Mar. 4; was perhaps deposed in 1544, and restored in 1557; d. 1568 or 1570.

1546. Henry Man. The see of Man was united with the province of York by Act of Parliament, 33 Hen. VIII. c. 31, A. D. 1542.

APPENDIX VII.

*Catalogues of British and Welsh Bishops before the union of the Welsh Sees
with the English province of Canterbury.*

THE following Lists are given in this place in order to clear away at once all questionable,
legendary matter from the subject. There is probably some little truth in each of them :
but so much that is simple fabrication, that I have thought it better to insert them whole
here, with what remarks I have to make on them, than to mix with undoubtedly true records any portion of what stands on so weak a foundation.

I. PROVINCE OF LONDON.

1. LIST OF THE METROPOLITANS OF LONDON.

The following List was formed by Jocelin of Furness, a Monk of the 12th century. It may
be found in Stow, Ussher, Godwin and the Fasti of Le Neve. Wharton unhesitatingly re-
jects the whole, and it is indeed a most uncritical performance : the compiler however evi-
dently acted in good faith, and put down no more than he found in his authorities.

I. Theonus or Theanus.	In the time of Lucius. He built the church of S. Peter, Cornhill.
II. Elvanus.	The messenger of Lucius to Rome ; consecrated by Pope Eleutherus.
III. Cadar or Cadoc.	He occurs also at Caer Leon.
IV. Obinus.	
V. Conan.	
VI. Palladius.	Plainly a mistake arising from Palladius's being called a Bishop of Britain.
VII. Stephanus.	
VIII. Iltutus.	He was Abbat of the school of Llandaff ; perhaps there is a confusion be-tween Landavensis and Londinensis.
Augulus.	A Saint and Bishop of Augusta ; commemorated Feb. 7.
IX. Theodwin or Dedwin.	Both these names have a Saxon look ; the latter is evidently a late Bishop who has been misplaced. Perhaps Dedwin may be a mistake for Bed-wini who was King Arthur's Bishop in Cornwall.
X. Theodred.	
XI. Hilarius.	
XII. Guitelinus.	Mentioned by Nennius (p. 77) as having quarrelled with Ambrosius. Geof-frey says he was sent to Armorica for aid against the Saxons.
XIII. Vodinus.	Put to death 453. He opposed the marriage of Vortigern and Rowena.
XIV. Theonus II.	He was translated from Gloucester in 542, and fled into Wales in 586 A. D.

To these are to be added,

I. Restitutus.	Bishop of London. He attended the Council of Arles in 314 A. D.
II. Fastidius.	Bishop of Britain in 431 A. D.

One of Merlin's prophecies was that the pall of London should be translated to Dorobernia. Gilbert Ffolliott, Bishop of London, in the 12th century attempted to reject the obedience of Canterbury on the ground that London was once the metropolitan see of Britain. S. Gregory seems to have designed that it should continue to be so.

2. SUFFRAGAN SEES.

1. Winchester.	
(a) Constans.	Bishop at the second consecration in A. D. 293. [Rudburn.]
(b) Diruvianus.	Appointed by King Arthur in 519. Geoffrey.
2. Gloucester.	
(a) Eldad.	Bishop cir. 488. Geoffrey.
(b) Theonus.	Translated to London 542.
3. Congresbury.	A see was founded here by Fagan and Duman which lasted till 721, when it was removed to a village called Tydenton, now Wells. Daniel the last Bishop was consecrated in 704 : doubtless the same as Daniel Bishop of Winchester.
4. Silchester.	
Mauganius.	Made Bishop in 519 A. D. Geoffrey.
5. Cornwall.	Whitaker makes Rumon, Mancus, Barnic, Conoglas, and Elidius, Bishops of Cornwall. Kenstec, Bishop of Cornwall, made his profession to Archbishop Ceolnoth.

II. PROVINCE OF YORK.

1. METROPOLITANS.

The following List is given by Godwin, and is probably a fabrication of his own age.

(a) Sampson.	Godwin says he was appointed by Lucius. William Harrison, quoted by Ussher, names Theodosius ; others Faganus. Ussher, 72.
(b) Taurinus.	He was Bishop of Evreux, Ebroicensis. Similarly, Eutropius Bishop of Saintonge has been placed at Canterbury.
(c) Eborius.	Was at Arles in 314 A. D.
(d) Sampson or Sanxo.	Was expelled by the Saxons, took refuge in Gaul, and, according to one account, transferred the pall to Dol, in Britanny. He was consecrated in 490, and flourishing in 507 A. D. Geoffrey.
(e) Piran.	Was appointed by King Arthur in the place of Sampson at Christmas 522 A. D.
(f) Thadiacus Thadiocenus or Cadiocenus.	Retired into Wales in 586 A. D.

2. ALCLUD OR DUMBARTON.

Eledanius.	Appointed by King Arthur in 519.

3. CANDIDA CASA. (WHITHERN.)

S. Ninian.	The Apostle of the Picts 412 A. D. He built a Church of stone. Retired to Ireland 420 ; d. Sept. 16, 432.

4. MAN.

(a) Amphibalus.
(b) Germanus.
(c) Conondrius. } 447. All consecrated by S. Patrick.
(d) Romulus.
(e) Machutus.   498 ; d. 553 or 554.
(f) Contentus.   Conan d. 648.
(g) Baldus.
(h) Malchus.
(i) Torkinus.
(j) Brandan.

III. PROVINCE OF CAER LEON.

1. METROPOLITANS.

The following List is from "The Chronicles of the Ancient British Church," Lond. 1851 : it is described as "taken from a MS. of the late Iolo Morganwg (Edward Williams) as given by the Rev. J. Williams in his Antiquities of the Cymry."

1. Dyfan. }	The missionaries of Eleutherus.
2. Ffagan. }	
3. Elldeyrn.	
4. Edelfeid.	Adelfius, who was at Arles 314. He is claimed also by Colchester and Lincoln.
5. Cadwr.	
6. Cynan.	
7. Ilan.	
8. Llewyr.	
9. Cyhelyn.	
10. Guitelin.	He appears also in the list for London.
11. Tremorinus.	Died about 490, and was succeeded by Dubritius of Llandaff: after this time the primacy seems to have wavered between Llandaff and Menevia.

2. BISHOPS OF MENEVIA.

The following List is formed from a collation of the two given by Godwin, one of which is from Giraldus. It will be remarked that there is much repetition of names, that some of them are claimed by Llandaff and Bangor, while others are obvious mistakes and interpolations. From the year 1023 the succession is ascertained from the Annales Cambriæ ; but even here are great difficulties.

1. S. David, Metropolitan.	Said to have been consecrated at Jerusalem, and elected to the see of Caer Leon on the death or retirement of Dubritius at the synod of Llandewi Brevi in 519. He died in 542. The Annales Cambriæ place his death in 601 A. D., which seems more likely, as he is not mentioned by Gildas.
2. Kenauc or Cynoc.	Bishop of Llanbadarn, translated to Menevia on S. David's death. He died 606. Annales Cambr. He was perhaps a suffragan. Ussher places his death in 597, and makes Teilo succeed him as metropolitan.
3. Teilo, Metropolitan.	Possibly succeeded to the metropolitan office on S. David's death. He was Bishop of Llandaff, which he retained, consecrating Ismael to Menevia. Ussher thinks him the same as Sampson, who is said to have taken the pall to Dol. He is called also Eliud. "Ἥλιος = Samson.
4. Ismael.	Consecrated by S. Teilo. Suffragan.
5. Morwal.	
6. Haerhunen.	

7. Elvaed.	Perhaps metropolitan, with see at Bangor. Flor. 768–807.
8. Gurnven.	
9. Lendivord.	See below under Lumbert.
10. Gorwyst.	
11. Gorgan.	
12. Cledauc.	
13. Anian.	
14. Elvoed.	See 7.
15. Eldunen.	
16. Elanc or Elvaeth.	See 7.
17. Mascoed.	
18. Sadernven.	See 20.
19. Catellus.	
20. Sulhaithnay.	Perhaps Satubin, who died 831. Ann. Camb.
21. Novis.	Regnavit 840, d. 873. The Brut says Meuric reigned 840, d. 873.
22. Etwal.	
23. *Asser.*	A Monk of S. David's, not Bishop of Menevia, but of Sherborn 889–909.
24. Arthuael.	
25. *Sampson.*	Placed here by Giraldus, who says that he retired to Dol with his pall. One Sampson was really Bishop of Dol, and died, according to Ussher, in 599. Perhaps Teilo was the person meant by Sampson.
26. Ruclin.	
27. *Rodherich.*	Died 961. Ann. Cambr. Misplaced.
28. Elguni.	
29. Lunverd.	Died 942 or 944. Consecrated by Ethelred of Canterbury.
30. Nergu.	Vercu, a good Bishop, d. 948.
31. Sulhidir.	
32. Eneuris.	Died 944 or 946. Ann. Cambr. and Brut.
Ritherch.	Died 961 or 962. Ib.
33. Morgenen.	Slain 998 or 1000 A.D. Ann. Cambr. Could he be the same as Tremerinus, who was consecrated by Siric of Canterbury? R. Diceto.
34. Nathan.	
35. Jevan.	
36. Argustie.	
37. Mergeneuth.	Died 1023 or 1025.
38. Ervin or Ernun.	Died 1038 or 1040.
39. Tramerin.	Died 1055. He was Suffragan to Ethelstan of Hereford.
40. Joseph.	Died 1061 or 1064.
41. Bleithud.	Died 1071. Consecrated by [Ethelnoth] the Archbishop of Canterbury. R. de Diceto.
42. Sulghein.	Resigned in 1076, returned in 1078, and died in 1088. Ann. Menev.
43. Abraham.	1076–1078.
44. Rithmarch.	1088–1096.
45. Wilfrid, or Griffith.	1096. He was suspended, and afterwards restored, by S. Anselm. Eadmer. Died 1115.

3. BISHOPS OF LLANDAFF.

1. Dubritius, Metropolitan.	Consecrated, according to Benedict of Gloucester, by Germanus in 449; according to Geoffrey in 490. He was Bishop of Llandaff, and kept his metropolitical seat there, as his successor did at Menevia. Resigned in 519 and d. 522, Geoff.; died 612, Ann. Cambr.

2. Teilo, Metropolitan.	Succeeded to Llandaff 519, to the metropolitan dignity in 542 A.D. Geoff. He was consecrated at Jerusalem with S. David. He retired into France during the prevalence of the ictericia pestis, and returned in 596 ; d. 604. Ussher.
3. Oudoceus.	Succeeded Teilo. He is said to have been consecrated at Canterbury.
4. Ubilwyn or Berthgwin.	Contemporary with King Brochmail. One Brocmail was at the massacre of Bangor in 613 ; one died in 662 A.D. R. Diceto says that "Bregwin" he consecrated Archbishop Britwald of Canterbury 693.
5. Aidan.	
6. Elgistil.	
7. Lunapeius.	A disciple of S. Teilo in 596. Ussher.
8. Comegern.	Contemporary with Ywyr King of Gwynedd.
9. Argustil.	
10. Guodoloiu.	
11. Edilbin.	
12. Grecielus.	
13. Berthguin.	
14. Trychan.	Contemporary with King Fernmail. One King of this name died 763, another 775, another flourished 880.
15. Elvogus.	See Menevia 7, and Bangor.
16. Catgwaret.	
17. Cerenhir.	
18. Novis.	Cf. Menevia 21.
19. Gulfrid.	
20. Nudd.	
21. Cimeliauc.	Consecrated by Ethelred of Canterbury ; d. 927.
22. Libiau.	Consecrated by Athelm or Wulfhelm of Canterbury ; d. 929.
23. Marchluith.	See Bangor. Died 943.
24. Pater.	Fl. 955.
25. Gucan or Gucaur.	Consecrated between 963 and 971 A.D. by S. Dunstan, Brihthelm, Alfwold, Ethelwold, Oswald. Liber Landav.
26. Bledri or Bedreu.	Consecrated after 993 by Alfric of Canterbury. Liber Landav.
27. Joseph.	Consecrated Oct. 1, 1022 or 1027, by Ethelnoth. Liber Landav. Died 1043 or 1046.
28. Herewald.	Consecrated at Pentecost 1056, at London, by Kinsy Abp. of York ; d. 1103.

On both the preceding lists we must remark—

1. That they abound with anachronisms.

2. That the names are repeated in a way that seems to show that there were a few well known ones, and that these were indefinitely varied to fill up a certain space in the lists.

3. That some names belong to other sees, as Elvod and Asser.

4. Some, as Catellus, may have been Princes, not Bishops.

5. But we must not be too critical ; the successive Bishops may have had similar names. The mischief is, that the historical portions are so corrupt as to throw suspicion on all that is known from these sources only.

4. SUFFRAGAN SEES.

These are given by Godwin as Llandaff, Bangor, Llanelwy, Exeter, Bath, Hereford, and
Ferns: from Hoveden as Llandaff, Bangor, S. Asaph, Worcester, Hereford, Chester, and
Llanbadarn.

1. S. Asaph or Llanelwy.	
(a) Kentigern.	A Briton, consecrated by an Irish Bishop for Glasgow; was in exile in Wales and founded a see at Llanelwy; cons. 540; 543 came to Llanelwy; d. 612. Ann. Cambr.
(b) S. Asaph.	Succeeded Kentigern in 560 A. D.
(c) Chebur.	940; temp. Howel Dha. See also Ann. Cambr. ad annum 501.
2. Bangor.	
(a) Daniel.	Consecrated by Dubritius or S. David about 522. He died 584. Ann. Cambr.
(b) Elvod.	Or Elbod, Archbishop of Gwynedd; fl. 768 to 809 A. D.
(c) Mordav.	Fl. 940. Perhaps the same as Marchluith of Llandaff, who died in 943.
3. Llanbadarn.	
(a) S. Patern.	Consecrated at Jerusalem with S. David about 518; ruled 21 years.
(b) S. Cynoc.	Succeeded at Menevia, on S. David's death.
(c) Idnerth.	Slain by his townspeople, (date unknown.) Was the last Bishop.
4. Anglesey. S. Kebius.	Corinnius, son of Solomon Duke of Cornwall, consecrated by S. Hilary of Poitiers; founded Holy Head, A. D. 369.

APPENDIX VIII.

Indexes of Bishops arranged under their Sees.

CANTERBURY.

	Conse-cration.	Accession.	First Signature.	Last Signature.	Death.
Augustine ..	597	597			604
Laurentius ..	604	604	604		619
Mellitus	604	619			624
Justus	604	624			627
Honorius ..	627	627			653
Deusdedit ..	655	655			664
Theodore ..	668	668	676	686	690
Brihtwald ..	693	693	693	706	731
Tatwin.... :	731	731	732		734
Nothelm	735	735	736	738	740
Cuthbert....	736	741	741	758	758
Bregwin	759	759	762	764	765
Jaenbert....	766	766	765	789	790
Ethelhard ..	793	793	793	805	805
Wulfred	805	805	805	831	832
Feologild....	832	832			832
Ceolnoth	833	833	833	868	870
Ethelred	870	870	875		889
Plegmund ..	890	890	895	910	914
Athelm	909	914			923
Wulfhelm ..	914	923	923	941	942
Odo	926	942	942	959	959
Dunstan	957	960	960	988	988
Ethelgar ..	980	988	988		989
Siric	985	990	994		994
Elfric	990	995	995	1005	1005
Elphege	984	1005	1007	1012	1012
Living	999	1013	1015	1019	1020
Ethelnoth ..	1020	1020	1020	1035	1038
Eadsige	1035	1038	1042	1052	1050
Robert......	1044	1051			1070
Stigand	1043	1052	1052		

CANTERBURY (Continued).

	Conse-cration.	Accession.		Conse-cration.	Accession.
Lanfranc	1070	1070	John Stafford	1425	1443
Anselm	1093	1093	John Kemp	1419	1452
Ralph d'Escures	1108	1114	Thomas Bouchier	1435	1454
William de Corbeuil ..	1123	1123	John Morton	1479	1486
*Theobald	1139	1139	Henry Dean	1496	1501
Thomas à Becket	1162	1162	William Warham	1502	1503
Richard	1174	1174	Thomas Cranmer	1533	1533
Baldwin	1180	1185	Reginald Pole	1556	1556
Hubert Fitzwalter....	1189	1193	Matthew Parker	1559	1559
Stephen Langton	1207	1207	Edmund Grindal	1559	1576
Richard Grant	1229	1229	John Whitgift	1577	1583
Edmund Rich........	1234	1234	Richard Bancroft	1597	1604
Boniface	1245	1245	George Abbot	1609	1611
Robert Kilwardby....	1273	1273	William Laud........	1621	1633
John Peckham	1279	1279	William Juxon	1633	1660
Robert Winchelsey ..	1294	1294	Gilbert Sheldon	1660	1663
Walter Reynolds	1308	1313	William Sancroft	1678	1678
Simon Mepeham	1328	1328	John Tillotson	1691	1691
John Stratford	1323	1333	Thomas Tenison	1692	1695
Thomas Bradwardine..	1349	1349	William Wake	1705	1716
Simon Islip	1349	1349	John Potter	1715	1737
Simon Langham......	1362	1366	Thomas Herring	1738	1747
William Whittlesey ..	1362	1368	Matthew Hutton	1743	1757
Simon Sudbury	1362	1375	Thomas Secker	1735	1758
William Courtenay ..	1370	1381	Frederick Cornwallis..	1750	1768
Thomas Arundel	1374	1397	John Moore	1775	1783
Roger Walden	1398	1398	Charles Manners Sutton	1792	1805
Thomas Arundel......	1374	1399	William Howley......	1813	1828
Henry Chicheley	1408	1414	John Bird Sumner....	1828	1848

LONDON.

	Conse-cration.	First Signat.	Last Signat.	Death.		Conse-cration.	First Signat.	Last Signat.	Death.
Mellitus	604				Wighed				
Cedda	654			664	Aldberht ..	767	775	785	
Wina	662			675	Eadgar		789		
Erkenwald ..	675	676	692	693	†Kenwalch..		793	793	
Waldhere ..	693	694	704		Eadbald				
Ingwald		706	737	745	Heathobert..	794	798	799	801
Egwulf	745	747	759		Osmund	802	803	805	

* To Theobald's consecrators may be added Robert of Bath and Bernard of S. David's,—from a letter of R. Bath in the Canterbury archives.
† The reference to Simeon of Durham after Bishop Kenwalch's name at page 8, col. 5, belongs to Archbishop Ethelhard in the line above.

LONDON (CONTINUED).

	Conse-cration.	First Signat.	Last Signat.	Death.		Conse-cration.	First Signat.	Last Signat.	Death.
Ethelnoth ..		811	816		Dunstan	957	959		
Ceolbert		824	839		Elfstan	961	961	995	
Deorwulf ..		860–2			Wulfstan II	996	997	1003	
Swithulf				898	Elfwin	1004	1004	1012	
Elfstan					Elfwy	1014	1015	1035	
Wulfsy	898	901	910		Elfweard....	1035	1035	1044	1044
Elfstan					Robert)				
Theodred ..		926	951		Champart }	1044	1046	1050	
Wulfstan ..					William	1051			1075
Brihthelm ..		953	959						

	Conse-cration.	Accession.		Conse-cration.	Accession.
Hugh d'Orivalle	1075	1075	Thomas Savage	1493	1496
Maurice	1086	1086	William Warham	1502	1502
Richard de Beames ..	1108	1108	William Barons	1504	1504
Gilbert Universalis ..	1128	1128	Richard Fitz James ..	1497	1506
Robert de Sigillo	1141	1141	Cuthbert Tunstall	1522	1522
Richard de Beames ..	1152	1152	John Stokesley	1530	1530
Gilbert Ffolliott......	1148	1163	Edmund Bonner	1540	1540
Richard Fitz Neal....	1189	1189	Nicolas Ridley	1547	1550
Wᵐ de S. Mere l'Eglise	1199	1199	Edmund Grindal	1559	1559
Eustace de Fauconberg	1221	1221	Edwin Sandys	1559	1570
Roger Niger	1229	1229	John Aylmer	1577	1577
Fulk Bassett	1244	1244	Richard Fletcher	1589	1595
Henry de Wengham ..	1260	1260	Richard Bancroft	1597	1597
Henry de Sandwich ..	1263	1263	Richard Vaughan	1596	1604
John Chishull........	1274	1274	Thomas Ravis	1605	1607
Richard Gravesend ..	1280	1280	George Abbot	1609	1610
Ralph Baldock	1306	1306	John King	1611	1611
Gilbert Segrave	1313	1313	George Mountain	1617	1621
Richard Newport	1317	1317	William Laud........	1621	1628
Stephen Gravesend ..	1319	1319	William Juxon	1633	1633
Richard Bintworth ..	1338	1338	Gilbert Sheldon	1660	1660
Ralph Stratford	1340	1340	Humfrey Henchman ..	1660	1663
Michael Northburgh ..	1355	1355	Henry Compton......	1674	1675
Simon Sudbury	1362	1362	John Robinson	1710	1714
William Courtenay ..	1370	1375	Edmund Gibson	1716	1723
Robert Braybrook....	1382	1382	Thomas Sherlock	1728	1748
Roger Walden	1398	1405	Thomas Hayter	1749	1761
Nicolas Bubwith	1406	1406	Richard Osbaldeston ..	1747	1762
Richard Clifford......	1401	1407	Richard Terrick......	1757	1764
John Kemp	1419	1421	Robert Lowth	1766	1777
William Gray........	1426	1426	Beilby Porteus	1777	1787
Robert Fitzhugh	1431	1431	John Randolph	1799	1809
Robert Gilbert	1436	1436	William Howley	1813	1813
Thomas Kemp	1450	1450	Charles J. Blomfield ..	1824	1828
Richard Hill	1489	1489	Archibald C. Tait	1856	1856

WINCHESTER.

	Conse-cration.	First Signat.	Last Signat.	Death.		Conse-cration.	First Signat.	Last Signat.	Death.
Birinus	634			650	Swithun	852	858	862	862
Agilbert	650				Alfred	862	868	871	
Wina	662				Tumbert			877	879
Leutherius ..	670		676	676	Denewulf ..	879	882	904	908
Hedda......	676	676	701	705	Frithstan....	909	909	931	933
Daniel......	705	705	737	745	Beornstan ..	931	931	934	934
Hunferth....	744	747	749		Elphege	934	934	951	951
Kynheard ..	754	755	766		Alfsin	951	952	958	
Ethelhard ..					Brihthelm ..	960	960	961	963
Egbald		778	781		Ethelwold ..	963	964	984	984
Dudda					Elphege	984	985	1005	
Kinbert		785	801		Kenulf	1005			1006
Alhmund ..	802	803	805		Ethelwold ..	1006	1007	1012	
Wigthen		811	828	833?	Alfsin	1014	1014	1033	
Herefrith ..	825	825	826	833?	Alwin	1032	1033	1046	1047
Eadmund ..	833?	836	838		Stigand	1043	1047	1053	
Helmstan ..	838	838	841						

	Conse-cration.	Accession.		Conse-cration.	Accession.
Walkelin	1070	1070	Stephen Gardiner	1531	1531
William de Giffard ..	1107	1107	John Poynet	1550	1551
Henry de Blois	1129	1129	John White	1554	1556
Richard Toclive	1174	1174	Robert Horne	1561	1561
Godfrey de Lucy	1189	1189	John Watson	1580	1580
Peter des Roches	1205	1205	Thomas Cowper.. ...	1571	1584
William de Raleigh ..	1239	1244	William Wickham....	1584	1595
Aylmer de Valence ..	1260	1260	William Day	1596	1596
John Gervais	1262	1262	Thomas Bilson	1596	1597
Nicolas Ely..........	1266	1268	James Montagu......	1608	1616
John of Pontoise	1282	1282	Launcelot Andrewes..	1605	1619
Henry Woodlock	1305	1305	Richard Neile	1608	1628
John Sendale	1316	1316	Walter Curll	1628	1632
Rigaud Asser........	1320	1320	Brian Duppa	1638	1660
John Stratford	1323	1323	George Morley	1660	1662
Adam Orlton	1317	1333	Peter Mews	1673	1684
William Edendon	1346	1346	Jonathan Trelawny ..	1685	1707
William of Wykeham	1367	1367	Charles Trimnell	1708	1721
Henry Beaufort......	1398	1405	Richard Willis	1715	1723
William of Wainfleet..	1447	1447	Benjamin Hoadly	1716	1734
Peter Courtenay	1478	1487	John Thomas	1747	1761
Thomas Langton	1483	1493	Brownlow North	1771	1781
Richard Fox	1487	1501	George Pretyman	1787	1820
Thomas Wolsey	1514	1529	Charles R. Sumner ..	1826	1827

ELY.

	Conse-cration.	Accession.		Conse-cration.	Accession.
Hervè	1092	1109	Richard Redman	1471	1501
Nigel	1133	1133	James Stanley	1506	1506
Geoffrey Riddell	1174	1174	Nicolas West	1515	1515
William Longchamp ..	1189	1189	Thomas Goodrich	1534	1534
Eustace	1198	1198	Thomas Thirlby	1540	1554
John Pherd	1220	1220	Richard Cox	1559	1559
Geoffrey de Burgh....	1225	1225	Martin Heaton	1600	1600
Hugh Norwold	1229	1229	Launcelot Andrewes..	1605	1609
William de Kilkenny .	1255	1255	Nicolas Felton	1617	1619
Hugh Belsham	1257	1257	John Buckeridge	1611	1628
John Kirby	1286	1286	Francis White	1626	1631
William de Lude	1290	1290	Matthew Wren	1635	1638
Ralph Walpole	1289	1299	Benjamin Laney	1660	1667
Robert Orford	1302	1302	Peter Gunning	1670	1675
John Keeton	1310	1310	Francis Turner	1683	1684
John Hotham........	1316	1316	Simon Patrick	1689	1691
Simon Montacute	1334	1337	John Moore	1691	1707
Thomas de Lisle......	1345	1345	William Fleetwood ..	1708	1714
Simon Langham......	1362	1362	Thomas Green	1721	1723
John Barnet	1362	1366	Robert Butts	1733	1738
Thomas Arundel	1374	1374	Thomas Gooch	1737	1747
John Fordham	1382	1388	Matthias Mawson	1739	1754
Philip Morgan	1419	1426	Edmund Keene	1752	1771
Lewis of Luxemburg ..	1415	1438	James Yorke	1774	1781
Thomas Bouchier	1435	1443	Thomas Dampier	1802	1808
William Gray........	1454	1454	Bowyer E. Sparke....	1810	1812
John Morton	1479	1479	Joseph Allen	1834	1836
John Alcock	1472	1486	Thomas Turton	1845	1845

LEICESTER AND DORCHESTER.

	Conse-cration.	First Signat.	Last Signat.	Death.		Conse-cration.	First Signat.	Last Signat.	Death.
Cuthwin	680			691	Alheard			888	897-8
Wilfrid [ad-ministered 692-705.]	664				Ceolwulf	909			
					Winsy		926	934	
					Oskytel	950	952	956	
The see was joined to Lichfield 705-737.					Leofwin			965	
					Eadnoth		975	975	
					Escwy		979	1002	
Torthelm ..	737	747	758	764	Alfhelm	1002	1002	1005	
Eadbert	764	764	781		Eadnoth	1006	1012	1012	1016
Unwona		785	799		Ethelric	1016	1020	1032	1034
Werenbert ..	802	803	814		Eadnoth	1034	1042	1046	1050
Hrethun	816	816	839		Ulf	1050	1050		
Aldred					Wulfwy	1053	1055		1067
Ceolred	840	840	869		Remigius....	1067			1092

LINDSEY.

	Conse-cration.	First Signat.	Last Signat.	Death.		Conse-cration.	First Signat.	Last Signat.	Death.
Eadhed	678				Ceolwulf	767	767	794	796
Ethelwin	680				Eadulf......	796	796	836	
Eadgar		706			Berhtred		838	869	
Kinbert				732					
Alwig	733	737	747	750	Leofwin		953	965	
Eadulf......	750	758			Sigeferth		997	1004	

LINCOLN.

	Conse-cration.	Accession.		Conse-cration.	Accession.
Robert Bloett........	1094	1094	Henry Holbeach	1538	1547
Alexander	1123	1123	John Taylor	1552	1552
Robert de Chesney ..	1148	1148	John White	1554	1554
Walter de Coutances..	1183	1183	Thomas Watson......	1557	1557
Hugh of Grenoble	1186	1186	Nicolas Bullingham ..	1560	1560
William of Blois......	1203	1203	Thomas Cowper	1571	1571
Hugh Wallis	1209	1209	William Wickham....	1584	1584
Robert Grosstête	1235	1235	William Chaderton ..	1579	1595
Henry Lexington	1254	1254	William Barlow......	1605	1608
Richard Gravesend ..	1258	1258	Richard Neile	1608	1614
Oliver Sutton	1280	1280	George Mountain	1617	1617
John d'Alderby	1300	1300	John Williams	1621	1621
Henry Burwash......	1320	1320	Thomas Winniffe	1642	1642
Thomas Bek	1342	1342	Robert Sanderson	1660	1660
John Gynwell........	1347	1347	Benjamin Laney	1660	1663
John Bokyngham	1363	1363	William Fuller	1663	1667
Henry Beaufort......	1398	1398	Thomas Barlow	1675	1675
Philip Repingdon	1405	1405	Thomas Tenison	1692	1692
Richard Fleming	1420	1420	James Gardiner	1695	1695
William Gray........	1426	1431	William Wake	1705	1705
William Alnwick	1426	1436	Edmund Gibson......	1716	1716
Marmáduke Lumley ..	1430	1450	Richard Reynolds	1721	1723
John Chadworth	1452	1452	John Thomas	1744	1744
Thomas Rotherham ..	1468	1472	John Green..........	1761	1761
John Russell	1476	1480	Thomas Thurlow	1779	1779
William Smith	1493	1496	George Pretyman	1787	1787
Thomas Wolsey	1514	1514	George Pelham	1803	1820
William Atwater	1514	1514	John Kaye	1820	1827
John Longlands......	1521	1521	John Jackson........	1853	1853

LICHFIELD, CHESTER AND COVENTRY.

	Consecration.	First Signat.	Last Signat.	Death.		Consecration.	First Signat.	Last Signat.	Death.
Diuma......	656			658	Herewin		816	817	
Ceollach	658				Ethelwald ..	818	822	825	828
Trumhere ..	659			662	Hunberht ..	828			
Jarumnan ..	662			667	Kynferth....		836	841	
Chad	664			672	Tunberht....		844	857	
Winfrid ...	672				Ella, or Elfwin		926	935	
Saxulf......	675	676		691	Algar, or Wulgar		941	948	
Hedda......	691	693	706		Kinsy		949	963	
Aldwin, Wor	721	727	736	737	Winsy		964	973	
Huitta......	737	747	749		Elphege	973	975	1002	
Hemele	752				Godwin		1004	1008	
Cuthfrith....	765		767		Leofgar	1020			
Berthun	768	774	777		Brihtmar....	1026	1026	1033	1039
Higbert	779	779	801		Wulfsy	1039	1039	1053	1053
Aldulf......		803	814		Leofwin	1053			1067

	Consecration.	Accession.		Consecration.	Accession.
Peter	1072	1072	Geoffrey Blyth	1503	1503
Robert de Limesey ..	1086	1086	Rowland Lee........	1534	1534
Robert Peche........	1121	1121	Richard Sampson	1536	1543
Roger de Clinton	1129	1129	Ralph Bayne	1554	1554
Walter Durdent......	1149	1149	Thomas Bentham	1560	1560
Richard Peche	1161	1161	William Overton	1580	1580
Gerard la Pucelle	1183	1183	George Abbot	1609	1609
Hugh Nonant........	1188	1188	Richard Neile........	1608	1610
Geoffrey Muschamp ..	1198	1198	John Overall	1614	1614
William Cornhill	1215	1215	Thomas Morton......	1616	1619
Alexander Stavenby..	1224	1224	Robert Wright	1622	1632
Hugh Pateshull......	1240	1240	Accepted Frewen	1644	1644
Roger Weseham......	1245	1245	John Hacket	1661	1661
Roger Longespée	1258	1258	Thomas Wood	1671	1671
Walter de Langton ..	1296	1296	William Lloyd	1680	1692
Roger Northburgh ..	1322	1322	John Hough	1690	1699
Robert Stretton......	1360	1360	Edward Chandler	1717	1717
Walter Skirlaw	1386	1386	Richard Smallbrooke..	1724	1731
Richard Scroope	1386	1386	Frederick Cornwallis..	1750	1750
John Burghill........	1396	1398	John Egerton........	1756	1768
John Catterick	1414	1415	Brownlow North	1771	1771
William Heyworth ..	1420	1420	Richard Hurd	1775	1775
William Booth	1447	1447	James Cornwallis	1781	1781
Nicolas Close........	1450	1452	Henry Ryder........	1815	1824
Reginald Boulers	1451	1453	Samuel Butler	1836	1836
John Hales..........	1459	1459	James Bowstead	1838	1840
William Smith	1493	1493	John Lonsdale	1843	1843
John Arundel	1496	1496			

SHERBORN.

	Conse-cration.	First Signat.	Last Signat.	Death.		Conse-cration.	First Signat.	Last Signat.	Death.
Aldhelm	705			709	Ethelbald ..				
Forthere	709	712	737		Sigelm......		926	932	933
Herewald ..	736	737	766		Alfred.....	933	933	943	943
Aethelmod ..		778	789		Wulfsy		943	958	958
Denefrith ..	793	794	796		Elfwold	958	961	975	978
Wigbert		801	816		Ethelsy	978	979	990	
Ealhstan....	824	824	862	867	Wulfsy	992	993	1001	
Heahmund ..	868	868	870	871	Ethelric	1001	1002	1009	
Etheleage ..	872		877		Ethelsy		1012	1014	
Alfsy, or } Wulfsy }	883	889	892		Brihtwy				
Asser		900	904	909	Elmer	1017	1020	1022	
Ethelward ..		910			Brihtwy	1023	1023	1045	
Werstan					Elfwold	1045	1046	1050	1058
					Herman succ.	1058			1078

RAMSBURY.

	Conse-cration.	First Signat.	Last Signat.	Death.		Conse-cration.	First Signat.	Last Signat.	Death.
Ethelstan ..	909	910			Wulfgar	981	982	984	
Odo........		927			Siric	985	985		
Aelric					Elfric	990		994	1005
Osulf		952	970	970	Brihtwold ..	1005	1005	1045	1045
Elfstan		974	980	981	Herman	1045	1045		1078

SALISBURY.

	Conse-cration.	Accession.		Conse-cration.	Accession.
Osmund	1078	1078	Robert Wyville	1330	1330
Roger	1107	1107	Ralph Erghum	1375	1375
Jocelin de Bailleul ..	1142	1142	John Waltham	1388	1388
Hubert Fitz Walter ..	1189	1189	Richard Mitford......	1390	1395
Herbert le Poore	1194	1194	Nicolas Bubwith	1406	1407
Richard le Poore	1215	1217	Robert Hallam	1407	1407
Robert Bingham	1229	1229	John Chandler	1417	1417
William of York	1247	1247	Robert Neville	1427	1427
Giles Bridport	1257	1257	William Aiscough	1438	1438
Walter de la Wyle..	1263	1263	Richard Beauchamp ..	1449	1450
Robert Wickhampton	1274	1274	Lionel Woodville	1482	1482
Walter Scammell	1284	1284	Thomas Langton	1483	1485
Henry Brandeston....	1287	1287	John Blyth..........	1493	1493
William de la Corner..	1289	1289	Henry Dean	1496	1500
Nicolas Longespee....	1292	1292	Edmund Audley	1480	1492
Simon de Gand	1297	1297	Lorenzo Campegio ..		1524
Roger Mortival	1315	1315	Nicolas Shaxton......	1535	1535

SALISBURY (CONTINUED).

	Conse-cration.	Accession.		Conse-cration.	Accession.
John Salcot, or Capon	1534	1539	William Talbot	1699	1715
John Jewell	1560	1560	Richard Willis	1715	1721
Edmund Gheast......	1560	1571	Benjamin Hoadly	1716	1723
John Piers	1576	1577	Thomas Sherlock	1728	1734
John Coldwell	1591	1591	John Gilbert	1740	1748
Henry Cotton........	1598	1598	John Thomas	1747	1757
Robert Abbot........	1615	1615	Robert H. Drummond	1748	1761
Martin Fotherby	1618	1618	John Thomas	1744	1761
Robert Townson	1620	1620	John Hume	1756	1766
John Davenant	1621	1621	Shute Barrington	1769	1782
Brian Duppa	1638	1641	John Douglas........	1787	1791
Humfrey Henchman ..	1660	1660	John Fisher	1803	1807
John Earle	1662	1663	Thomas Burgess......	1803	1825
Alexander Hyde	1665	1665	Edward Denison	1837	1837
Seth Ward	1662	1667	Walter K. Hamilton..	1854	1854
Gilbert Burnet	1689	1689			

WELLS.

	Conse-cration.	First Signat.	Last Signat.	Death.		Conse-cration.	First Signat.	Last Signat.	Death.
Athelm	909				Alfwin......	997	997	998	
Wulfhelm ..	914				Living......	999	999	1012	
Elphege	923	930	937		Ethelwin.. ⎰	1013	1018	1023	
Wulfhelm ..	938	938	955		Brihtwin.. ⎱	1013	1018		
Brihthelm ..	956	956	973	973	Merewit	1027	1031	1032	1033
Kyneward ..	973	975		975	Duduc	1033	1042	1050	1060
Sigar	975	979	995	997	Giso	1061	1061		1088

BATH AND WELLS.

	Conse-cration.	Accession.		Conse-cration.	Accession.
John of Tours........	1088	1088	Walter Hasleshaw....	1302	1302
Godfrey	1123	1123	John Drokensford	1309	1309
Robert	1136	1136	Ralph of Shrewsbury..	1329	1329
Reginald Fitz Jocelin .	1174	1174	John Barnet	1362	1363
Savaric	1192	1192	John Harewell	1366	1366
Jocelin Troteman	1206	1206	Walter Skirlaw	1386	1386
Roger	1244	1244	Ralph Erghum	1375	1388
William Button	1248	1248	Henry Bowett	1401	1401
Walter Giffard	1265	1265	Nicolas Bubwith	1406	1407
William Button	1267	1267	John Stafford	1425	1425
Robert Burnell	1275	1275	Thomas Beckington ..	1443	1443
William de March	1293	1293	Robert Stillington....	1466	1466

BATH AND WELLS (CONTINUED).

	Conse-cration.	Accession.		Conse-cration.	Accession.
Richard Fox	1487	1491	Walter Curll	1628	1629
Oliver King	1493	1495	William Piers........	1630	1632
Hadrian de Castello ..		1504	Robert Creighton	1670	1670
Thomas Wolsey	1514	1518	Peter Mews	1673	1673
John Clerk..........	1523	1523	Thomas Ken	1685	1685
William Knight......	1541	1541	Richard Kidder	1691	1691
William Barlow	1536	1549	George Hooper	1703	1704
Gilbert Bourne	1554	1554	John Wynne	1715	1727
Gilbert Berkeley	1560	1560	Edward Willes	1743	1744
Thomas Godwin......	1584	1584	Charles Moss	1766	1774
John Still	1593	1593	Richard Beadon......	1789	1802
James Montagu.....	1608	1608	George Henry Law ..	1812	1824
Arthur Lake	1616	1616	Richard Bagot	1829	1845
William Laud	1621	1626	Robert John Eden....	1847	1854
Leonard Mawe	1628	1628			

CREDITON.

	Conse-cration.	First Signat.	Last Signat.	Death.		Conse-cration.	First Signat.	Last Signat.	Death.
Eadulf......	909	926	934	934	Elfwold	988	988	1008	
Ethelgar	934	934	953	953	Eadnoth		1012	1019	
Elfwold		953	970	972	Living......	1027	1027	1045	1046
Sideman	973	974	975	977	Leofric	1046	1046	1065	1072
Elfric	977	979	985						

CORNWALL.

	Conse-cration.	First Signat.	Last Signat.	Death.		Conse-cration.	First Signat.	Last Signat.	Death.
Conan		931	934		Ealdred		993	1002	
Comoere					Burwold		1018		
Wulfsy		967	980		Living......		1027		1046

EXETER.

	Conse-cration.	Accession.		Conse-cration.	Accession.
Osbern	1072	1072	John Fitz Luke	1186	1186
* William Warelwast ..	1107	1107	Henry Marshall......	1194	1194
Robert Chichester	1138	1138	Simon of Apulia	1214	1214
Robert Warelwast....	1155	1155	William Brewer......	1224	1224
Bartholomew	1162	1162	Richard Blondy	1245	1245

* W. W. died 1137 Oct. 1. Reg. Plympton.

EXETER (CONTINUED).

	Conse-cration.	Accession.		Conse-cration.	Accession.
Walter Bronscomb ..	1258	1258	Gervas Babington	1591	1595
Peter Wyville	1280	1280	William Cotton	1598	1598
Thomas Button	1292	1292	Valentine Cary	1621	1621
Walter Stapleton	1308	1308	Joseph Hall	1627	1627
James Berkeley......	1327	1327	Ralph Brownrigg	1642	1642
John Grandison	1327	1327	John Gauden	1660	1660
Thomas Brentingham .	1370	1370	Seth Ward	1662	1662
Edmund Stafford	1395	1395	Antony Sparrow	1667	1667
John Catterick	1414	1419	Thomas Lamplugh....	1676	1676
Edmund Lacy	1417	1420	Jonathan Trelawny ..	1685	1689
George Neville	1458	1458	Offspring Blackall	1708	1708
John Booth	1465	1465	Launcelot Blackburn .	1717	1717
Peter Courtenay	1478	1478	Stephen Weston......	1724	1724
Richard Fox	1487	1487	Nicolas Claggett	1732	1742
Oliver King	1493	1493	George Lavington	1747	1747
Richard Redman	1471	1496	Frederick Keppel	1762	1762
John Arundel........	1496	1502	John Ross	1778	1778
Hugh Oldham	1505	1505	William Buller	1792	1792
John Harman,or Voysey	1519	1519	Henry R. Courtenay..	1794	1797
Miles Coverdale......	1551	1551	John Fisher	1803	1803
James Turberville	1555	1555	George Pelham	1803	1807
William Alley	1560	1560	William Carey	1820	1820
William Bradbridge ..	1571	1571	Christopher Bethell ..	1824	1830
John Wolton	1579	1579	Henry Phillpotts	1831	1831

DUNWICH.

	Conse-cration.	First Signat.	Last Signat.	Death.		Conse-cration.	First Signat.	Last Signat.	Death.
Felix	630			647	Aldberht....				
Thomas	647			652	Eglaf				
Boniface	652			669	Heardred ..		781	789	
Bisi	669				Aelhun	790	790	793	797
Etti	673				Tidferth	798	798	816	
Astwulf					Weremund ..		824		
Eadulf......		747			Wilred	825	825	845	
Cuthwin					Ethelwulf ..				

ELMHAM.

	Conse-cration.	First Signat.	Last Signat.	Death.		Conse-cration.	First Signat.	Last Signat.	Death.
Bedwin	673	693			Eanferth		758		
Nothbert ..		706			Ethelwulf ..		781		
Heatholac ..					Alheard		785	811	
Ethelfrith ..	736				Sibba		814	816	

ELMHAM (CONTINUED).

	Conse-cration.	First Signat.	Last Signat.	Death.		Conse-cration.	First Signat.	Last Signat.	Death.
Hunferth ..					Algar		1001	1018	1021
Humbert....		824	838	870	Alwin	1016	1019	1022	
Eadulf......		956	964		Elfric				1038
Elfric					Elfric	1038			
Theodred ..		975			Stigand	1043		1046	
Theodred ..			995		Ethelmar ..	1047		1055	
Elfstan	995	997	1001						

THETFORD AND NORWICH.

	Conse-cration.	Accession.		Conse-cration.	Accession.
Herfast	1070	1070	John Hopton	1554	1554
William de Beaufeu ...	1086	1086	John Parkhurst	1560	1560
Herbert de Losinga ..	1091	1091	Edmund Freke	1572	1575
Everard	1121	1121	Edmund Scambler....	1561	1585
William de Turbe	1146	1146	William Redman	1595	1595
John of Oxford	1175	1175	John Jegon	1603	1603
John de Gray	1200	1200	John Overall	1614	1618
Pandulf Masca	1222	1222	Samuel Harsnett	1609	1619
Thomas Blunville	1226	1226	Francis White	1626	1629
William de Raleigh ..	1239	1239	Richard Corbett......	1628	1632
Walter Suffield, or Calthorp	1245	1245	Matthew Wren	1635	1635
			Richard Montagu	1628	1638
Simon de Wanton, or Walton	1258	1258	Joseph Hall	1627	1641
			Edward Reynolds	1661	1661
Roger Skirving	1266	1266	Antony Sparrow	1667	1676
William Middleton ..	1278	1278	William Lloyd	1675	1685
Ralph Walpole	1289	1289	John Moore ......:.	1691	1691
John Salmon	1299	1299	Charles Trimnell	1708	1708
William Ayermin	1325	1325	Thomas Green	1721	1721
Antony Bek	1337	1337	John Leng	1723	1723
William Bateman	1344	1344	William Baker	1723	1727
Thomas Percy	1356	1356	Robert Butts	1733	1733
Henry Spenser	1370	1370	Thomas Gooch	1737	1738
Alexander Tottington.	1407	1407	Samuel Lisle	1744	1748
Richard Courtenay ..	1413	1413	Thomas Hayter	1749	1749
John Wakering	1416	1416	Philip Young........	1758	1761
William Alnwick	1426	1426	Lewis Bagot	1782	1783
Thomas Brown	1435	1436	George Horne	1790	1790
Walter le Hart	1446	1446	Charles Manners Sutton	1792	1792
James Goldwell	1472	1472	Henry Bathurst......	1805	1805
Thomas Jane	1499	1499	Edward Stanley	1837	1837
Richard Nykke	1501	1501	Samuel Hinds........	1849	1849
William Repps, or Rugg	1536	1536	John Thomas Pelham .	1857	1857
Thomas Thirlby	1540	1550			

z

WORCESTER.

	Conse-cration.	First Signat.	Last Signat.	Death.		Conse-cration.	First Signat.	Last Signat.	Death.
Bosel	680				Ethelhun ..	915			922
Oftfor	692	693			Wilferth	922			929
Egwin	693		716	717	Kinewold ..	929	930	957	957
Wilfrid	717	718	743	743	Dunstan	957	958		
Milred	743	743	774	775	Oswald	961	961	991	992
Weremund ..	775	775			Aldulf	992	994	1001	1002
Tilhere	777	777	780	781	Wulfstan....	1003	1004	1022	1023
Heathored ..	781	781	798	798	Leofsin	1016	1016	1022	1033
Deneberht ..	798	801	817	822	Brihteag	1033	1033		1038
Eadberht....	822	822	845	848	Living (succ.)	1038	1027	1045	1046
Aelhun	848	848	869	872	Ealdred . ..	1044	1044		
Werefrith ..	873	873	904	915	Wulfstan....	1062			1095

	Conse-cration.	Accession.		Conse-cration.	Accession.
Samson	1096	1096	Tideman de Winchcomb	1393	1395
Theulf	1115	1115	Richard Clifford	1401	1401
Simon	1125	1125	Thomas Peverell	1397	1407
John of Pageham	1151	1151	Philip Morgan	1419	1419
Alfred	1158	1158	Thomas Polton	1420	1426
Roger	1164	1164	Thomas Bouchier	1435	1435
Baldwin	1180	1180	John Carpenter	1444	1444
William Northall	1186	1186	John Alcock	1472	1476
Robert Fitz Ralph ..	1191	1191	Robert Morton	1487	1487
Henry de Soilli	1193	1193	John de Gigliis	1497	1497
John of Coutances....	1196	1196	Silvester de Gigliis ..	1498	1498
Mauger	1200	1200	Julius de Medicis		1521
Walter Gray	1214	1214	Jerome Ghinucci		1522
Silvester of Evesham ..	1216	1216	Hugh Latimer	1535	1535
William of Blois	1218	1218	John Bell	1539	1539
Walter Cantilupe	1237	1237	Nicolas Heath	1540	1543
Nicolas of Ely	1266	1266	John Hooper	1551	1552
Godfrey Giffard	1268	1268	Richard Pates	1554	1554
William Gainsbrough .	1302	1302	Edwin Sandys	1559	1559
Walter Reynolds	1308	1308	Nicolas Bullingham ..	1560	1571
Walter Maidstone....	1313	1313	John Whitgift	1577	1577
Thomas Cobham	1317	1317	Edmund Freke	1571	1584
Adam Orlton	1317	1327	Richard Fletcher	1589	1593
Simon Montacute	1334	1334	Thomas Bilson	1596	1596
Thomas Hemenhale ..	1337	1337	Gervas Babington	1591	1597
Wulstan Bransford ..	1339	1339	Henry Parry	1607	1610
John Thoresby	1347	1350	John Thornborough ..	1593	1616
Reginald Brian	1350	1352	John Prideaux	1641	1641
John Barnet	1362	1362	George Morley	1660	1660
William Whittlesey ..	1362	1364	John Gauden	1660	1662
William de Lynn	1362	1368	John Earle	1662	1662
Henry Wakefield	1375	1375	Robert Skinner	1636	1663

WORCESTER (Continued).

	Conse-cration.	Accession.		Conse-cration.	Accession.
Walter Blandford	1665	1671	James Johnson	1752	1759
James Fleetwood	1675	1675	Brownlow North	1771	1774
William Thomas	1678	1683	Richard Hurd	1775	1781
Edward Stillingfleet ..	1689	1689	Ffolliott H. W. }	} 1797	1808
William Lloyd	1680	1699	Cornewall }		
John Hough	1690	1717	Robert James Carr ..	1824	1831
Isaac Maddox	1736	1743	Henry Pepys	1840	1841

HEREFORD.

	Conse-cration.	First Signat.	Last Signat.	Death.		Conse-cration.	First Signat.	Last Signat.	Death.
Putta (succ. } 676)	669			688	Beonna	823	824	825	
					Eadulf......		836		
Tyrhtel	688		693		Cuthwulf ..	837	838	857	
Torhthere .	710		727		Mucel				
Wahlstod ..					Deorlaf		866	884	
Cuthbert....	736	737			Cynemund ..	888			
Podda	741		747		Edgar		901	930	
Hecca		758			Tidhelm		930	934	
Ceadda			770		Wulfhelm ..		939	940	
Aldberht....	777	777	781		Alfric		941	951	
Esne		785			Athulf......		973	1012	
Ceolmund ..		788	793		Ethelstan ..	1012	1012	1052	1056
Utel		798	799		Leofgar	1056			1056
Wulfhard ..	800	801	822		Walter	1061			1079

	Conse-cration.	Accession.		Conse-cration.	Accession.
Robert de Losinga ..	1079	1079	Richard Swinfield	1283	1283
Gerard	1096	1096	Adam Orlton	1317	1317
Reinhelm	1107	1107	Thomas Charlton	1327	1327
Geoffrey de Clive	1115	1115	John Trilleck	1344	1344
Richard	1121	1121	Lewis Charlton	1361	1361
Robert de Bethune ..	1131	1131	William Courtenay ..	1370	1370
Gilbert Ffolliott......	1148	1148	John Gilbert	1372	1375
Robert de Maledon ..	1163	1163	John Trevenant......	1389	1389
Robert Ffolliott......	1174	1174	Robert Mascall	1404	1404
William de Vere	1186	1186	Edmund Lacy	1417	1417
Giles de Bruce	1200	1200	Thomas Polton	1420	1420
Hugh de Mapenore ..	1216	1216	Thomas Spofford	1422	1422
Hugh Ffolliott	1219	1219	Richard Beauchamp ..	1449	1449
Ralph Maidstone	1234	1234	Reginald Boulers	1451	1451
Peter d'Acquablanca..	1240	1240	John Stanbery	1448	1453
John Breton	1269	1269	Thomas Milling	1474	1474
Thomas Cantilupe	1275	1275	Edmund Audley	1480	1492

HEREFORD (CONTINUED).

	Consecration.	Accession.		Consecration.	Accession.
Hadrian de Castello ..		1502	Herbert Croft........	1662	1662
Richard Mayew......	1504	1504	Gilbert Ironside......	1689	1691
Charles Booth	1516	1516	Humfrey Humphries..	1689	1701
Edward Fox	1535	1535	Philip Bisse	1710	1713
John Skip	1539	1539	Benjamin Hoadly	1716	1721
John Harley	1553	1553	Henry Egerton	1724	1724
Robert Parfew, or ⎱ Wharton ⎰	1536	1554	James Beauclerk	1746	1746
			John Harley	1787	1787
John Scory..........	1551	1559	John Butler	1777	1788
Herbert Westfaling ..	1586	1586	Ffolliott H. W. ⎱ Cornewall ⎰	1797	1803
Robert Bennett	1603	1603			
Francis Godwin......	1601	1617	John Luxmoore......	1807	1808
Augustine Lindsell ..	1633	1634	George Is. Huntingford	1802	1815
Matthew Wren	1635	1635	Edward Grey	1832	1832
Theophilus Field	1619	1635	Thomas Musgrave....	1837	1837
George Coke	1633	1636	Renn D. Hampden ..	1848	1848
Nicolas Monk	1661	1661			

SELSEY.

	Consecration.	First Signat.	Last Signat.	Death.		Consecration.	First Signat.	Last Signat.	Death.
Eadbert	709				Bernege	909	926	929	
Eolla		714			Wulfhun....		931	940	
Sigga	733	737	747		Alfred		944	953	
Aluberht....					Eadhelm		963	979	
Osa		765	770		Ethelgar	980	980	987	
Gislehere....		780	781		Ordbriht	989	990	1008	1009
Totta		785			Elmer	1009	1012	1031	
Wiohthun ..		789	805		Ethelric	1032	1032	1033	1038
Ethelwulf ..		811	816		Grimketel ..	1039	1042	1046	1047
Cenred		824	838		Hecca	1047	1050		1057
Gutheard ..		860	862		Ethelric ...	1058			

CHICHESTER.

	Consecration.	Accession.		Consecration.	Accession.
Stigand	1070	1070	Simon de Wells*......	1204	1204
Gosfrid	1087	1087	Richard le Poor......	1215	1215
Ralph Luffa	1091	1091	Ralph of Wareham ..	1218	1218
Seffrid d'Escures	1125	1125	Ralph Neville	1224	1224
Hilary..............	1147	1147	Richard de Wych	1245	1245
John Greenford	1174	1174	John Climping	1254	1254
Seffrid..............	1180	1180	Stephen Berksted	1262	1262

CHICHESTER (CONTINUED).

	Conse-cration.	Accession.		Conse-cration.	Accession.
Gilbert de S. Leofard .	1288	1288	Thomas Bickley	1586	1586
John Langton	1305	1305	Antony Watson	1596	1596
Robert Stratford	1337	1337	Launcelot Andrewes . .	1605	1605
William de Lynn	1362	1362	Samuel Harsnett	1609	1609
William Reade	1368	1368	George Carleton	1618	1619
Thomas Rushook	1383	1385	Richard Montagu	1628	1628
Richard Mitford	1390	1390	Brian Duppa	1638	1638
Robert Waldby	1387	1396	Henry King	1642	1642
Robert Reade	1394	1397	Peter Gunning	1670	1670
Stephen Patrington . .	1415	1417	Ralph Brideoake	1675	1675
Henry de la Ware	1418	1418	Guy Carleton	1672	1678
John Kemp	1419	1421	John Lake	1683	1685
Thomas Polton	1420	1421	Simon Patrick	1689	1689
John Rickingale	1426	1426	Robert Grove	1691	1691
Simon Sydenham	1431	1431	John Williams	1696	1696
Richard Praty	1438	1438	Thomas Manningham .	1709	1709
Adam Moleyns	1446	1446	Thomas Bowers	1722	1722
Reginald Peacock	1444	1450	Edward Waddington . .	1724	1724
John Arundel	1459	1459	Francis Hare	1727	1731
Edward Story	1468	1478	Matthias Mawson	1739	1740
Richard Fitz James . .	1497	1503	William Ashburnham .	1754	1754
Robert Sherborn	1505	1508	John Buckner	1798	1798
Richard Sampson	1536	1536	Robert James Carr . .	1824	1824
George Day	1543	1543	Edward Maltby	1831	1831
John Scory	1551	1552	William Otter	1836	1836
John Christopherson . .	1557	1557	Phil. N. Shuttleworth .	1840	1840
William Barlow	1536	1559	Ashurst T. Gilbert	1842	1842
Richard Curteis	1570	1570			

ROCHESTER.

	Conse-cration.	First Signat.	Last Signat.	Death.		Conse-cration.	First Signat.	Last Signat.	Death.
Justus	604	604			Weremund . .		785	803	
Romanus	624			627	Beornmod . .		805	842	
Paulinus	625			644	Tatnoth . . .	844	844		
(succ. 633)					Badenoth . .				
Ithamar	644				Weremund . .		860	862	
Damian	655			664	Cuthwulf . .		868		
Putta	669				Swithulf			880	897
Cuichelm	676				Ceolmund . .		904	909	
Gebmund . .	678		693		Kynferth . .		926	931	
Tobias	693	706		726	Burrhic		934	946	
Eadulf	727	735	738		Elfstan		964	995	
Dunno	741		747		Godwin	995	995		
Eardulf	747	747	765		Godwin			1046	
Diora		775	781		Siward	1058	1058		1075

ROCHESTER (CONTINUED).

	Conse-cration.	Accession.		Conse-cration.	Accession.
Arnostus	1076	1076	Edmund Audley	1480	1480
Gundulf	1077	1077	Thomas Savage	1493	1493
Ralph d'Escures	1108	1108	Richard Fitz James ..	1497	1497
Ernulf	1115	1115	John Fisher	1504	1504
John	1125	1125	John Hilsey	1535	1535
John (v. Wharton)....		1137	Nicolas Heath	1540	1540
Asceline	1142	1142	Henry Holbeach	1538	1544
Walter	1148	1148	Nicolas Ridley	1547	1547
Waleran	1182	1182	John Poynet	1550	1550
Gilbert Glanville	1185	1185	John Scory	1551	1551
* Benedict de Sansetun	1215	1215	Maurice Griffin	1554	1554
Henry Sandford	1227	1227	Edmund Gheast	1560	1560
Richard Wendover ..	1238	1238	Edmund Freke	1572	1572
Laurence de S. Martin	1251	1251	John Piers	1576	1576
Walter de Merton....	1274	1274	John Young	1578	1578
John Bradfield	1278	1278	William Barlow	1605	1605
Thomas Ingaldsthorpe	1283	1283	Richard Neile	1608	1608
Thomas of Wouldham.	1292	1292	John Buckeridge	1611	1611
Haymo Heath	1319	1319	Walter Curll	1628	1628
John Sheppey	1353	1353	John Bowle	1630	1630
William Whittlesey ..	1362	1362	John Warner	1638	1638
Thomas Trilleck	1364	1364	John Dolben	1666	1666
Thomas Brinton	1373	1373	Francis Turner	1683	1683
William Bottlesham ..		1389	Thomas Spratt	1684	1684
John Bottlesham	1400	1400	Francis Atterbury....	1713	1713
Richard Young	1400	1404	Samuel Bradford	1718	1723
John Kemp	1419	1419	Joseph Wilcocks	1721	1731
John Langdon	1422	1422	Zachary Pearce	1748	1756
Thomas Brown	1435	1435	John Thomas	1774	1774
William Wells	1437	1437	Samuel Horsley	1788	1793
John Lowe ...	1433	1444	Thomas Dampier	1802	1802
Thomas Rotherham ..	1468	1468	Walker King	1809	1809
John Alcock	1472	1472	Hugh Percy	1827	1827
John Russell	1476	1476	George Murray	1814	1827

OXFORD.

	Conse-cration.	Accession.		Conse-cration.	Accession.
Robert King		1545	John Howson	1619	1619
Hugh Curwen	1555	1567	Richard Corbet	1628	1628
Vacant 1568–1589.			John Bancroft	1632	1632
John Underhill	1589	1589	Robert Skinner	1637	1641
Vacant 1592–1604.			William Paul	1663	1663
John Bridges	1604	1604	Walter Blandford	1665	1665

* Died 1226 Dec. 18. Chron. Dover.

OXFORD (CONTINUED).

	Conse-cration.	Accession.		Conse-cration.	Accession.
Nathanael Crewe	1671	1671	Robert Lowth	1766	1766
Henry Compton	1674	1674	John Butler	1777	1777
John Fell	1676	1676	Edward Smallwell....	1783	1788
Samuel Parker	1686	1686	John Randolph	1799	1799
Timothy Hall........	1688	1688	Charles Moss	1807	1807
John Hough	1690	1690	William Jackson	1812	1812
William Talbot	1699	1699	Edward Legge	1816	1816
John Potter	1715	1715	Charles Lloyd........	1827	1827
Thomas Secker	1735	1737	Richard Bagot	1829	1829
John Hume	1756	1758	Samuel Wilberforce .	1845	1845

PETERBOROUGH.

	Conse-cration.	Accession.		Conse-cration.	Accession.
John Chamber	1541	1541	Thomas White	1685	1685
David Poole	1557	1557	Richard Cumberland..	1691	1691
Edmund Scambler....	1561	1561	White Kennett	1718	1718
Richard Howland	1585	1585	Robert Clavering	1725	1729
Thomas Dove........	1601	1601	John Thomas	1747	1747
William Piers........	1630	1630	Richard Terrick......	1757	1757
Augustine Lindsell ..	1633	1633	Robert Lambe	1764	1764
Francis Dee	1634	1634	John Hinchcliffe	1769	1769
John Towers	1639	1639	Spencer Madan	1792	1794
Benjamin Laney	1660	1660	John Parsons........	1813	1813
Joseph Henshaw	1663	1663	Herbert Marsh	1816	1819
William Lloyd	1675	1679	George Davys	1839	1839

BRISTOL.

	Conse-cration.	Accession.		Conse-cration.	Accession.
Paul Bush	1542	1542	Thomas Howell	1644	1644
John Holyman	1554	1554	Gilbert Ironside......	1661	1661
Richard Cheyney	1562	1562	Guy Carleton	1672	1672
John Bullingham	1581	1581	William Gulston	1679	1679
Richard Fletcher	1589	1589	John Lake	1683	1684
Vacant 1593-1603.			Jonathan Trelawny ..	1685	1685
John Thornborough ..	1293	1603	Gilbert Ironside......	1689	1689
Nicolas Felton	1617	1617	John Hall	1691	1691
Rowland Searchfield ..	1619	1619	John Robinson	1710	1710
Robert Wright	1623	1623	George Smallridge....	1714	1714
George Coke	1633	1633	Hugh Boulter	1719	1719
Robert Skinner	1637	1637	William Bradshaw....	1724	1724
Thomas Westfield	1642	1642	Charles Cecil	1733	1733

BRISTOL (CONTINUED).

	Conse-cration.	Accession.		Conse-cration.	Accession.
Thomas Secker	1735	1735	Henry R. Courtenay ..	1794	1794
Thomas Gooch	1737	1737	Ffoll. H. W. Cornewall	1797	1797
Joseph Butler	1738	1738	George Pelham	1803	1803
John Conybeare......	1750	1750	John Luxmoore......	1807	1807
John Hume	1756	1756	William L. Mansell ..	1808	1808
Philip Young........	1758	1758	John Kaye..........	1820	1820
Thomas Newton......	1761	1761	Robert Gray	1827	1827
Lewis Bagot	1782	1782	Joseph Allen	1834	1834
Christopher Wilson ..	1783	1783	James Henry Monk ..	1830	1836
Spencer Madan	1792	1792	Charles Baring	1856	1856

GLOUCESTER.

	Conse-cration.	Accession.		Conse-cration.	Accession.
John Wakeman......	1541	1541	Richard Willis	1715	1715
John Hooper	1551	1551	Joseph Wilcocks	1721	1721
James Brooks........	1554	1554	Elias Sydall	1731	1731
Richard Cheyney	1562	1562	Martin Benson	1735	1735
John Bullingham	1581	1581	James Johnson	1752	1752
Godfrey Goldsbrough .	1598	1598	William Warburton ..	1760	1760
Thomas Ravis	1605	1605	James Yorke	1774	1779
Henry Parry	1607	1607	Samuel Hallifax......	1781	1781
Giles Thompson	1611	1611	Richard Beadon......	1789	1789
Miles Smith	1612	1612	George Is. Huntingford	1802	1802
Godfrey Goodman	1625	1625	Henry Ryder	1815	1815
William Nicolson	1661	1661	Christopher Bethell ..	1824	1824
John Pritchett	1672	1672	James Henry Monk ..	1830	1830
Robert Frampton	1681	1681	Charles Baring	1856	1856
Edward Fowler	1691	1691			

S. DAVID'S.

	Conse-cration.	Accession.		Conse-cration.	Accession.
Bernard	1115	1115	Henry Gower........	1328	1328
David Fitzgerald	1148	1148	John Thoresby	1347	1347
Peter de Leia........	1176	1176	Reginald Brian	1350	1350
Geoffrey Henlaw	1203	1203	Thomas Fastolf	1352	1352
Gervas..............	1215	1215	Adam Houghton	1362	1362
Anselm le Gras	1231	1231	John Gilbert	1372	1389
Thomas Wallensis	1248	1248	Guy de Mohun	1397	1397
Richard de Carew	1256	1256	Henry Chicheley	1408	1408
Thomas Bek	1280	1280	John Catterick	1414	1414
David Martin........	1296	1296	Stephen Patrington ..	1415	1415

S. DAVID'S (CONTINUED).

	Conse-cration.	Accession.		Conse-cration.	Accession.
Benedict Nicolls	1408	1418	William Thomas	1678	1678
Thomas Rudborne	1434	1434	Laurence Womock	1683	1683
William Linwood	1442	1442	John Lloyd	1686	1686
John Langton	1447	1447	Thomas Watson	1687	1687
John De la Bere	1447	1447	George Bull	1705	1705
Robert Tully	1460	1460	Philip Bisse	1710	1710
Richard Martin	1482	1482	Adam Ottley	1713	1713
Thomas Langton	1483	1483	Richard Smallbrooke	1724	1724
Hugh Pavy	1485	1485	Elias Sydall	1731	1731
John Morgan	1496	1496	Nicolas Claggett	1732	1732
Robert Sherborn	1505	1505	Edward Willes	1743	1743
Edward Vaughan	1509	1509	Richard Trevor	1744	1744
Richard Rawlins	1523	1523	Antony Ellis	1753	1753
William Barlow	1536	1536	Samuel Squire	1761	1761
Robert Ferrar	1548	1548	Robert Lowth	1766	1766
Henry Morgan	1554	1554	Charles Moss	1766	1766
Thomas Young	1560	1560	James Yorke	1774	1774
Richard Davies	1560	1561	John Warren	1779	1779
Marmaduke Middleton	1579	1582	Edward Smallwell	1783	1783
Antony Rudd	1594	1594	Samuel Horsley	1788	1788
Richard Milbourne	1615	1615	William Stuart	1794	1794
William Laud	1621	1621	George Murray	1801	1801
Theophilus Field	1619	1627	Thomas Burgess	1803	1803
Roger Mainwaring	1636	1636	John B. Jenkinson	1825	1825
William Lucy	1660	1660	Connop Thirlwall	1840	1840

LLANDAFF.

	Conse-cration.	Accession.		Conse-cration.	Accession.
Urban	1107	1107	William Bottlesham		1386
Uhtred	1140	1140	Edmund Bromfield	1389	1389
Nicolas ap Gurgant	1148	1148	Tideman de Winchcomb	1393	1393
William Saltmarsh	1186	1186	Andrew Barrett	1395	1395
Henry of Abergavenny	1193	1193	John Burghill	1396	1396
William of Goldclive	1219	1219	Thomas Peverell	1397	1398
Elias of Radnor	1230	1230	John de la Zouch	1408	1408
William de Burgh	1245	1245	John Wells	1425	1425
John de la Ware	1254	1254	Nicolas Ashby	1441	1441
William of Radnor	1257	1257	John Hunden	1458	1458
William de Bruce	1266	1266	John Smith	1476	1476
John of Monmouth	1297	1297	John Marshall	1478	1478
John Eaglescliffe		1323	John Ingleby	1496	1496
John Pascall		1347	Miles Salley	1500	1500
Roger Cradock	1350	1361	George de Athequa	1517	1517
Thomas Rushook	1383	1383	Robert Holgate	1537	1537

A a

LLANDAFF (Continued).

	Conse-cration.	Accession.		Conse-cration.	Accession.
Antony Kitchin, or Dunstan	1545	1545	Robert Clavering	1725	1725
			John Harris	1729	1729
Hugh Jones	1566	1566	Matthias Mawson	1739	1739
William Blethin......	1575	1575	John Gilbert	1740	1740
Gervas Babington	1591	1591	Edward Cressett	1749	1749
William Morgan	1595	1595	Richard Newcome....	1755	1755
Francis Godwin	1601	1601	John Ewer	1761	1761
George Carleton	1618	1618	Jonathan Shipley	1769	1769
Theophilus Field	1619	1619	Shute Barrington	1769	1769
William Murray	1622	1627	Richard Watson......	1782	1782
Morgan Owen	1640	1640	Herbert Marsh	1816	1816
Hugh Lloyd	1660	1660	William Van Mildert .	1819	1819
Francis Davies	1667	1667	Charles R. Sumner ..	1826	1826
William Lloyd	1675	1675	Edward Copleston....	1828	1828
William Beaw	1679	1679	Alfred Ollivant	1849	1849
John Tyler..........	1706	1706			

BANGOR.

	Conse-cration.	Accession.		Conse-cration.	Accession.
Hervè	1092	1092	John Stanbery	1448	1448
David the Scot	1120	1120	James Blakedon	1442	1453
Maurice	1140	1140	Richard Edenham	1465	1465
Guy Rufus	1177	1177	Henry Dean	1496	1496
Alban	1195	1195	Thomas Pigott	1500	1500
Robert of Shrewsbury	1197	1197	John Penny	1505	1505
Martin or Cadogan ..	1215	1215	Thomas Skirvington ..	1509	1509
Richard	1237	1237	John Salcot	1534	1534
Anian	1267	1267	John Bird	1537	1539
Griffin ap Yorwerth ..	1307	1307	Arthur Bulkeley	1542	1542
Anian Seys..........	1309	1309	William Glynne......	1555	1555
Matthew Englefield ..	1328	1328	Rowland Meyrick	1559	1559
Thomas Ringsted	1357	1357	Nicolas Robinson	1566	1566
Gervas de Castro	1366	1366	Hugh Bellott	1586	1586
Howel ap Grono	1371	1371	Richard Vaughan	1596	1596
John Gilbert	1372	1372	Henry Rowlands	1598	1598
John Swaffham	1363	1376	Lewis Bayly	1616	1616
Richard Young	1400	1400	David Dolben	1632	1632
*Benedict Nicolls ...	1408	1408	Edmund Griffith	1634	1634
William Barrow......	1418	1418	William Roberts	1637	1637
John Cliderow	1425	1425	Robert Morgan	1666	1666
Thomas Cheriton	1436	1436	Humfrey Lloyd	1673	1673

* Lewis Bifort was appointed Bishop of Bangor by the interest of Owen Glendower soon after 1400, but was never recognised by the English church. The Pope translated him to another see in 1408, but he appeared as "Ludovicus Bangorensis" at the Council of Constance.

BANGOR (CONTINUED).

	Consecration.	Accession.		Consecration.	Accession.
Humfrey Humphries ..	1689	1689	Zachariah Pearce	1748	1748
John Evans	1702	1702	John Egerton........	1756	1756
Benjamin Hoadly	1716	1716	John Ewer	1761	1769
Richard Reynolds	1721	1721	John Moore	1775	1775
William Baker	1723	1723	John Warren	1779	1783
Thomas Sherlock	1728	1728	William Cleaver	1788	1800
Charles Cecil	1733	1734	John Randolph	1799	1807
Thomas Herring	1738	1738	Henry W. Majendie ..	1800	1809
Matthew Hutton	1743	1743	Christopher Bethell ..	1824	1830

S. ASAPH.

	Consecration.	Accession.		Consecration.	Accession.
Gilbert	1143	1143	Thomas Goldwell	1555	1555
Geoffrey Arthur	1152	1152	Richard Davies	1560	1560
Richard	1154	1154	Thomas Davis	1561	1561
Geoffrey	1160	1160	William Hughes	1573	1573
Adam	1175	1175	William Morgan	1595	1601
John	1183	1183	Richard Parry	1604	1604
Reiner..............	1186	1186	John Hanmer........	1624	1624
Abraham............	1225	1225	John Owen..........	1629	1629
Hugh	1235	1235	George Griffith	1660	1660
Howel ap Ednevet ..	1240	1240	Henry Glemham	1667	1667
Anian	1249	1249	Isaac Barrow	1663	1670
John	1267	1267	William Lloyd	1680	1680
Anian Schonaw	1268	1268	Edward Jones	1683	1692
Leoline Bromfield	1293	1293	George Hooper	1703	1703
David ap Blethyn	1315	1315	William Beveridge....	1704	1704
John Trevor	1352	1352	William Fleetwood ..	1708	1708
Leoline ap Madoc	1357	1357	John Wynne	1715	1715
William Spridlington .	1376	1376	Francis Hare	1727	1727
Laurence Child	1382	1382	Thomas Tanner	1732	1732
Alexander Bache	1390	1390	Isaac Maddox	1736	1736
John Trevor	1395	1395	Samuel Lisle	1744	1744
Robert Lancaster	1411	1411	Robert H. Drummond	1748	1748
John Lowe..........	1433	1433	Richard Newcome....	1755	1761
Reginald Peacock	1444	1444	Jonathan Shipley	1769	1769
Thomas Knight	1451	1451	Samuel Hallifax	1781	1789
Richard Redman	1471	1471	Lewis Bagot	1782	1790
Michael Deacon......	1496	1496	Samuel Horsley	1788	1802
David ap Yorwerth ..	1500	1500	William Cleaver	1788	1806
David ap Owen	1504	1504	John Luxmoore	1807	1815
Edmund Birkhead....	1513	1513	William Carey	1820	1830
Henry Standish	1518	1518	Thomas Vowler Short	1841	1846
Robert Wharton	1536	1536			

YORK.

	Conse-cration.	First Signat.	Last Signat.	Death.		Conse-cration.	First Signat.	Last Signat.	Death.
Paulinus	625				Wulfhere ..	854			900
Ceadda	664				Ethelbald ..	900			
Wilfrid	664			709	Rodewald ..		928	930	
Bosa	678			705	Wulfstan ..		931	955	956
John of Beverley, (succ. 705)	687			721	Oskytel (succ. 958)	950	958	969	971
Wilfrid II ..	718			732	Oswald (succ. 972)	961		991	992
Egbert	734			766	Aldulf	992	995	1001	1002
Ethelbert, or Cœna	767			780	Wulfstan II	1003	1004	1022	1023
Eanbald	780			796	Elfric	1023	1033	1049	1051
Eanbald II ..	796		808		Kinsy	1051			1060
Wulfsy					Ealdred (succ. 1061)	1044			1069
Wigmund ..	837								

	Conse-cration.	Accession.		Conse-cration.	Accession.
Thomas	1070	1070	Thomas Savage	1493	1501
Gerard	1096	1101	Christopher Bainbridge	1507	1508
Thomas II	1109	1109	Thomas Wolsey	1514	1514
Thurstan...........	1119	1119	Edward Lee	1531	1531
William Fitz Herbert	1143	1153	Robert Holgate	1537	1545
Henry Murdac	1147	1147	Nicolas Heath	1540	1555
Roger de Pont l'Evêque	1154	1154	Thomas Young	1560	1561
Geoffrey Plantagenet .	1191	1191	Edmund Grindal	1559	1570
Walter Gray	1214	1215	Edwin Sandys	1559	1577
Sewall de Bovill......	1256	1256	John Piers	1576	1589
Godfrey de Ludham ..	1258	1258	Matthew Hutton	1589	1595
Walter Giffard	1266	1265	Tobias Matthew	1595	1606
William Wikwan	1279	1279	George Monteigne ..	1617	1628
John Romain........	1286	1286	Samuel Harsnett	1609	1628
Henry Newark	1298	1298	Richard Neile	1608	1632
Thomas Corbridge....	1300	1300	John Williams	1621	1641
William Greenfield ..	1306	1306	Accepted Frewen	1644	1660
William de Melton ..	1317	1317	Richard Sterne	1660	1664
William de la Zouch ..	1342	1342	John Dolben	1666	1683
John Thoresby	1347	1352	Thomas Lamplugh ..	1676	1688
Alexander Neville ..	1374	1374	John Sharpe	1691	1691
Thomas Arundel	1374	1388	William Dawes	1708	1714
Robert Waldby	1387	1397	Launcelot Blackburn .	1717	1724
Richard Scroope......	1386	1398	Thomas Herring	1738	1743
Henry Bowet........	1401	1407	Matthew Hutton	1743	1747
John Kemp	1419	1426	John Gilbert	1740	1757
William Booth	1447	1452	Robert H. Drummond	1748	1761
George Neville	1458	1464	William Markham ..	1771	1777
Laurence Booth......	1457	1476	Edward V. Vernon ..	1791	1808
Thomas Rotherham ..	1468	1480·	Thomas Musgrave....	1837	1847

LINDISFARNE.

	Conse-cration.	Death.		Conse-cration.	Death.
Aidan	635	651	Ethelwold	724	740
Finan	651	661	Cynewulf	740	782
Colman	661	676	Higbald	781	802
Tuda	664	664	Egbert	803	
Eata	678		Heathored	821	
Cuthbert............	685	687	Egred	830	
Eadberht........	687	698	Eanbert	845	
Eadfrith	698	721	Eardulf	854	899

CHESTER LE STREET. 883.

	Conse-cration.	Death.		Conse-cration.	Death.
Cutheard	900		Sexhelm	947	
Tilred	915		Ealdred	957	968
Wigred	928	944	Elfsy	968	990
Uhtred	944				

HEXHAM.

	Conse-cration.	Death.		Conse-cration.	Death.
Eata	678	686	Alhmund	767	781
Trumbert	681		Tilbert......	781	789
Eata (restored 685) ..		686	Ethelbert (succ. 789) ..	777	797
John of Beverley	687		Heardred	797	797
Wilfrid (succ. 705)	664	709	Eanbert	800	
Acca	709	740	Tidferth	806	821
Frithobert	734	766			

DURHAM.

	Conse-cration.	Accession.		Conse-cration.	Accession.
Aldhun	990	990	Hugh de Puisac......	1153	1153
Edmund	1020	1020	Philip of Poitou	1197	1197
Eadred	1041	1041	Richard Marsh	1217	1217
Ethelric	1042	1042	Richard le Poore	1215	1229
Ethelwin............	1056	1056	Nicolas Farnham	1241	1241
Walcher	1071	1071	Walter Kirkham	1249	1249
William of S. Carileph	1081	1081	Robert Stichill	1261	1261
Ralph Flambard	1099	1099	Robert of Holy Island	1274	1274
Geoffrey Rufus	1133	1133	Antony Bek	1284	1284
William de S. Barba ..	1143	1143	Richard Kellaw	1311	1311

DURHAM (CONTINUED).

	Conse-cration.	Accession.		Conse-cration.	Accession.
Lewis de Beaumont ..	1318	1318	Tobias Matthew......	1595	1595
Richard of Bury	1333	1333	William James	1606	1606
Thomas Hatfield	1345	1345	Richard Neile	1608	1617
John Fordham	1382	1382	George Monteigne ..	1617	1628
Walter Skirlaw	1386	1388	John Howson........	1619	1628
Thomas Langley	1406	1406	Thomas Morton	1616	1632
Robert Neville	1427	1438.	John Cosin..........	1660	1660
Laurence Booth......	1457	1457	Nathanael Crewe	1671	1674
William Dudley......	1476	1476	William Talbot	1699	1721
John Sherwood	1484	1484	Edward Chandler	1717	1730
Richard Fox	1487	1494	Joseph Butler........	1738	1750
William Senhouse	1496	1502	Richard Trevor	1744	1752
Christopher Bainbridge	1507	1507	John Egerton	1756	1771
Thomas Ruthall......	1509	1509	Thomas Thurlow	1779	1787
Thomas Wolsey......	1514	1523	Shute Barrington	1769	1791
Cuthbert Tunstall	1522	1530	William Van Mildert .	1819	1826
James Pilkington	1561	1561	Edward Maltby	1831	1836
Richard Barnes	1567	1577	Charles T. Longley ..	1836	1856
Matthew Hutton	1589	1589			

CARLISLE.

	Conse-cration.	Accession.		Conse-cration.	Accession.
Adelulf	1133	1133	Richard Scroope	1464	1464
Bernard	1189	1203	Edward Story	1468	1468
Hugh	1219	1219	Richard Bell	1478	1478
Walter Mauclerc	1224	1224	William Senhouse	1496	1496
Silvester Everdon	1247	1247	Roger Layburn	1503	1503
Thomas Vipont	1255	1255	John Penny	1505	1509
Robert Chause	1258	1258	John Kite	1513	1521
Ralph Ireton	1280	1280	Robert Aldrich	1537	1537
John Halton	1292	1292	Owen Oglethorpe	1557	1557
John Ross	1325	1325	John Best	1561	1561
John Kirkby	1332	1332	Richard Barnes	1567	1570
Gilbert Welton	1353	1353	John May	1577	1577
Thomas Appleby	1363	1363	Henry Robinson	1598	1598
Robert Reade	1394	1396	Robert Snowden	1616	1616
Thomas Merks	1397	1397	Richard Milbourne ..	1615	1621
William Strickland ..	1400	1400	Richard Senhouse	1624	1624
Roger Whelpdale	1420	1420	Francis White	1626	1626
William Barrow......	1418	1423	Barnabas Potter	1629	1629
Marmaduke Lumley..	1430	1430	James Usher	1621	1642
Nicolas Close	1450	1450	Richard Sterne	1660	1660
William Percy	1452	1452	Edward Rainbow	1664	1664
John Kingscote	1462	1462	Thomas Smith	1684	1684

CARLISLE (CONTINUED).

	Conse-cration.	Accession.		Conse-cration.	Accession.
William Nicholson....	1702	1702	Edmund Law........	1769	1769
Samuel Bradford	1718	1718	John Douglas........	1787	1787
John Waugh	1723	1723	Edw. Venables Vernon	1791	1791
George Fleming......	1735	1735	Samuel Goodenough ..	1808	1808
Richard Osbaldeston ..	1747	1747	Hugh Percy	1827	1827
Charles Lyttelton	1762	1762	Henry Montagu Villiers	1856	1856

CHESTER.

	Conse-cration.	Accession.		Conse-cration.	Accession.
John Bird	1537	1541	Thomas Cartwright ..	1686	1686
George Coates	1554	1554	Nicolas Stratford	1689	1689
Cuthbert Scott	1556	1556	William Dawes	1708	1708
William Downham ..	1561	1561	Francis Gastrell......	1714	1714
William Chaderton ..	1579	1579	Samuel Peploe	1726	1726
Hugh Bellott	1586	1595	Edmund Keene	1752	1752
Richard Vaughan	1596	1597	William Markham....	1771	1771
George Lloyd........	1600	1605	Beilby Porteus	1777	1777
Thomas Morton......	1616	1616	William Cleaver......	1788	1788
John Bridgman	1619	1619	Hen. W. Majendie....	1800	1800
Brian Walton........	1660	1660	Bowyer E. Sparke....	1810	1810
Henry Fern	1662	1662	George Henry Law ..	1812	1812
George Hall	1662	1662	Charles J. Blomfield..	1824	1824
John Wilkins	1668	1668	John Bird Sumner ..	1828	1828
John Pearson.... ...	1673	1673	John Graham........	1848	1848

RIPON.

	Conse-cration.	Accession.
Charles T. Longley ..	1836	1836
Robert Bickersteth ..	1857	1857

MANCHESTER.

	Conse-cration.	Accession.
James Prince Lee	1848	1848

SODOR AND MAN.

	Conse-cration.	Accession.		Conse-cration.	Accession.
Henry Man	1546	1546	John Philips	1605	1605
Thomas Stanley (p. 151)			William Forster......	1634	1634
John Salisbury	1536	1571	Richard Parr	1635	1635
John Meyrick	1576	1576	Samuel Rutter	1661	1661
George Lloyd........	1600	1600	Isaac Barrow	1663	1663

SODOR AND MAN (Continued).

	Conse-cration.	Accession.		Conse-cration.	Accession.
Henry Bridgman	1671	1671	George Murray	1814	1814
John Lake	1683	1683	William Ward	1828	1828
Baptist Levinz	1685	1685	James Bowstead	1838	1838
Thomas Wilson	1698	1698	Henry Pepys	1840	1840
Mark Hildersley	1755	1755	Thomas Vowler Short	1841	1841
Richard Richmond ..	1773	1773	Walter A. Shirley	1847	1847
George Mason	1780	1780	Robert John Eden ..	1847	1847
Claudius Crigan......	1784	1784	Horace Powys	1854	1854

WHITHERN IN GALLOWAY.

	Conse-cration.		Conse-cration.
Trumwin............	681	Christian	1154
Pecthelm	730	John	1189
Frithwald	735	Walter	1209
Petwin	763	Gilbert	1235
Ethelbert	777	Henry..............	1255
Badulf	791	Thomas Dalton	1294
		Simon of Wedehale ..	1317
Gilaldanus	1133	Michael Malconhalgh .	1355

INDEX TO APPENDIX VIII.

	Page.		Page.
Bangor	178	London	159
Bath and Wells	166	Manchester	184
Canterbury	158	Norwich, &c.	168
Carlisle	182	Oxford	174
Chester	183	Peterborough	175
Chichester, &c.	172	Ripon	183
Durham, &c.	181	Rochester	173
Ely	162	Salisbury, &c.	165
Exeter, &c.	167	S. Asaph..............	179
Gloucester and Bristol ..	175	S. David's	176
Hereford	171	Sodor and Man	184
Lichfield..............	164	Winchester	161
Lincoln, &c.	162	Worcester	170
Llandaff	177	York	180

THE END.

www.ingramcontent.com/pod-product-compliance
Ingram Content Group UK Ltd.
Pitfield, Milton Keynes, MK11 3LW, UK
UKHW042153280225
455719UK00001B/317